Performing Shakespeare in India

Shakespeare *Performing*
in India

EXPLORING INDIANNESS, LITERATURES and CULTURES

Edited by
SHORMISHTHA PANJA
BABLI MOITRA SARAF

Los Angeles | London | New Delhi
Singapore | Washington DC | Melbourne

First published in 2016 by

 SAGE Publications India Pvt Ltd
B1/I-1 Mohan Cooperative Industrial Area
Mathura Road, New Delhi 110 044, India
www.sagepub.in

SAGE Publications Inc
2455 Teller Road
Thousand Oaks, California 91320, USA

SAGE Publications Ltd
1 Oliver's Yard, 55 City Road
London EC1Y 1SP, United Kingdom

SAGE Publications Asia-Pacific Pte Ltd
3 Church Street
#10-04 Samsung Hub
Singapore 049483

Published by Vivek Mehra for SAGE Publications India Pvt. Ltd, typeset in 10/12 pts Times New Roman by Diligent Typesetter India Pvt Ltd, Delhi and printed at Chaman Enterprises, New Delhi.

Library of Congress Cataloging-in-Publication Data

Names: Panja, Shormishtha, author. | Saraf, Babli Moitra, author.
Title: Performing Shakespeare in India : exploring indianness, literatures and cultures / Shormishtha Panja, Babli Moitra Saraf.
Description: New Delhi, India ; Thousand Oaks, California : SAGE Publications India Pvt Ltd, 2016. | Includes bibliographical references and index.
Identifiers: LCCN 2016013840| ISBN 9789351509745 (hardback : alk. paper) | ISBN 9789351509738 (epub) | ISBN 9789351509752 (ebook)
Subjects: LCSH: Shakespeare, William, 1564-1616—Stage history—India. | Shakespeare, William, 1564-1616—Appreciation—India. | English drama—Appreciation—India. | Theater—India—History.
Classification: LCC PR3109.I4 P36 2016 | DDC 792.9/50954—dc23 LC record available at https://lccn.loc.gov/2016013840

ISBN: 978-93-515-0974-5 (HB)

The SAGE Team: Shambhu Sahu, Guneet Kaur Gulati, Shobana Paul and Vinitha Nair

Contents

SHAKESPEARE AND INDIAN ICONS

Acknowledgements

The editors acknowledge with thanks Dr Nita Kumar, the then Secretary of the Shakespeare Society of India, for coordinating the process of procuring the essays from the contributors for this book and for her expertise in their revision and screening for publication, and also for keeping meticulous records of all correspondence and documents.

An international conference, "Revisiting Shakespeare in Indian Literatures and Cultures," held in March 2013, with Principal, Dr Babli Moitra Saraf, and Professor Shormishtha Panja, the then President, Shakespeare Society of India, as joint chairpersons, was collaboratively organized by Indraprastha College for Women (I.P. College) and the Shakespeare Society of India. This was the germ of this volume. Grateful thanks are owed to the Governing Body of I.P. College, University of Delhi, for providing the entire financial support and the extensive infrastructure of the college, as collaborators with the Shakespeare Society of India, to host this international conference.

We thank Dr Poonam Trivedi, the I.P. College academic co-ordinator of the conference supported by the Department of English of the College and Professor Rajiva Verma, Ms Nivedita Basu, Ms Davinder Mohini Ahuja, Dr Vandana Agrawal and Dr Vikram Chopra of the Shakespeare Society of India for their invaluable input and guidance.

We especially thank Dr Manasvini Yogi from the Department of Philosophy of I.P. College and her team of student and teacher volunteers for organizing the formidable logistical support for the three-day international conference. We also thank the Principal's Office of the college which liaisoned with all external agencies, and the support staff of the college.

We acknowledge Bangiya Sahitya Parisad, Kolkata, for visuals of illustrations in the Rakshit and the Dutta translations of Shakespeare.

We acknowledge Tara Arts and the photographer Tallulah Shepherd for visuals of the Tara Arts' productions of *The Merchant of Venice* and *The Tempest*.

1

Introduction

Shormishtha Panja and
Babli Moitra Saraf

This book is envisaged as an important intervention in the ongoing explorations in social and cultural history, into the questions of what constitutes Indianness and the meaning of being Indian, for the colonial and the postcolonial subject. This collection of essays is in the nature of a socio-historical and socio-cultural engagement with the agenda of identity formation in India across the cultural artefacts of productions and expositions around Shakespeare. Even as the conscious project of dismantling colonization and its intellectual apparatus in various forms was on from the nineteenth century onwards, the Indian literati, intellectuals, scholars and dramaturges were engaged in deconstructing the ultimate icon of colonial presence: Shakespeare. This project was both the text and the subtext of cultural enterprise like translation and stage performance and later, cinema. The essays in this collection, here revised and elaborated upon, were originally papers presented by scholars, theatre persons and translators in an international conference on Shakespeare in India held in March 2013, jointly organized by Indraprastha College for Women, University of Delhi and the Shakespeare Society of India. The combined narrative of the essays in this collection is connected by the common thread of extraordinary negotiations of postcolonial identity issues, be they in language, in social and cultural practices or in art forms. Further, these developments intertwined literary and cultural giants from various regions in India whose interventions in the cultural history of the period are indisputable. Given the fact that 2016 is the 400th anniversary of Shakespeare's death, this collection would be in the nature of both a retrospective appraisal as well as an anticipatory homage.

Shakespeare is implicated in the biggest and most significant colonial construct in India—the English language—with all its cultural baggage. The language issue is an inevitable refrain in all considerations of Shakespeare in India, mainly through the two modes of the literary translation and the innovations and adaptations in performance. The question of language is both unavoidable and inescapable in a region where vast numbers of theatre and cinema audience were, and still are, illiterate and/or unschooled in the English language. The agenda of a people's education is almost always a hegemonic exercise and, in a linguistically diverse context like India, the instrumentalization of Shakespeare for education is fascinating because it yields results that are divergent and go far beyond the colonial goal of showcasing the best of the English language or imperial culture.[1]

Why Shakespeare? Shakespeare for whom? Who knows Shakespeare? What is the use of Shakespeare? How is Shakespeare deployed? Each of these questions (and many more around Shakespeare) is an enterprise unto itself, embedded in the long history of colonial rule, the struggle against it and the negotiation of postcolonial identities, which in the case of India also imply the emergence of regional identities around questions of language and linguistic empowerment. To complicate matters, the regional identities and languages are very often internal contestations of political and social power in the struggle for supremacy. Why is it that many nineteenth-century Bengali intellectuals term Shakespeare a *bishwokobi* (world poet) but Indians from other regions are not convinced? What does this say about the reaction and resistance to colonial rule in different parts of India? Does the knowledge of Shakespeare add to the Bengali *bhodrolok*'s (gentleman) aura of civility or diminish it? Translation has always been a site for transactions of culture, both of the foreign and the domestic. The history of translation of Shakespeare's works alone would provide a fascinating insight, on the one hand, into the appropriation of both Shakespeare and the English language, and, on the other hand, into the ways in which local and regional languages were affected by the source text. Malayalam literary history notes how translating the blank verse of Shakespeare, an entirely novel poetic form, infused traditional verse with new energy. Indeed, Shakespeare has been identified by Malayalam literary historians as one of the five sources that influenced the literary trajectory of Malayalam literature. In that movement, the realism of Shakespeare's conception of the human condition and the richness of his characterization and language are all matched by the resistance evident over more than a century in this country's reception of Shakespeare. India received Shakespeare and "did things to it," in much the same way as it did to all else that it received from foreign shores in its extended history. Its intellectuals harnessed Shakespeare's verse and the issues explored in his works to indigenous cultural enterprises. We may refer to this phenomenon as the impact of Shakespeare or the appropriation of Shakespeare depending on where one wants to locate the agency, except that the two are not mutually exclusive. Thus, when Shakespeare is "exported" from India and received by a mixed audience which also contains the Indian diaspora, the energy fields often change and are reconfigured in interesting ways, and these should be accounted for in the scholarship on and around Shakespeare.

There are many schools of thought on the presence of Shakespeare in India and, as an instance of the varied approaches to Shakespeare, we consider two of those here. The first is the notion of Shakespeare the bishwokobi or world poet, a writer to whom all Indians feel a natural affinity. The other is that there is nothing timeless or universal about Shakespeare. His works are not those to which Indians automatically relate. There is nothing natural or spontaneous about Indians' love of Shakespeare. Shakespeare is, in fact, a sign of neocolonial hegemony, something that the colonial rulers slyly used to make their Indian subjects docile and obedient.[2] The latter school believes that the Shakespeare text cannot be separated from its historical moorings. It cannot be disassociated from the social and political upheavals of the post-colonial world.[3] They argue that Shakespeare enters India as a colonial tool and ends up as a sign of market forces in academia and cultural phenomena.

Intersecting this larger debate and often moving in tandem with it is the exploration, experimentation and exposition of cultural forms by individuals and groups for whom the exposure to European modes of cultural production is both exciting and challenging. The creative interface between Shakespeare and the existing as well as emerging art forms in India continue to produce fresh points of entry into the Shakespearean text. The "Shakespearean moment" in India is thus marked by a release of energy in various directions. Technological advances and newer art forms such as cinema have only enriched the experience. Vishal Bhardwaj's treatment of Hamlet as Haider, in the film of the same name, demonstrates the latest innovation in this trajectory in its deployment of the famous tragic hero, to focus on what is "rotten" in the state of Jammu and Kashmir. Bhardwaj's other films project different trajectories, such as

Omkara (based on *Othello*) that is located in the badlands of Uttar Pradesh with its murky politics and violent social tensions and *Maqbool* (based on *Macbeth*) that unfolds in the scenario of the Mumbai underworld and its gang wars. All these films resonate with the familiar in Shakespeare and are indigenous and domestic in their focus. Though Hindi cinema and Bollywood have had a very long history of Shakespearean moorings, Vishal Bhardwaj acknowledges Shakespeare's influence in the opening title of *Maqbool*. This is an important cultural event as it displays a comfort level with both the original and the recreation/adaptation, which marks the emergence of an Indianness in the public space that is bold, global, unabashed and unapologetic.

Recent stage performances such as *Piya Behrupiya* (Chameleon Lover) performed by Atul Kumar's Company Theatre, based on *Twelfth Night*, have reinvented both the text and its exposition. *Piya Behrupiya* is, in fact, an excellent example of intercultural theatre—it proves that the less fidelity the adaptation demonstrates to the Shakespeare text, the more vital the performance becomes. It also challenges the settled hierarchies of the literary text being superior to the performance and the original against which the performance must be measured. The cheeky asides that the actor playing Sebastian addresses to the audience where he protests that Shakespeare gets all the credit and he, as translator, none, also destabilize the hierarchies of colonial master text and postcolonial performance. Shakespeare continues to excite. The confidence of producers both in the fields of cinema and theatre is a remarkable shift away from the sacred cow of the Shakespearean text, as significant as the developments in the use of the English language in the former colonies or among the formerly colonized peoples all over the world.

A crucial thing to be kept in mind while discussing Shakespeare in India is that Shakespeare comes to India through a different route from the one it takes to China, Japan or Korea. Indians read Shakespeare in English and not just in translation. His texts are part of the curriculum of schools and universities. As a result of the victory of the Anglicists over those who thought Indian universities should teach the classics, as was the case in England, the colonial Indian curriculum was mainly humanities-based and included Shakespeare. Thus, English literature, including Shakespeare, was taught in India before it was introduced in the English universities. In the latter, the curriculum consisted of Greek and Latin classics. It comes as no surprise, then, that Sukanta Chaudhuri claims that "[o]utside the Western world, India has the longest and most intense engagement with Shakespeare of any country anywhere."[4] As Gauri Vishwanathan argues in

Masks of Conquest: Literary Study and British Rule in India, Shakespeare and Milton were seen as appropriate secular channels by the English colonial administrators of English values and beliefs to be imparted to the colonial subjects. Shakespeare, as Jyotsna Singh suggests, has thus been used as an educational tool by colonial rulers often as a means of intellectual manipulation.[5]

Early Shakespeare in India[6]

Shakespeare is not an "accommodating ideal" as Jyotsna Singh puts it,[7] erasing or eliding all traces of cultural difference. Indigenous theatrical performance could challenge, consciously or unconsciously and through adaptation, the status of Shakespeare as a marker of universal cultural value on the Indian stage. In this land of diverse regional languages and cultures, it is vital to note that translations and adaptations of Shakespeare appear in all corners of the country, demonstrating the ease and willingness of troupes and players to adopt Shakespeare and nurture him within prevalent traditions of the theatrical spectacle. The production of "different vernacular Shakespeares [are] mediated by heterogeneous forces of race, language," according to Singh,[8] and, one might add, by regional cultures with very strong traditions of indigenous folk and classic theatre. Shakespeare is neither a "transcendentally benevolent or non-political" influence,[9] nor is he an influence to be treated with reverence and whose works are left pristine. Some of the major regional Shakespeare productions and translations merit a brief mention.[10] The plays were translated and staged all over the country, be it in Bengali, Hindi, Urdu or Marathi, in the north-eastern language Assamese or in the south Indian languages Telugu, Kannada, Malayalam and Tamil. Be it the dubbing of Shakespeare as "Sulapani" in Telugu[11] or a Hamlet singing songs in the so-called "Indian Shakespeare" Agha Hashr's melodramatic poetic-prose Urdu translation of *Hamlet*,[12] Shakespeare was both omnipresent and inflected with a local identity.

Shakespeare was particularly big in Calcutta (modern Kolkata), the first capital of British India. Two famed actor–directors staging Bengali Shakespeare were Girish Chandra Ghosh (1844–1912) and Amarendranath Dutta (1876–1916). While Ghosh preferred remaining true to the original and lost the audience's interest quite speedily, Amarendranath chose adaptations. His *Horiraj* (c. 1896), an adaptation of *Hamlet*, proved quite popular while Ghosh's expensive *Macbeth* (1893), "staged in the European style," was a box-office disaster.[13] Of note is the performance of Boishnob Choron Addy as the first Indian Othello in the Sans Souci Theatre, Calcutta, in 1848. A letter in *The Calcutta Star* (1848) used the racist phrase "unpainted nigger Othello" for Addy besides distorting his name almost beyond recognition to Baboo Bustomchurn Addy. Besides *Othello*, there were twenty-three productions of Shakespeare in Bengali, mostly tragedies and romances, between 1852 and 1899.

Another major area of Shakespeare's influence was in Parsi theatre. There, Shakespeare's place was paramount. Around a dozen Shakespeare plays were adapted and staged, using Hindi, Urdu, Gujarati and even English, the medium being prose, verse and rhyming couplets. The playwrights were both Hindu and Muslim, a noteworthy fact that points to a period of communal and religious harmony and interaction, not always the case in present-day India. This has remained the case in one contemporary cultural formation, however, and that is cinema. It should be no surprise that Parsi theatre is an important precursor of Hindi commercial cinema. The Parsi plays were free and popular adaptations, with new characters, situations and plot lines added keeping in mind Indian social mores and entertainment preferences, including the penchant for music and dance. The famous Victoria Natak Mandali company had thirty-five plays as part of its repertoire. It toured throughout the Far East—Mandalay, Rangoon, Bangkok, Java—and then London. Among the twenty dramatic clubs in Bombay in the 1860s, there was one called the Shakespeare Natak Mandali. The majority of their unprinted scripts are unfortunately lost.[14]

Between 1919 and 1947, there was a lull in Shakespeare performances on the Indian stage. A possible cause for this could be that the national movement against the British colonial rulers was gaining momentum. Gandhi's Quit India movement, for example, was fully operational by 1942. Performing the works of an iconic English playwright on the Indian stage while fighting for independence against the British could not have been seen as compatible exercises.

Indian Shakespeare After 1947[15]

India became independent in 1947. Post-independence, Shakespeare performance falls into two major categories: productions in English and adaptations of Shakespeare in the Indian languages.[16] The latter may be further subdivided into performances that follow Shakespeare's text faithfully with literary translations, as in Ebrahim Alkazi's production of *King Lear* (1964) in Hindi and *Othello* (1969) in Urdu, and productions that adapt the Shakespearean text radically. Since the focus in this volume is on the creation of Indianness, it is important to state that Indianness through theatre is seen as a heterogeneous condition and is not limited to any specific language, region, religion or class. Shakespeare is adapted into as varied folk forms as Kathakali (from Kerala), Nautanki (from Uttar Pradesh with emphasis on music), Yakshagana (from Karnataka) and Jatra (from Bengal with emphasis on dialogue). There may also be a combination of one or more of these forms within a single performance. The adaptations may modify the characters and situations and completely transform the source text to such an extent that it may appear unfamiliar even to those Indians in the audience who know their Shakespeare but not the folk form in which it is enacted. And, of course, the addition of music, dance, colourful costumes and the ritualized folk performance makeup can make the source play unrecognizable to a non-Indian audience. Some brilliant examples of Shakespeare adaptations in indigenous forms are *Barnam Vana* (Birnam Forest, 1979) based on *Macbeth, Othello* (1996 onwards) and *King Lear* in Kathakali (1989) and *Kamdeo ka Apna Basant Ritu ka Sapna* (The Love God's Own, a Spring Reverie, 1993) based on *A Midsummer Night's Dream.* As all these have been discussed in detail elsewhere, that ground will not be gone over again here.[17]

It should be mentioned, however, that these productions were not without their controversies. The Kathakali *King Lear*, for example, satisfied neither the audience in the West nor the Indian audience. Uninitiated Western audiences or critics were left mystified while Malayalam-language critics felt that the Kathakali codes had been violated with a woman performing Cordelia (the French actor–dancer Annette Leday), since traditionally Kathakali was an all-male performance. They also protested that the removal of Lear's customary headdress in the storm scene denuded him of the grandeur associated with a protagonist. As Phillips wisely observes, the betrayal of the laws of intercultural performance is the condition of its existence.[18] It is pointless to expect a Kathakali adaptation of any Shakespeare play to remain entirely true to both English source text and Indian folk form. Loss and gain work hand in hand. Hybridity rather than purity is the objective of any successful intercultural performance.[19]

Kamdeo ka Apna Basant Ritu ka Sapna is an adaptation of *A Midsummer Night's Dream* directed by Habib Tanvir (1923–2009) who was trained at the Royal Academy of Dramatic Art and the Old Vic and was the founder of the Naya Theatre. This successful adaptation actually originated in a catastrophe. Tanvir was supposed to collaborate with an English theatre company which was supposed to supply the Athenian characters. However, that company folded. Tanvir bravely went ahead with his abbreviated performance, dealing almost exclusively with the "rude mechanicals," apart from an opening and closing scene with the courtly characters. The play proved to be a hit. For Bottom and his band, Tanvir enlisted tribal performers speaking in the Bastar dialect. Tanvir was a pioneer in the combination of folk theatre and politics. The language used in the play is a hybrid of Hindi and the Bastar dialect of the tribals. Tanvir's art abolishes the hierarchies between folk and classic forms. Even though he was trained at the Old Vic, Tanvir espouses complete confidence in the tribal performers' instinctive histrionic flair. Tanvir is not interested in producing authentic folk theatre. Like the pastoral poets of the classical tradition, Theocritus and Virgil, Tanvir is a thoughtful and highly sophisticated urban artist, one who is deeply influenced by Brecht and one who takes a conscious ideological stance. He chooses folk improvisational techniques and music, and combines them with his own socialist and comic look at the Indian socio-political situation. In *Kamdeo,* the commitment to a certain ideology, a sense of faith in tribal performance and ethos and Tanvir's loyalty to Shakespeare's language and humour, all find equal expression.

In Bengal, Utpal Dutt's (1929–93) Calcutta-based Little Theatre Group produced a variety of Shakespeare's plays, including *The Merchant of Venice* (1953), *Macbeth* (1954), *Julius Caesar* (1957), *Romeo and Juliet* (1964) and *A Midsummer Night's Dream* (*Choitali Rater Shopno* in Bengali, 1964).[20] However, in the light of the violence that had gripped the politics of Bengal in the 1960s and 1970s, to "stick to Shakespeare or Bernard Shaw was unbearable," writes Dutt. When he returned to Shakespeare, he did ninety-eight performances of *Macbeth* in the Jatra style for Bengal's villagers. Jatra is an exaggerated folk form with an emphasis on declamatory dialogue and dramatic gestures. It is performed all night, out in the open. The Jatra style is very different from Dutt's earlier restrained proscenium productions. This *Macbeth* showcased not a timeless universal Shakespeare as propagated by Dutt's guru Geoffrey Kendal, but one that took into account class, education and cultural moorings.[21] It rouses the audience from "unthinking stupor by sensation, visual surprise, songs, dances, colour."[22] Dutt's Jatra *Macbeth,* some critics argue, comes closer to Elizabethan theatre with its proximity to the groundlings than the serious proscenium productions on the Calcutta stage mounted by Dutt for an elite audience.[23]

Manipur has been the site of a number of hugely innovative adaptations which have effectively combined Meiteilon language, attire, music, dance and spectacle with Shakespeare's characters and plotlines. Lokendra Arambam's *Chingkhei Napa* (Manipuri Macbeth) (1997), Ratan Kumar Singh's *Julius Caesar* (2003), Ratan Thiyam's Chorus Repertory Theatre, Imphal's *Macbeth* (2014) and Ranbir Mangang's 2015 adaptation of the same play present powerful visual appropriations replete with spectacle. Ratan Thiyam's *Macbeth* was performed at the inauguration of the National School of Drama's annual international theatre festival, Bharat Rang Mahotsav, in Delhi in February 2016. The audience was held spellbound by a performance, the words of which were incomprehensible to almost all in the audience as the language used was Meiteilon. Thiyam made Lady Macbeth a towering figure in whose presence Macbeth fades into inconspicuousness. The use of swords, tribal costumes, mostly black and red, headgear and beads made the play a visual spectacle even though there were very few props and no backdrop. In addition, the use of Manipuri music and song, particularly the use of drums and a keening, wailing lament, created the haunting atmosphere of a remote civilization and enhanced the tragic ethos. It is significant that in these productions Shakespeare lives on in the strength of a strong, indigenous Manipuri theatre tradition that includes both tribal and imaginative elements created by the respective directors. The introduction of Shakespeare produces a hybrid performance that appeals both to those who are familiar with the original Shakespeare text and to lay theatregoers who have never heard of Shakespeare.

Roysten Abel's *Othello: A Study in Black and White* (1999–2000) is a sensitive and insightful production of the United Players' Guild that embeds *Othello* in a contemporary English play about a group of Indian actors rehearsing Shakespeare's play and foregrounds tensions, other than racial, in contemporary Indian society, be they related to class, the urban versus rural divide, the metropolis versus small town battle and/or the Westernized versus *desi* (indigenous) tussle. Shakespeare becomes the site on which the tensions of the non-homogeneous contemporary Indian society erupt.[24] The languages used are English, Hindi and Assamese, the last the language of Adil Hussain, the actor who plays Othello. One of the most effective scenes is when Adil breaks into Assamese while rehearsing a scene with Lushin Dubey (Desdemona), thereby merging Othello's otherness in Venice with the otherness of regional Assamese identity versus a supposed but illusory pan-Indian identity.

Piya Behrupiya by Atul Kumar and The Company Theatre, which was performed at the London Globe in April 2012 and then all across India to full houses, brings Shakespeare performance in India to a new high with respect to the confidence essayed in the matter of hybridity and heterogeneity. It is a hilarious mix of colour, music (folk and *qawwali*), dance, language and meta-theatricality, with English words liberally thrown in for comic and meta-theatrical effects. The actor who plays Sebastian, who is also the translator of the play, complains that the translator gets no credit (everyone says "*Wah* Shakespeare"). He also shares with the audience the usual actor's woes of being sidelined. This cheeky, thumb-your-nose-at-a-classic production aptly illustrates W.B. Worthen's idea of performance as iteration, rather than a reconstitution of a superior literary artefact. Kumar has also staged *Nothing like Lear*, a one-man show, and *Hamlet the Clown Prince*. One may not agree with his statement that Shakespeare "is always a super hit" in India "because Shakespeare's tales and human conditions are quite timeless, space-less and cultureless—they are simply human" (Vincent 2012) which strays dangerously close to the nineteenth-century notion of Shakespeare as a bishwokobi (world poet,) but Kumar is not guilty of bardolatry. His attitude to Shakespeare is the opposite of reverential: in his own words, "[T]he comedy works very well when you disrespect it and shake hands readily with the audience."[25] As mentioned earlier, in Kumar's production, the brassy and spectacular infidelities to the supposed master text, Shakespeare, vociferously challenge the settled hierarchies of literary text and performance, of English source text and of Indian adaptation. As Worthen observes, the hallmark of a successful intercultural production is the extent of its departure from the source text. Infidelity is the very condition and prerequisite of a performance that brings together diverse cultures.[26]

Shakespeare and Films

Shakespeare's influence on the genre of cinema had directly descended from the Parsi theatre of the late nineteenth and early twentieth centuries as mentioned earlier. From the days of *Dil Farosh* (one who sells his heart), a 1927 silent film based on *The Merchant of Venice* which is probably the earliest example of Shakespeare in Indian cinema, to Sohrab Modi's *Khoon ka Khoon* (Blood for blood) in 1935 based on *Hamlet* and *Romeo and Juliet* (1948) starring Nargis who was favourably compared to Norma Shearer who played Juliet in a 1936 Hollywood version of the play, and from Kishore Sahu's sombre *Hamlet* (1954) down to the recent Malayalam *Kaliyattam* (Play of God, 1997) based on *Othello* which turns the racial conflict into a caste-based conflict and situates the story among a group of Kathakali performers, Shakespeare has had an enormous influence on Indian cinema. The Bengali *Bhranti Bilash* (1963) directed by Manu Sen, starring the screen legend Uttam Kumar and based on Ishwar Chandra Vidyasagar's excellent translation, was a delightful rendition of *The Comedy of Errors*. It was a box office hit and is viewed with pleasure even today. Gulzar's Hindi *Angoor* (Grapes, 1982) based on the same play, was also a hit. In recent times, the many adaptations of *Romeo and Juliet*, such as, *Ek Duje Ke Liye* (Made for each other, 1981), directed by K. Balachander and addressing the love between a man from Tamil Nadu and a North Indian woman, *Qayamat se Qayamat Tak* (From catastrophe to calamity, 1988) directed by Mansoor Khan and based on two warring and arch-conservative Thakur families in Rajasthan and *Ishaqzaade* (Children of love, 2012) directed by Habib Faisal about the children of two warring political families, the Hindu Chauhans and the Muslim Qureshis, have all been box office successes, usually starring fresh new actors. The landmark contribution of Vishal Bhardwaj's trilogy, *Maqbool* (2003), *Omkara* (2006) and *Haider* (2014), has already been mentioned.

Performing Shakespeare

Let us now move on to the essays in this collection. This book consists of an Introduction and thirteen essays written by national and international scholars, working in India and elsewhere, and subdivided into the following categories: Shakespeare and Indian visual culture; contemporary Shakespeare performance onstage in India and the diaspora; Shakespeare and Indian films; translation and issues of language and politics in regional Shakespeares; identity and the politics of language; and the cultural capital of Shakespeare as assessed by various Indian cultural icons. The emphasis is on Shakespeare as one of the catalysts for the entrance of the Indian nation into modernity. The critical approaches in the essays are manifold. They include socio-historical analysis, political commentary, translation studies, literary criticism, visual culture studies, and performance and film studies. Unlike other volumes on Shakespeare and India,[27] this volume makes forays into yet unexamined terrain like Shakespearean influence on visual art, the diasporic experience of Shakespeare, the implications of playing Shakespeare in the public sphere of theatre and the interface of Shakespeare and other icons of Indian literatures and cultures, including critics and commentators who shaped critical studies and sensibilities in various Indian languages.

Shakespeare and Indian Visual Culture

Shormishtha Panja's essay, "'To Confine the Illimitable': Visual and Verbal Narratives in Two Bengali Retellings of Shakespeare," is unique in the sense that it discusses illustrations of Shakespeare's plays. It demonstrates how in the early years of the nineteenth century Charles Lamb complained that the artists, Henry Fuseli and Joshua Reynolds among them, who had painted characters and scenes from Shakespeare's plays for The Boydell Shakespeare Gallery (1789), which was to result in "A Most Magnificent and Accurate" illustrated edition of Shakespeare's plays (1802), "confine[d] the illimitable." The essay examines how, contrary to Lamb's opinion, paintings and illustrations of Shakespeare's works or their retellings tell us a great deal about the culture in which they were created and the reception and readership of his works. Panja closely analyzes a few illustrations in two Bengali prose retellings of Shakespeare's plays: one late nineteenth century, the other mid-twentieth century, both books predating the year of Indian independence. The role of Shakespeare in not merely the colonial enterprise but also in reform movements spearheaded by Bengalis, Shakespeare and the rise of the new woman in Bengal, the transition from stage to page, the influence of Charles and Mary Lamb's *Tales from Shakespeare* and the vexing question of the universal versus local identity of Shakespeare are some of the issues that are explored in the course of the discussion. Panja argues that the illustrations in these works often have a narrative of their own which is independent of the verbal text, a narrative that adds another dimension to the debate about the perceived timelessness and omnipresence of Shakespeare.

Contemporary Shakespeare Performance on Stage in India and the Diaspora

Paromita Chakravarti in "Urban Histories and Vernacular Shakespeares in Bengal: *Kolkatar Hamlet, Hemlat* and *Hamlet 2011*" examines how some Indian adaptations of Shakespearean drama have helped to forge, among other things, a particular sense of the "urban"—a heightened consciousness of the history, politics and feel of specific Indian cities and cityscapes. Shakespearean tragedies, *King Lear, Macbeth* and *Hamlet* primarily, have been deployed to evoke urban angst, the layered histories of particular Indian cities and their changing maps of violence, crime and politics. In films like *Maqbool,* based on Shakespeare's *Macbeth,* contemporary Mumbai emerges as a central protagonist. Rituparno Ghosh, director of the English-language film *The Last Lear,* stated that the Kolkata setting of his film was meant to evoke the empire and its erstwhile capital, as well as the history of Kolkata's English-language theatre and love of Shakespeare.

However, within the Bengali theatre tradition, Shakespeare's *Hamlet* has been used to forge a very different history of Kolkata and its politics, argues Chakravarti. In Asit Basu's *Kolkatar Hamlet* (1973), set against the Naxal movement of the 1970s, the figure of Hamlet stands as an icon of youthful rebellion against unjust regimes, inspiring the young revolutionaries of the city. Hamlet's association with the players represents a tradition of progressive theatre associated with Kolkata. Using Shakespeare's *Hamlet,* Bratya Basu's *Hemlat* (2007) articulates a very different Kolkata of the twenty-first century. Staged 34 years after *Kolkatar Hamlet, Hemlat* portrays the failure of the revolution and of Left politics. *Hemlat* is no prince—he is a lumpenized, lower middle-class protagonist with an intimate connection to the city and its subaltern lives. The play takes an unforgiving look at a Kolkata in decline, brokering away its stately buildings to a criminal land mafia which is hand in glove with the government, constructing malls and apartments to bring a new city into existence on the ruins and corpses of its past. Bibhash Chakraborty production of *Hamlet* in 2011 is based in a city pub on Park Street, representing the new spaces which are emerging in a changing city. In the framing meta-play, we are told that the performance of *Hamlet* to celebrate the opening of the pub is dedicated to a man who was killed in a police encounter several years ago. The reference sets up an intertextual dialogue with *Kolkatar Hamlet* and the context of city youths dying in police encounters. Chakravarti's essay uses these three plays to examine how Shakespeare's *Hamlet* provides the context of mapping the changing contours of the city and what it means for prison-like Denmark to become the Kolkata of the 1970s or of the first decade of the twenty-first century, two points of extreme political crisis in West Bengal. Further, the essay explores possibilities of intertextual readings of the cityscape through these plays.

Claire Cochrane in "Shakespeare and the Re/vision of Indian Heritage in the Postcolonial British Context" discusses British Asian theatre-makers operating outside the theatrical mainstream and their refashioning of Shakespeare, with particular reference to the company Tara Arts. What Cochrane explores in this essay is the way in which that complexity of heritage has been brought to bear on the re-visioning of Shakespeare by British Asian theatre-makers operating outside the theatrical mainstream. In general, because of the social, economic and institutional challenges facing British Asian theatre artists, the number of independent professional companies is comparatively small and, for the most part, their work has focused on creating drama which interrogates thorny questions of identity formation and contemporary cultural practices within the "new" British Asian communities. Nevertheless, for artists born and/or educated in the UK, the Western classical canon, including Shakespeare, is as much part of their heritage as the classical Indian narratives and performance traditions which so powerfully evoke collective memories of the lost "home" of their elders. Cochrane discusses examples of Tara productions in the light of the manner in which Shakespeare's plays have been used to forge both creative synergies between parallel cultures, and provide a means of addressing the ontological ruptures and dislocations associated with the colonial past.

Thea Buckley in "Indian Shakespeare in the World Shakespeare Festival" examines three Shakespearean productions as adapted into Indian contexts and performed at the World Shakespeare Festival (WSF), part of the 2012 Cultural Olympics in the UK. She gives a first-person view as a non-Indian of the transformations and absorption into an Indian context of *Much Ado About Nothing*, *Twelfth Night* and *All's Well That Ends Well*, to examine whether the experience could be called truly "intercultural." The first of these productions was performed by an Indo-British cast in conjunction with the Royal Shakespeare Company and the latter two were performed at the Globe Theatre by visiting troupes from Mumbai's Company and Arpana Theatres, respectively. In comparing and contrasting the approaches taken to these adaptations, drawing on evidence including directorial interviews, the essay problematizes the continuing "global" dialogue between Shakespeare's source and the host cultures of Britain and India, arguing that the term is a simplistic representation of an intercultural relationship that involves interaction and negotiation on multiple levels. The variables involved comprise not only those layers of space or geographical distance and time or historical distance, but also shades of cultural and linguistic variations, whether between individuals, states or nations. The essay concludes by exploring the question of whether these productions—English, Hindi and Gujarati—fuse not only languages and literatures but also cultures, unifying their audiences through a shared love of Shakespeare.

Shakespeare and Indian Cinema

Trisha Mitra in "The Othello-figure in Three Indian Films: *Kaliyattam, Omkara and Saptapadi*" explores the appropriation of the figure of Othello in these films located in different sociological contexts. Mitra examines the characteristics of the original text which have been adopted by directors/scriptwriters and the variations which have been introduced to add layers of meaning.

The primary themes and motifs providing intertextual frames (racism, transgressive romance and sexual jealousy) have been borrowed, only to be dislocated and employed in the plots of these films. The figure of Othello provokes anxieties related to race and miscegenation which have been transposed onto caste, class and communal anxieties in this postcolonial location.

Mitra's essay looks at the development of the reformulations of Othello's "otherness" in order to understand their relocation and inter-communal or caste dynamics. While in *Omkara* and *Saptapadi* racial relations are explored, *Kaliyattam* carefully and subtly circumnavigates the issue.

Paramita Dutta in "Shakespeareana to *Shakespeare Wallah*: Selling or Doing Shakespeare in India" examines the film *Shakespeare Wallah* and the life and career of Geoffrey Kendal. Apart from an analysis of how Shakespeare becomes the true protagonist in the ways in which he inflects characters and relationships, she also discusses the economies of Shakespeare performance. *Shakespeare Wallah*, the Merchant Ivory Productions film of 1965, depicts the events in the life of a British theatrical troupe that was touring and performing Shakespeare in various regions in post-independence India. Ismail Merchant, the producer of the film, explicates that the "Wallah" in the title of the film means a tradesman or one who sells something (here Shakespeare) whereas the director James Ivory wishes to stress that it actually implies one who is associated with something and, here, one who "does" Shakespeare. As a result of the pervasive influence of Shakespeare in the film, Dutta concludes that Shakespeare remains the true protagonist in *Shakespeare Wallah*.

Translation and Issues of Language and Politics in Regional Shakespeares

T.S. Satyanath, in "Mapping Shakespearean Translations in Indian Literatures," argues for the need to see theatre as a potential platform for discursive exchanges between a play, its audience, theatre artists, playwrights and the subsequent discussions. As the discussions and debates pertaining to the performance continue in print, conversations and mass media that includes scripto-centric, phono-centric and body-centric representations, the theatrical public sphere may be considered, Satyanath states, as one of the most effective public spheres for the communication and circulation of ideas. Theatre as a public sphere is actually a modification of the public sphere theory from a focus on the political accomplishment of a single economic class to a potential situation or an institution in which diverse aesthetic and social epistemologies are present simultaneously.

Sayantan Roy Moulick and Sandip Debnath in "'Murmuring your Praise': Shakespearean Echoes in Early Bangla Drama" present a comparative analysis of the texts *Kirttibilash* (1852) by Jogindro Chandro Gupto and *Bhanumoti Chittobilash* (1853) by Hurro Chunder Ghose as emblematic of the covert and overt reception of Shakespeare in early modern Bengal and explore how these works reacted to, manipulated or resisted the ideological content of British literary education. Any cultural transaction occupies a "third space," they argue. Roy Moulick and Debnath's essay traces the "absent presence" of Shakespeare in Jogindro Chandro Gupto's *Kirttibilash* and closely examines Ghose's adaptation of Shakespeare's *Merchant of Venice* to unravel the said discursive paradigm. While the preface to Ghose's play reveals the author's bardolatry, it also avows a "heterodiegetic transposition"/"transculturation" of Shakespeare "to suit the native taste." On the other hand, the preface to Gupto's play reveals not only his reverence for Shakespeare, but also his defence of the Western mode of dramatic traditions.

Jatindra K. Nayak in "A Future Without Shakespeare" looks at an Odia translation of fourteen of Charles and Mary Lamb's twenty tales of Shakespeare published in 1977. The translator, a teacher of English literature, seeks to place his decision to translate the tales in the context of the changing role of English in India after independence and explores the possibility of Shakespeare being ousted from the English syllabus. He perceives his translation as more than a mere linguistic effort and presents it as a way of keeping the readers' interest alive in Shakespeare, as and when English will be reduced to a mere tool of communication. He goes a step further and visualizes a new role for English teachers in India who can enrich Indian literatures through their knowledge of English literature. Thus, his meditations on a future without Shakespeare open new ways of looking at using Shakespeare to vitalize local cultures.

Identity and the Politics of Language

Preti Taneja in "Does Shakespeare's Text Even Matter?" considers whether Shakespeare's text will cease to matter as audiences with no familiarity with the plays watch them in languages they do not understand, languages "other" to Shakespeare's revered idiom. "Does this in itself matter?" she asks. By examining how the translations were effected and presented in the Globe festival of 2012 which featured thirty-seven plays in as many languages, and through an analysis of audience and critical response, Taneja exposes some of the underlying politics of perception that still surround cross-cultural approaches to Shakespeare's text. The alchemical space, the space between original text and translation, where text meets performance, such attitudes, she argues, are challenged. As fresh linguistic and cultural understandings are forged, the text itself is both subverted and renewed. Paradoxically, even as its importance seems to disintegrate, it endures through endless permutations.

Naina Dey in "Utpal Dutt and *Macbeth* Translated" looks at the issues involved in Dutt's translation of *Macbeth* into Bengali and whether changes were wrought for the sake of stageworthiness or political ideology. Dey states that Bengal's preoccupation with Shakespeare's plays is nothing new considering that Indian universities ran Honours and Masters courses in English literature well before Britain, with Shakespeare as staple fare.

Utpal Dutt's *Macbeth* was staged on 27 September 1975, by People's Little Theatre, exactly three months after the Emergency of 26 June 1975, at Robindra Shodon in Calcutta as a cultural retaliation against the erstwhile Congress regime under Indira Gandhi. Dey's essay examines all the stage directions and end notes incorporated by Dutt in his translation of *Macbeth,* directions and notes that indicate specific movements, emotions, locations and language for the actors of his group. She poses questions about the presence of these directions—are they related to Dutt's political convictions, to the unstable and repressive political conditions of the times, to his minute and scholarly knowledge of Shakespeare or to all of the above?

Shakespeare and Indian Icons

Radha Chakravarty in "Tagore and Shakespeare: A Fraught Relationship" explores the complex relationship between the two. Rabindranath Tagore's complex relationship with Shakespeare, from his early translation of *Macbeth* to his later pronouncements on life and literature, raises larger contextual and theoretical issues. These issues range from questions of stagecraft (such as the use of backdrops and stage props) to literary matters such as characterization or the author's bid for "impersonality" and to broader socio-political arguments about the relationship between the cultures of the East and the West. At every stage, the evolution of his attitude to Shakespeare charts Tagore's internal struggle to construct and establish his own creative identity.

Himani Kapoor in "Mapping Shakespeare and Kalidasa: Early Indian Translations" argues that this comparison became the site for the intersection of colonial modernity and Indian tradition. Kapoor maps the processes of negotiating Shakespeare and Kalidasa as modernity versus tradition as well as examining the hybridization attempts in Indian literary and critical representations of Shakespeare through a study of the nineteenth- and early twentieth-century translations and criticisms. Kapoor argues that contrary to European modernism that was opposed to realism, Indian modernism opposed traditionality. It is the attempt to negotiate this conflict, she opines, that appears to be at the centre of translating Shakespeare and Kalidasa. Kapoor states that the nineteenth and early twentieth centuries were crucial eras for both the reception of Shakespeare as well as Kalidasa for Indian literary scholars and translators. The use of medieval verse, songs and contemporary prose were common elements seen in the translations of both. Moreover, the hybridization attempted in the Shakespearean drama by the Indian translators and drama companies (chiefly the Parsi theatre) is also noteworthy. Being itinerant performing groups, the play-production companies had to cater to the constantly changing and divergent sensibilities of the audience and, hence, the plays had to be perpetually indigenized, reformed and re-interpreted for Indian audiences consisting mostly of average, everyday folk. This entire process, Kapoor attests, could be looked at as an attempt at negotiating Indian tradition and Western modernity.

As can be seen from the discussion above, this volume is an important intervention on Shakespeare studies in India, discussing the author's presence on the Indian stage and screen and in visual culture, the icon's habitation in translation and adaptation, and his omnipresence in both regional Indian literatures and the diaspora. The co-existence of a confident, even cheeky adaptation of Shakespeare's works, be it onstage in *Piya Behrupiya* or on screen in Bhardwaj's *Haider*, can be seen as an outcome of the conflicting relationship that Indian literary greats like Rabindranath Tagore have had with the works of Shakespeare. The bishwokobi of the nineteenth century, while living on in Odia and Kannada translations, has become indigenized as the Kalidasa of the West and the public sphere of performance makes this apparent. The reverence and irreverence, in equal share, that Indian cultural forms have for Shakespeare, live on in productions in the diaspora and in India's engagement with Shakespeare as the English writer is redeployed and reinvented in as many ways as there exist cultural variations in India. Shakespeare is a site that makes possible the celebration in India of the local and the regional, the particular and the minute and the heterogeneous and the remote, as opposed to the mainstream, the homogeneous and the readily accessible. From the murmur of praise we now move to the shout of adaptation. This all but silences the Shakespearean source text in the clamour of music, dance, local language and identity politics and indigenous folk theatre forms in illustration, in translation, on stage and on screen.

Notes

1. Thus, in one of the early receptions of Shakespeare in Bengal carried in this volume, renaming Hamlet as Hemlat is not a mere act of domestication, but also making the familiar foreign, in that the particle "lat" evokes "*laat* sahib," not just as in the technical title in the vernacular of the English head of a region, but also as the derogatory term in Bengali referring to an Indian one who parades and postures as an Englishman.

2. See Gauri Vishwanathan, *Masks of Conquest: Literary Study and British Rule in India* (1989; repr., London: Faber and Faber, 1990) and Jyotsna Singh, "Different Shakespeares: The Bard in Colonial/Postcolonial India," *Theatre Journal* 41, no. 4 (1989): 445–58.

3. See Ania Loomba, *Gender, Race, Renaissance Drama* (1989; repr., Delhi: Oxford UP, 1992) and Singh, "Different Shakespeares."

4. See "Introduction: Shakespeare in India" by Sukanta Chaudhuri in *The Shakespearean International Yearbook,* vol. 12: Special Section, "Shakespeare in India" eds. Tom Bishop and Alexander C.Y. Huang (Farnham: Ashgate, 2012), 3–6.

5. See Shormishtha Panja, "Intercultural Theatre and Shakespeare Productions in India," in *Routledge Handbook of Asian Theatre,* ed. Siyuan Lee (London: Routledge, 2016), 504–09.

6. See Panja, "Intercultural Theatre and Shakespeare Productions in India," 504–09.

7. Jyotsna Singh, "Different Shakespeares: The Bard in Colonial/Postcolonial India," *Theatre Journal* 41 no. 4 (1989): 458.

8. Jyotsna Singh, "Different Shakespeares," 447.

9. Jyotsna Singh, "Different Shakespeares," 450.

10. See Panja "Intercultural Theatre and Shakespeare Productions in India," 504–09 for a more elaborate discussion.

11. P. V. Rajamannar, "Shakespeare in Telegu," *Indian Literature* 7, no. 1 (1964): 127–31.

12. Mohammad Hasan, "Shakespeare in Urdu," *Indian Literature* 7, no. 1(1964): 132–39.

13. See Shormishtha Panja, "Shakespeare on the Indian Stage: Resistance, Recalcitrance, Recuperation," in *Transnational Exchange in Early Modern Theater,* eds. Robert Henke and Eric Nicholson (Aldershot: Ashgate, 2008), 215–24.

14. See Chandravan C. Mehta, "Shakespeare and the Gujarati Stage," *Indian Literature* 7, no. 1 (1964): 41–50 and Panja, "Intercultural Theatre and Shakespeare Productions in India," 504–09.

15. See Panja, "Intercultural Theatre and Shakespeare Productions in India," 504–09.

16. See Panja, "Shakespeare on the Indian Stage," 215–24.

17. See Panja, "Shakespeare on the Indian Stage," 215–24 and Panja, "Intercultural Theatre and Shakespeare Productions in India," 504–09.

18. John W.P. Phillips, "Shakespeare and the Question of Intercultural Performance," in *Shakespeare in Asia: Contemporary Performance*, eds. Dennis Kennedy and Yong Li Lan (Cambridge: Cambridge UP, 2010), 249–50.

19. See Panja, "Intercultural Theatre and Shakespeare Productions in India," 504–09.

20. See Shormishtha Panja, "Lebedeff, Kendal, Dutt: Three Travellers on the Indian Stage," in *Transnational Mobilities in Early Modern Theater*, eds. Robert Henke and Eric Nicholson (Farnham, Surrey and Burlington, Vermont: Ashgate, 2014), 245–61 for a detailed discussion of the contribution of Utpal Dutt.

21. See Jyotsna Singh, "Different Shakespeares," 455.

22. See Nandini and Pradipta Bhattacharya, "A Weapon of Change: Interview with Utpal Dutt," *Sunday*, 3 November 1985, quoted by Singh, "Different Shakespeares," 454.

23. See Rustom Bharucha, *Rehearsals for Revolution: The Political Theatre of Bengal* (Honolulu: University of Hawaii Press, 1983), 242–43.

24. See Shormishtha Panja, "Not Black and White but Shades of Grey: Shakespeare in India," in *Shakespeare Without English: The Reception of Shakespeare in Non-Anglophone Countries*, eds. Sukanta Chaudhuri and Chee Seng Lim (New Delhi: Pearson Longman, 2006), 102–16, for a detailed discussion of this particular adaptation.

25. Nidhi Gupta, "A Masala-tinged Poem, Sung to Perfection," *Sunday Guardian*, 2 September 2012.

26. See W.B. Worthen, "Drama, Performativity and Performance," *PMLA* 113, no. 5 (October 1998): 1093–1107 and Phillips, "Shakespeare and the Question of Intercultural Performance," 234–52. See also Panja, "Intercultural Theatre and Shakespeare Productions in India," 504–09.

27. See Poonam Trivedi and Dennis Bartholomeusz, eds., *India's Shakespeare: Translation, Interpretation and Performance* (Delhi: Dorling Kindersley, 2005,) largely based on papers presented at an international conference organized by the Shakespeare Society of India and the Department of English, University of Delhi, in 1998; Sukanta Chaudhuri and Chee Sen Lim, eds., *Shakespeare Without English: The Reception of Shakespeare in Non-Anglophone Countries* (Delhi: Dorling Kindersley, 2006); and *The Shakespearean International Yearbook*, vol. 12: Special Section, "Shakespeare in India," eds. Tom Bishop and Alexander C.Y. Huang (Farnham: Ashgate, 2012).

Shakespeare and Indian Visual Culture

2

"To Confine the Illimitable"
Visual and Verbal Narratives in Two Bengali Retellings of Shakespeare[1]

Shormishtha Panja

I

In this essay I shall examine the illustrations in two Bengali retellings of Shakespeare's plays. I argue that on the one hand the illustrations express the debates about the new woman and a new notion of romantic love in Bengal, both of which stem in part from Shakespeare's influence, and on the other hand the visual narrative of the illustrations has its own identity at times independent of the verbal text, a narrative that critiques the notion of the non-contingent, acultural and eternal value of Shakespeare.

Elsewhere I have discussed in detail the strong presence of Shakespeare in colonial Bengal, both on the page and on the stage, and how Shakespeare was used as a gentle tool for subjugation and the enforcement of a certain ideology by the colonial rulers.[2] I shall not go over the same terrain once again here. Suffice it to say that English literature was not just used to create colonial administrators and docile subjects: certain Bengalis found in it inspiration to launch reform movements within Bengal addressing matters of religion and education, including women's education and marriage. Nineteenth-century Bengali literature heavyweights like Bankim Chandra Chattopadhyay (Chatterjee) who wrote his first novel in English (*Rajmohan's Wife*) read Shakespeare with enthusiasm, but more of that later. Shakespeare's heroines obviously made a great impression on the Bengali imagination: in the second

volume of the 1896 Rakshit translation that I shall examine, many
of the retellings of Shakespeare's plays are named after the heroines
rather than the actual titles of the plays or their Bengali equivalent.
For example, *The Winter's Tale* is titled "Hermione," *The Taming of
the Shrew* "Katherine," and *The Tempest* "Miranda." The education of
the Bengali woman in modernity was on the agenda of the nineteenth-
century Bengali *bhodrolok*—the word means not just "gentleman" but
carries within it connotations of civility, courtesy, respectability and
bourgeois gentility. Partha Chatterjee and Tanika Sarkar have observed
that many affluent, middle-class Bengali men wanted their wives to be
educated. They were enamoured of the concept of the companionate
marriage, knowledge of which came from the West, in part, no doubt,
from English literature.[3] One can draw a parallel with the Lambs' Preface
to *Tales from Shakespeare,* most of which was apparently written by
Mary Lamb, where they exhort young British boys to read selections of
the plays aloud to their sisters who did not have the benefit of accessing
their fathers' libraries as early as their brothers:

> For young ladies too, it has been the intention chiefly to write; because boys
> being generally permitted the use of their fathers' libraries at a much earlier
> age than girls are, they frequently have the best scenes of Shakespeare by
> heart before their sisters are permitted to look into this manly book; and,
> therefore, instead of recommending these Tales to the perusal of young
> gentlemen who can read them so much better in the originals, their kind
> assistance is rather requested in explaining to their sisters such parts as are
> hardest for them to understand: and when they have helped them to get
> over the difficulties, then perhaps they will read to them (carefully selecting
> what is proper for a young sister's ear) some passage which has pleased
> them in one of these stories, in the very words of the scene from which it
> is taken; and it is hoped they will find that the beautiful extracts, the select
> passages, they may choose to give their sisters in this way will be much
> better relished and understood from their having some notion of the general
> story from one of these imperfect abridgments;[4]

II

The first of the two books that I shall discuss is simply called *Shakespeare*
Part 1 (with an introduction, the date missing and a brief *atmakatha* or
account of the author/translator and an account of Shakespeare's life)
translated by Haran Chandra Rakshit, published by Sri Bipin Bihari

Rakshit, Mojilpur, 24 Parganas, (now a part of Kolkata) in c.1896 (four volumes published between 1896 and 1902). Its price is ₹1.25. The illustrator's name is not mentioned. Part 1 has 242 pages and 21 illustrations. There is no frontispiece and no captions for the illustrations. Some illustrations are vertical, like the verbal text, others horizontal, so that one has to turn the book around in order to get a view. Part 1 contains the following works, the titles written in Bengali and English: *Otello* [sic], *Merchant of Venice, Romeo and Juliet, Pericles, Twelfth Night, Timon of Athens, Cymbeline* and *King Lear. The Merchant of Venice* has one illustration, a line drawing. *Romeo and Juliet* has three illustrations, all part of a page, none full page. The illustrations are not half-tone but they are finely drawn.

I shall discuss two of the illustrations for *Romeo and Juliet* given in the first volume by Rakshit.

The second illustration, occupying part of a page, is on page 90 (Figure 2.1). It shows Romeo kissing Juliet under an arch. Trees and a building form the backdrop. The architecture, with the arch and the design of the moulding, is completely Indian. Romeo kisses Juliet ardently, if somewhat clumsily, as he is leaving, clambering over the balcony. The illustration comes exactly at the point in the story when Romeo leaves Juliet after they have spent a night together. Juliet's hair is loose, a sign of the passion that the two have just shared—whereas in the earlier illustration it had been tied in a decorous bun—and she seems to kiss him back just as enthusiastically, although the illustrator depicts only her back. From this illustration it is evident that this is not a book meant for young Bengali readers in the nineteenth century. The resemblance is to Ford Madox Brown's 1867 painting of Romeo and Juliet on the balcony with Romeo ardently kissing Juliet's neck rather than to the restrained and decorous illustration Arthur Rackham provides for *Lambs' Tales from Shakespeare* with the caption "At the cell of Friar Lawrence" where the two lovers merely join hands and gaze at one another, with Friar Lawrence as vigilant chaperone. Note how the Bengali illustration spills out of the frame. Rackham's illustrations always have a border around them, differentiating the spaces of verbal and visual very distinctly. In Rakshit's book, however, the flowers in a vase on the floor and the drapery swell out of the picture frame on to the printed page, mirroring the sway of Juliet's body. Perhaps this is the artist's way of emphasizing the tumultuous passion of the two protagonists.

The third illustration, again part of a page, on page 102, depicts Juliet sprawled on Romeo's sleeping body (Figure 2.2). She has just killed herself. There is a figure at the back carrying a staff, the friar. There

Figure 2.1

Romeo and Juliet illustration, *Shakespeare Pratham Bhag o Ditiya Bhag* Sri Haran
Chandra Rakshit, Mojilpur, 24 Parganas, Poush, 1303

Source: Bangiya Sahitya Parisad, Kolkata.

is an erotic abandon in the two bodies plastered on one another, again
emphasizing the fact that illustrations give one a clue to the target audience
of the book. This illustration does not coincide with the verbal text that
talks about Romeo and Paris's duel. The significance of this is that the

Figure 2.2

Romeo and Juliet illustration, *Shakespeare Pratham Bhag o Ditiya Bhag* Sri Haran Chandra Rakshit, Mojilpur, 24 Parganas, Poush, 1303

Source: Bangiya Sahitya Parisad, Kolkata.

ending of the story of the star-crossed lovers is probably already known to most of the Indian readers.

However, where does this passionate young girl come from and how does the illustrator depict her so adroitly? I should like to argue that the figure of Juliet and the depiction of the couple is, in fact, the result of long debates about the nature of women and of romantic love (*prem*) in nineteenth-century Bengal. Let us take the woman question first, by looking at two essays by Bankim. In his essay *"Prachina O Nobina"* (the woman of old and the new woman) Bankim writes wittily of the new woman who has emerged in Bengal as a result of colonial rule.[5] While the *"Purush probhu stree dashi"* (man the master, woman the slave) ethos of the old age has been replaced by opportunities for education for women, it has also led to the idleness of the nobina; as a result of their sloth their children are neglected and their houses unkempt. An even more grave crime is their change of religious affiliation. Does the prachina's religion of *pativrata* (the wife's devoted worship of the husband) still exist? "But is that still the case," asks Bankim rhetorically, swiftly disclaiming, "Such questions cannot be answered easily."[6] He says he has nothing against education and praises its powers of demystification: it sifts the true from the false in matters of religion. But what of incomplete education, asks Bankim. It reveals the frailties of religion, but not its strengths. The irony and humour of this essay does not entirely conceal the underlying tone of sadness and wistfulness. Bankim feels a real sense of bereavement at the disappearance of the prachina who so willingly surrendered her own hopes on the altar of her lord and husband and her children's well-being.

Where does Bankim find a true pativrata? Let us turn to another essay by Bankim, "Shakuntala, Miranda *ebong* Desdemona" (1875). Here, in Shakespeare, Bankim finds his true pativrata. He praises Desdemona's fidelity to her husband, unchanged through insults, violence and death, calling her a true pativrata, even more so than Kalidasa's heroine who publicly criticizes her husband. Miranda's frank and spontaneous nature is also praised by Bankim. Bankim opines that, for the most part, Shakuntala's feelings have to be wrung out of her; they are expressed only by signs. Miranda, however, openly expresses her thoughts and is curious about the world around her. Like Desdemona, she is never shy: "I might call him/A thing divine; for nothing natural/I ever saw so noble"[7] she says after she glimpses Ferdinand.[8] Desdemona is equally forthright about her physical needs: "If I be left behind,/A moth of peace, and he go to the war,/The rites for which I love him are bereft me"[9] (these specific lines from Shakespeare are not quoted by Bankim, but he would have them in mind). Bankim implies that Shakespeare's heroines may provide a new model for Bengali women—a new kind of nobina who assimilates Western influences in a positive way.

Bankim in this essay also hints at a new kind of language that would give expression to this new woman who would combine Miranda's candour with Desdemona's selfless devotion. In this essay Bankim is advocating a style of writing hitherto unknown in Bengali, a style that he recognized in Shakespeare, a style that plumbs characters, particularly those of women, to their depths: while Shakuntala was a garden, Desdemona, in the complexity and profundity of her characterization, is an ocean. It was Tagore who nuanced the portrayal of the new woman suggested by Bankim even further by introducing Binodini in *Chokher Bali* (1903,) a woman who combines the virtues of the prachina and the nobina but who also has agency and boldly expresses her own sexuality despite being a widow (something that Bankim hinted at in "Shakuntala, Miranda *ebong* Desdemona").[10] Tagore eschews practically all outward sensationalism, be it in racy plots or somewhat simplified characterization, the former being something that Bankim cannot resist in his novels. Tagore's aim is the creation of what Dipesh Chakravarty calls "interiority" that is crucial to the birth of the self-reflexive subject in the Bengali novel, a subject that acts and feels, that is an agent and not a puppet and that is not just the recipient of the gaze but observes himself/herself and others.[11] This may be related to what Tagore says in a letter written to Indira Devi Choudhurani from London in May 1913: "What people here call 'reality' is essential in writing. We in Bengal deal very little in this particular commodity—and so we neither recognize its presence nor feel its absence."[12] As Tagore boasted in a 1921 letter written to Prashanta Chandra Mahalanobis, "My own conviction is that I was the first to introduce the land of Bengal to Bengalis as a subject fit for literature—neither Michael nor Nabin Sen or Bankim did that."[13]

III

Let us now take the question of romantic love or *prem*.

The woman's question in nineteenth-century Bengal was tied up with the notion of the conjugal marriage and the related question of widow rehabilitation, either through remarriage or other means. Tanika Sarkar observes that the conjugal marriage was one of the ways in which the Bengali Babu tried to introduce an element of romance or prem into an arranged marriage. The Brahmo Marriage Act of 1873, the proposals to introduce divorce in the 1880s and the Age of Consent Act of 1891 were all indications, she argues, of the colonized subject's attempt to introduce love as a means of self-fulfillment in the private domain when the public one was the space of being browbeaten and insulted at the hands of the British.

Dipesh Chakravarty, citing Bankim's essay "Vidyapati *o* Jaidev," (Vidyapati and Jaidev) suggests that the Vaishnav model of love being either physical or spiritual as described through the poems about Radha and Krishna, Jaidev's expressing *bahiprakriti* (outward beauty, sensuality) and Vidyapati's *antaprakriti*, (spirituality/interiority,) formed an important model for Bengali literary romantic love. Arranged marriages, often between two people who hardly knew one another and with a wide disparity in age, was the norm in nineteenth-century Bengal. However, my contention is, could a love that combined the physical and the non-physical (which Bankim avows stays separate in the works of Jaidev and Vidyapati,) not be found in Shakespeare in plays such as *Romeo and Juliet*? Could not an impetus for a new discussion in Bengal about romantic heterosexual love as opposed to lust be inspired by Shakespeare's works?

It was in part through the study of Shakespeare, I argue, that this transition from stereotypical women characters to complex female characters with physical desires and a sense of agency, this notion of prem or romantic love that could combine the physical with the non-physical, were introduced in Bengali fiction. The portrayal of Romeo and Juliet in these illustrations is very much a result of the debates about the nature of love, prem, and of the new woman.

IV

The second book I discuss is called *Shakespearer golpo tragedy o comedy ekotre* (Shakespeare's stories, tragedies and comedies together) by Shri Bimal Dutta MA, published by B. Sarkar & Co. I looked at the second edition, published in 1940–45. This translation was published in the tumultuous years leading up to Indian independence in 1947, but there is no reference to this in the Preface. This is very significant. This suggests that Shakespeare is almost a Bengali author. His association with the colonial ruler in the years of greatest conflict requires no explanation or apology.

The book is of 197 pages with eight illustrations, and six half-tone and two line drawings. All the illustrations are full page illustrations. There is a frontispiece depicting Hamlet and his father's ghost. The illustrators are mentioned in the following, non-alphabetical order: Shri Shumukh Nath Mitra and Shri Ashwini Kormokar. Mitra is the superior artist; his signature is visible. Kormokar's illustrations carry only his initials, if that. The book retells the four great tragedies as well as *Romeo and Juliet* and *Julius Caesar*: All these plays are there in the Lambs' book, except *Julius Caesar*. The latter must have been included because it was part of the Indian curriculum and had also been performed on stage and in school performances. The book also contains seven comedies, of which I shall look at the illustration for *The Merchant of Venice*. The Lambs' collection has, of course, many more, retold by Mary Lamb. In the Preface, Dutta rejoices in the fact that the first edition sold so rapidly that he has now been able to publish a second in which he has corrected the errors of the first, and added an account of Shakespeare's life and the story of a new play, *Julius Caesar*, complete "with half-tone illustration." The fact that the illustration gets special mention and the fact that all the illustrations are full-page signify that Bengali authors and publishers have realized the increasing importance of illustrations to attract readers. The price, Dutta boasts, remains the same: ₹1. He mentions Charles and Mary Lamb in his Preface; he hopes that his stories will continue to be as loved as theirs. However, this is not a mere translation of *Tales from Shakespeare*. The inclusion of plays like *Julius Caesar* and the fact that Dutta does not refer to the edifying nature of Shakespeare's stories as do the Lambs ("enrichers of the fancy, strengtheners of virtue, a withdrawing from all selfish and mercenary thoughts, a lesson of all sweet and honourable thoughts and actions, to teach courtesy, benignity, generosity, humanity; for of examples, teaching these virtues, his [Shakespeare's] pages are full" as the Lambs put it in the Preface to the *Tales*) proves that this is not a slavish imitation of the Lambs' work. Dutta also states that he has used *shadhubhasha*, non-colloquial language, free of regional inflections and dialectical deviations, so that the work is accessible to all in Bengal. He claims that while the stories have been edited, in order to make them fit for young readers, no crucial events have been omitted out of sloppiness or haste. More importantly, the illustrations too are sanitized and do not have the sexual abandon of the Rakshit illustrations. Dutta mentions the fact that many others have brought out such collections and will continue to do so, but he hopes that his book will survive the test of time as has *Tales from Shakespeare*.

I want to analyze the conflicting visual and verbal narratives in this retelling. While the translation is seamless and there is no attempt to culturally annotate/inflect the English text, the illustrations tell a different story—they highlight the struggle to familiarize and own something intrinsically, even insuperably, foreign.

Let us begin with the frontispiece. As Stuart Sillars has observed, frontispieces have tremendous significance.[14] This one pulls the reader in with a startling scene. It makes a statement even before the reader has read a single line. It usurps, if temporarily, the power of the written word. In this case, it does not spoil the suspense because this is a scene that occurs very early in the play *Hamlet*. Rather, it whets the reader's appetite. The artist is Shumukh Nath Mitra.

The caption of this frontispiece is "Hamlet and his father's ghost" (Figure 2.3). The word used, the dignified *pretatma* rather than the common *bhoot*, carries the suggestion of an unquiet spirit, a spirit in search of something. The page is divided vertically into black and white. Hamlet, clean-shaven, is clothed in a hat, a cloak held by a brooch, hose, and there is a faint suggestion of a ruff at the throat: there is an effort to create a quasi-Elizabethan costume. He carries a sword. There is a vague

Figure 2.3

Hamlet and his Father's Ghost illustration, *Shakespearer Golpo, Tragedy o Comedy Ekotre* Sri Bimal Dutta, B. Sarkar & Co., 15 College Square, Calcutta, 2nd Sanskaran, Magh 1347

Source: Bangiya Sahitya Parisad, Kolkata.

outline of sandals (not appropriate, given the location or time—it is as if the artist's exhausted imagination finally gave up creating culturally appropriate clothing when it came to the footwear). The ghost is a very interesting figure. It is the same size as Hamlet; it seems to have the same right to space as a living being. It does not hover in the background as if unsure of its welcome. It wears a conical cap, meant to suggest a helmet perhaps. Its eyes stare upwards; it does not make eye contact with Hamlet. Hamlet looks at the ghost but the ghost looks upward. It has luxuriant whiskers and a windblown beard. Its torso seems bare. Its right hand is crossed over its chest—perhaps signifying its own truthfulness? The shoes that it wears are the common Indian *nagra*. It wears no armour, apart from the headgear, which is a significant departure from the text. The ghost's genitalia are not illustrated proving that this is a sanitized edition that children can safely read, unlike the erotic abandon of Romeo and Juliet in the Rakshit illustrations. The ghost is a spectral figure in a tradition very different from the one to which Bengali readers are accustomed. If one looks at the ghosts in Bengali folk tales and children's tales one sees that they are invariably hideous creatures. One may recall the creature in Dakshina Ranjan Mitra Majumdar's enormously popular collection of folk tales, *Thakurmar Jhuli* (Grandma's Bag, *c*. 1907). The ghost poses a real challenge to Mitra. It has made a deep impression on his imagination. Mitra is trying to create something otherworldly without necessarily following details in the text (e.g., the ghost wears no armour) or borrowing from the Indian tradition. Between the two figures is a building, but not a castle; it is an oriental building with a minaret and a dome.

The illustration for *The Merchant of Venice*, the last one that I shall examine, is also a full-page one (Figure 2.4). It is by the same artist: Shumukh Nath Mitra. It is on the right side of the page, depicts the trial scene and carries the caption, "*Ore yehudi darao aaro kichu baki achche*" (wait, Jew, there's something else). The illustration runs concurrent with the text. It intensifies the reader's pleasure: she sees the illustration right when she is reading about the trial. It also depicts a pivotal moment in the trial. Portia and Shylock dominate the scene as protagonist and antagonist. The other figures hover behind them. Shylock, with white hair, beard and a big mole, dressed in a dark habit with an embroidered border, a brooch and a belt, and his money pouch suspended at his waist, has his knife out and is about to clutch Antonio in order to extract his pound of flesh. The purse indicates not just his profession or his attachment to wealth but hints that he is about to lose all. Antonio wears an ornate knee-length tunic with puffed and embroidered sleeves, very similar to the Elizabethan knights in their jousting costumes. His hand covers his face. In the play Antonio is stoic; here, the illustrator employs a dramatic gesture that would appeal to the Bengali readers' fondness for emotional display as something appropriate to the situation. Unlike Shylock and Antonio, Portia, arm dramatically outstretched and holding a paper, is dressed in a light-coloured cap, rather

Figure 2.4

Merchant of Venice Trial Scene illustration, *Shakespearer Golpo, Tragedy o Comedy Ekotre* Sri Bimal Dutta, B. Sarkar & Co., 15 College Square, Calcutta, 2nd Sanskaran, Magh 1347

Source: Bangiya Sahitya Parisad, Kolkata.

like a beret, and a gown. The most interesting feature of the illustration is not the figures, however. At the centre of the illustration is a picture of the Madonna and Child, presumably a painting hanging in the court. Mitra imaginatively and economically refers through this painting, entirely his own creation and not mentioned in the Shakespeare text, to the option of mercy that has been offered to Shylock and which he rejects.[15] In other words, the story of *Merchant of Venice* is so familiar to Mitra, unlike the story and setting of *Hamlet*, that he can refer to events or speeches that do not occur in the scene he chooses to illustrate. In this essay I have analyzed how illustrations in two Bengali retellings of Shakespeare reflect the age and concerns of the age, the debates about the nature and portrayal of women and of romantic love current in nineteenth-century Bengal. I have also discussed the tension between the verbal and visual narratives, and how in their mixture of Western and Indian details in costume, prop and gesture, the illustrators express their conflicting attitude towards Shakespeare, a figure at once familiar and alien. If one looks closely at the illustrations, I argue, the notion of the universal Shakespeare, Shakespeare the bishwokobi (world poet) in the Bengali imagination, is challenged. We can see that Charles Lamb's fears about the illustrations of Shakespeare vainly trying "to confine the illimitable"[16] are actually unfounded. Rather than limiting Shakespeare, the illustrations open up new vistas of interpretation.

Notes

1. After seeing the Boydell Shakespeare Gallery, Charles Lamb wrote to Samuel Rogers on 21 December 1833, "What injury did not Boydell's Shakespeare Gallery do me with Shakespeare. To have…light-headed Fuseli's Shakespeare…deaf-headed Reynolds' Shakespeare, instead of my and everybody's Shakespeare. To be tied down to an authentic face of Juliet!.... To confine the illimitable!" (In his works, vol. vii, 1903–04). William Jaggard, *Shakespeare Bibliography: A Dictionary of Every Known Issue of the Writings of our National Poet and of Recorded Opinion Thereon in the English Language* (Stratford upon Avon: Shakespeare P, MCMXI, 1911), 187.

2. See Shormistha Panja, "Shakespeare on the Indian Stage: Resistance, Recalcitrance, Recuperation," in *Transnational Exchange in Early Modern Theater*, eds. Robert Henke and Eric Nicholson (Aldershot: Ashgate, 2008), 215–224 and "'In Search of a Local Habitation and a name': Illustrations in 19th and 20th Century Bengali Prose Retellings of Shakespeare," in *The Shakespearean International Yearbook 13: Special Section, Macbeth*, ed. Stuart Sillars (Farnham: Ashgate, 2013), 35–52. In the latter essay, I confine my discussion to the *Macbeth* illustrations in Rakshit and Dutta.

3. See Partha Chatterjee, *The Nation and its Fragments: Colonial and Postcolonial Histories* (Princeton: Princeton UP, 1993) and Tanika Sarkar, *Hindu Wife, Hindu Nation: Community, Religion and Cultural Nationalism* (Delhi: Permanent Black, 2001).

4. See preface to Charles and Mary Lamb's *Tales from Shakespeare*, accessed 7 March 2016, http://www.gutenberg.org/files/573/573-h/573-h.htm

5. All translations from this essay are mine.

6. Bankim Chandra Chatterjee, "Prachina o Nobina," in *Bankim Rachanabali*, vol. 2. (Kolkata: Tuli Kolom, 1986), 249–254.

7. *Tempest* 1.2. 420–422.
8. All quotations from Shakespeare are from *The Norton Shakespeare* eds. Stephen Greenblatt et al. (New York and London: Norton, 1997).
9. *Othello* 1.3. 255–257.
10. See Shormishtha Panja, "Rabindranath Tagore's *Chokher Bali*: the New Woman, Conjugality and the Heterogeneity of Home," in *Signifying the Self: Women and Literature,* eds. Malashri Lal, Shormishtha Panja and Sumanyu Satpathy (2004; repr., Delhi: Macmillan, 2007), 211–225 for a detailed discussion of Bankim and Tagore's *Chokher Bali* in light of the new thoughts about the role and identity of women in Bengal.
11. See Dipesh Chakrabarty, "Witness to Suffering: Domestic Cruelty and the Birth of the Modern Subject in Bengal," in *Questions of Modernity,* ed. Timothy Mitchell (Minneapolis: University of Minnesota Press, 2000), 49–86.
12. Krishna Dutta and Andrew Robinson, eds. *Selected Letters of Rabindranath Tagore* (Cambridge: Cambridge University Press, 1997).
13. See Dutta and Robinson, *Selected Letters*. Perhaps Tagore is pigeonholing Bankim as the writer of historical romances like *Anondomoth,* the Indian Walter Scott as he was popularly known, rather than the Bankim of domestic novels like *Bishobrikkho* (Poison Tree), *Krishnokanter Will* (Krishnokanto's Will) and *Indira*. Partha Chatterjee in his essay "Two Poets and Death: On Civil and Political Society in the Non-Christian World," in *Questions of Modernity*, ed. Timothy Mitchell (Minneapolis: U of Minnesota P, 2000), 35–48 refers to Tagore's speech at a condolence meeting held after Bankim's death. There he says that as a result of the presence of Europe both "external conditions and subjective feelings were undergoing a change" in Bengal (Chatterjee, "Two Poets," 36). Hence there is nothing artificial about mourning the death of a poet in public as Nabinchandra Sen had protested there was. Earlier Bengal was a "domestic society" but now that society was flooded by "the public" (Chatterjee, "Two Poets," 37).
14. See Stuart Sillars, *The Illustrated Shakespeare 1709–1875* (Cambridge: Cambridge UP, 2008) and his excellent essay on frontispieces, "Image, Word, Authority in the Early Modern Frontispiece" in *Word, Image, Text: Studies in Literary and Visual Culture*, eds. Shormishtha Panja, Shirshendu Chakrabarti and Christel R. Devadawson (Delhi: Orient Blackswan, 2009), 10–21. I am indebted to Sillars' insights on how to interpret the significance of illustrations.
15. Again, one could compare Rackham's less ambitious illustration of Shylock sharpening his knife on his shoe, with the caption, "Shylock was sharpening a long knife." Shylock leans against a table, his brow is furrowed in concentration, and not, one imagines, in anxiety at the prospect of extracting a pound of flesh. Rackham dresses him in the usual Jewish garb, including a cap. He has a beard and a moustache. The illustration, like the monochromatic colouring, is somewhat bland and lacking in drama. Rackham does not even bother to make the pattern of the floor tiles perfectly symmetrical.
15. See note 1.

Contemporary Shakespeare Performance On stage in India and the Diaspora

3
Urban Histories and Vernacular Shakespeares in Bengal
Kolkatar Hamlet, Hemlat and Hamlet 2011

Paromita Chakravarti

Bibhash Chakraborty's production of the Bengali *Hamlet* in 2011 is set in a city pub on Park Street, the leisure artery of Kolkata.[1] The framing narrative tells us that the pub is reopening after being closed for "extremist activities" and Shakespeare's *Hamlet* would be performed to celebrate the occasion. The performance would be dedicated to the memory of a man, a friend of the pub owner, who was killed in a police "encounter" several years ago. This reference immediately sets up an intertextual dialogue between Chakraborty's play and a vernacular theatrical tradition of Calcutta *Hamlet*s as it does with the imaginary of violent clashes between the police and youth on Kolkata streets that remains an intrinsic part of our urban history. This essay will explore how Shakespeare's *Hamlet* is repeatedly used to map a political cartography of Kolkata from the 1970s to contemporary times through a reading of Asit Basu's *Kolkatar Hamlet* (1973), Bratya Basu's *Hemlat* (2006) and Bibhash Chakraborty's *Hamlet* (2011).

The reference to the "encounter" in Chakraborty's *Hamlet* evokes Utpal Dutt's[2] essay "Dharmatollar *Hamlet*" first published in 1971,[3] at the peak of the Naxal movement,[4] when Kolkata had turned into a nightmare city, a *Duswapner Nagari* (the title of a Dutt play). The essay starts with a scene that had become chillingly common in the contemporary urbanscape—that of an unclaimed corpse of a young man on the streets, dumped by a police vehicle, after an early morning "encounter." However, the setting of "Dharmatollar *Hamlet*" evokes an earlier history of colonial Kolkata, that of the Indian National Army (INA) uprising of the mid-1940s against the British.[5] By connecting a familiar city sight with an older event, Dutt locates the contemporary in a longer *durée*, opening up a vista of the city's revolutionary past condensed in a moment of intense theatricality. The dramatic description of the crowd surrounding the corpse, bullets being fired in the distance, trams burning and slogans being hurled against the British Empire leads to Japenda's (Dutt's fictional mouthpiece) ruminations about revolutionary theatre, class struggle and Shakespeare's plays. Japenda admits that the young men in radical movements may be misguided, yet they were the heroes of the contemporary people's theatre. Plays cannot be written nor songs sung about parliamentarians—these cultural expressions need armed revolutionaries like these reckless boys, such as a Surya Sen or a Subhash Bose.[6] Characterizing Hamlet as representing the protest of a generation, Japenda analyzes the play as an image of class conflict in which the hero emerges as a youthful voice of resistance against the greed and corruption of a rising bourgeoisie. Criticizing the schematic oversimplification of contemporary Left theatre, Japenda advises his young interlocutor to learn from the classics—"The proletarian hero should be today's Hamlet. He is at once simple yet complex. He is complex in his many personal failings and in his uncompromising hatred for the class enemy he is simple, upright and without doubts."[7] Japenda's injunction inaugurates a tradition of Bengali *Hamlet*s in which the protagonist is represented as a revolutionary who dies a martyr's death in an often doomed political struggle. He is an action hero rather than the brooding intellectual uneasy with killing, familiar in the Western tradition of criticism and performance.

Politicizing *Hamlet*: The Soviet Tradition

Japenda/Dutt's political reading of *Hamlet* appears to be indebted to the socialist performative and critical tradition, particularly the Soviet one. In the cold war era, when India and the Soviet Union shared strategic and cultural ties, there was a regular exchange of ideas between the Left intellectuals of Bengal and the Russian writers and artists.

Shakespeare was a well-loved playwright in pre-revolutionary Russia and *Hamlet* remained a popular play. In 1912, Stanislavsky and Gordon

Craig collaborated in a landmark *Hamlet* production for the Moscow Art theatre. In the Stalinist regime, there was an unofficial moratorium on the play for over a decade. This was triggered by Stalin's casual remark in 1941 questioning the performance of the play by the Moscow Art Theatre. Although Stalin's reservations against the play were never publicized, they perhaps had to do with a distrust of an over critical, self-doubting and indecisive hero unable to take action.[8] This seemed particularly unsuited to the mood of the early 1940s when Russian people needed to be inspired with courage and optimism in the war against Fascism.[9]

However, the silencing of the play rendered it more political.[10] Performances of *Hamlet* were revived in 1953 after Stalin's death. The most significant among these was Grigori Kozintsev's 1954 production at the Pushkin Theatre in Leningrad using Boris Pasternak's translation. It was a bold play that underlined Hamlet's role as a questioning and resistant figure; he became a "'brother-in-arms,'...in the arduous and tortuous efforts of Soviet society to liquidate Stalinism."[11]

In subsequent productions, Hamlet represented the voice of youthful conscience in a society rendered corrupt and impotent by the tyrannical exercise of power. The image of Denmark as a prison became emblematic of the totalitarian state. The grand sets of Okhlopkov's 1954 operatic *Hamlet* underlined through its rattling lattices the ambience of a prison house. "The cold prison of life surrounding Hamlet has made him its prisoner, but the prisoner has become a rebel."[12]

Criticizing Laurence Olivier's 1948 *Hamlet* film for cutting "the theme of government which I find the most interesting,"[13] Kozintsev in his 1964 film on the play emphasized the sense of coercive menace that Elsinore represents. Through it he tried to capture the surveillance and secret police haunted air of Stalinist Russia.

> The architecture of Elsinore-not walls, but ears in the walls. There are doors so that one can eavesdrop behind them, windows so that one can spy through them. The guards are the walls. Every sound gives birth to echoes, reverberations, whispers, rustling.... Fear...is the very air of Elsinore.[14]

Through the 1960s and 1970s, directors like Voldemar Panso and Yuri Lyubimov staged *Hamlet* in the tradition of Brechtian political theatre.[15] While Panso's *Hamlet* portrayed characters as pawns of a larger political machine, Lyubimov's 1971 production at the Moscow Taganka theatre was marked by the symbolic "curtain" that dominated the stage, representing a power which, like a giant spider's web, captured victims in its net.[16] In this production, Vladimir Vysotsky, an iconic rebellious poet-intellectual, played Hamlet. His persona brought to the role great courage, impatience with mediocrity and corruption, as well as his preference for an "honest death" over a "tortured life."[17] This tradition of politicizing the play helped to reverse the charges of "Hamletism," of self-regarding navel-gazing that the play and protagonist were once accused of.

The Russian critical and performative practice of portraying Hamlet as a young rebel under an authoritarian regime appears to have influenced the Bengali *Hamlet* adaptations under discussion. This could be seen as the impulse behind locating *Hamlet* within political events like the INA or the Naxal uprisings and on the bloodied streets of 1940s or 1970s Kolkata.

"Comrade Hamlet":[18] Asit Basu's *Kolkatar Hamlet*

Japenda's advice at the end of Dutt's essay, "Dharmatollar *Hamlet*," "Learn from the classics, learn from what you have seen in Dharmatolla—the bloody conflict of two unnatural hatreds and lying between them, a young man's corpse. This is the basic structure of great dramatic creations,"[19] rings through subsequent Bengali re-workings of *Hamlet*. This is echoed most clearly in Asit Basu's 1973 *Kolkatar Hamlet* that opens with two drunks discovering a bullet ridden corpse lying on the street. Kolkata is more a protagonist than a setting of the play that uses the figure of Hamlet to read and map the city at a moment of historical crisis and rupture.

The unclaimed body of a dead theatre activist on the streets becomes a marker of the city's decay and indifference. Even before the drunks come on stage, Basu's play presents a city photographer. In a city where people are afraid to bear witness, the camera becomes the objective recorder of events. The photographer promises the audience a play on Kolkata, as captured by his impersonal camera:

> Kolkata...Kolkata...the controversial metropolis or the necropolis or...the great, dead city of rallies! Here festivals are celebrated in homes in complete indifference even while there is a corpse lying on the road. Here the streets are steeped in sweat, blood, bullets, sticks and bombs. Right next to them are *pujas*, loudspeakers, subscriptions, concerts, films and culture! Here there is hunger, famine and epidemic, the obscene excesses of the lords of wealth. Kolkata holds all these things together in her breast—my city does not flinch, is numb to pain. Strange, strange, strange, my city Kolkata.[20,21]

While the 1970s represent a unique moment, stark in its unprecedented violence both perpetrated by and against the youth, yet (as Dutt suggests in "Dharmatollar *Hamlet*") the events evoke earlier episodes in the city's history. The photographer's description of Kolkata stokes memories of the Bengal famine of 1943 in which two million people died of hunger and the corpses were piled on the city streets. Bijan Bhattacharya's *Nabanno* (the harvest festival) produced by the Indian People's Theatre under the direction of Sombhu Mitra in 1944 is set against this backdrop and depicts the debilitating effects of the famine on peasants who were driven by hunger to migrate to Kolkata. The play portrays their subhuman existence, huddled in pavements, begging for starch, scavenging in rubbish heaps and dying of starvation while the urban rich continue their lavish celebrations of weddings and feasts. The play maps a cityscape of stark class contrasts defined by indifference. It is this refusal of the denizens to take responsibility for the city's dead or to bear witness to its brutalities that the photographer chastises.[22]

The corpse rises from the dead and introduces himself as the socially committed theatre director, Avi, to the numb audience of Kolkata. The scene shifts in flashback to a rehearsal room with Avi's troupe practicing a play on Abhimanyu's death. The story from the Mahabharata about the unjust killing of Arjuna's young and valiant son through the intrigue of family elders sets the scene for what follows.[23] The play merges into contemporary political reality as a youth, a present day Abhimanyu, rushes into the rehearsal space, chased by the police. He briefly finds shelter among the actors before he is forced out and killed. This young Naxalite, referred to as "the boy," one among the throng of Kolkata's anonymous dead, is then replaced by a surrogate from the repertory of classic theatre—Shakespeare's Hamlet whose entry has been carefully prepared for. Earlier in the play, Avi remarks that he felt he was living in a prison: "Like Hamlet: Denmark is a prison." When Falguni, an actor, says that it was not Claudius' Denmark, "the boy" responds: "Claudiuses are spread across all times and spaces. Poor Laertes and Hamlet were fighting and killing each other. They didn't even know that their weapons had been poisoned by Claudius."[24] Later, when "the boy" is hunted down and killed, Avi remarks that he has left for "the undiscovered country from whose bourn no man returns."[25,26]

These references materialize in the figure of Hamlet who appears in the rehearsal room, declaring he is a changeless and deathless twenty-six-year-old, renewed through every performance of Shakespeare's play, familiar with every language in which *Hamlet* is acted. He takes on an iconic role in the play, representing youthful rebellion against a corrupt and entrenched political order. He also stands for the inevitable failures of such movements by Hamlets armed only with stage foils, destined to die. As such he is like Abhimanyu and the Naxal revolutionary killed in a street encounter. At the end of the play when Hamlet reassures Avi that he should die in peace knowing that Hamlet would carry forth his legacy and avenge his death (speaking the lines from the play: "From this time forth, my thoughts be bloody...or nothing worth"[27]), Avi grips him by the collar and remonstrates:

> Fool! You have been moving in the labyrinth of "bloody thoughts" for four hundred years but have learnt nothing...the air is heavy with the smell of gunpowder, firearms are roaring through the breeze, the ground beneath the feet is slippery with blood...the Claudiuses have smeared Denmark with "bloody deeds"...now take that sword from its scabbard.... Can't you see that it...has no sharpness?

To this grand and dramatic call for action, Hamlet responds somewhat poignantly: "It never had any sharpness. It is a stage foil! How can I win a battle with that?"[28] These lines point towards both the tragic ineffectuality of radical movements as well as that of the theatre.

Hovering between a real character and symbolic figure made up of familiar lines from Shakespeare's play, Hamlet enters Basu's play announcing his literary existence "Words, words, words/Like a whore unpacking my heart with words" and conflating two separate utterances of Hamlet.[29] He claims a place in the revolutionary struggles in the theatre and politics of 1970s Kolkata since he sees his city and Denmark within the same continuum of political corruption:[30] "I see that Denmark has spread like an infectious sore all over the world! I can see that your country is my Denmark!"[31,32]

This universalizing impulse runs through Basu's play, connecting the political imperative of committed Left theatre to classic texts and authors like the Mahabharata and *Cyrano de Bergerac*, and Shakespeare and Calderon. This also links Basu's play with Japenda's injunction to follow the classics in "Dharmatollar *Hamlet*." But the mapping of Denmark onto contemporary Kolkata does not dilute the specificity of the latter. It emerges as a powerful presence intensified through the appropriation of Shakespeare's play. "Kolkatar *Hamlet*" ends by returning to the opening scene of the city streets. The actors have now been evicted from their rehearsal space and have turned into an itinerant theatre company like the roaming players in *Hamlet*. Avi remarks with satisfaction that now truly the actors have become one with the homeless of history—refugees and exiles. Only an unhoused theatre can serve the needs of the deprived proletariat.[33]

Avi's lines about actors turned outdoors are also a comment on the contemporary experiments of moving out of the proscenium stage into the public arena. Dutt's Jatra productions[34] and Badal Sircar's third-theatre movement emphasized the need to perform in unconventional spaces, such as the streets or in courtyards (Sircar's *Anganmanch*), on makeshift wooden platforms, so that ordinary people who could not afford to buy theatre tickets could be involved.[35] The new socially committed, democratic theatre movement of 1970s Kolkata sought to take plays to the masses by making the urban public spaces their stage. Both the spectacle of political violence and the drama of protest were being played out on Kolkata's streets.

Kolkatar Hamlet closes as it began with images of the city, but with images of a revolutionary rally and of a beggar-child dancing in joy. The final lines of the play are "Kolkata—beautiful, Kolkata-ugly, Kolkata—revolutionary Kolkata."[36] Kolkata claims and indigenizes Hamlet. Hamlet speaks not only Bangla but also a colloquial street Bangla full of expletives. He expostulates when Avi is shocked: "Am I not a man just because I am the poet's invention? Did I eat poetry? Did I float verses in response to nature's call?...Scoundrel!" He characterizes his creator as: "The great bard...my creator...was he any less roguish? Such scoundrels were rare in Elizabethan London! If he wasn't such a rogue he would not have survived in that London." Hamlet redefines vulgarity for Avi: "In such a time and environment would not refined words sound vulgar? The Claudiuses have completely wiped poetry out of the world."[37]

Basu's play distances itself from the tradition of liberal, humanist bardolatry and commits itself to a material and revolutionary engagement with Shakespeare inspired by the socialist tradition of political readings of the plays.

Hamlet, Class Struggle and the City

Within the Bengali vernacular tradition, Utpal Dutt's readings helped to establish Shakespeare as a playwright with a radical social consciousness. In his essay, "*Hamlet* and Popularity,"[38] Dutt characterizes Shakespeare's play as a study of class struggle that reflects the social mobility and volatility of London society at a historical juncture when the aristocracy was being threatened by the rising bourgeoisie. His essay dwells on contemporary accounts of London that describe it as a flashpoint of conflict between the old property owning feudal classes and the emerging mercantile nouveau riche who spent their newly acquired money on leisure, at taverns, brothels and theatres. The latter class was supported by the new working class, the young apprentices from workshops, who made up the bulk of the theatre audience. They were perceived as a source of social disorder since they rioted and attacked aristocrats frequently. The new urban milieu of London provided public spaces and recreational sites that brought diverse people together leading to new hostilities. Dutt reads Hamlet's lines as referring to this phenomenon:

> By the Lord, Horatio, these three years I have taken note of it, the age is grown so picked, that the toe of the peasant comes so near the heel of our courtier, he galls his kibe.[39]

Dutt's reading of *Hamlet* locates it within the city, characterized as a space that crystallizes class struggle. In *The Country and the City*, Williams shows how the nineteenth-century city is an expression of industrial capital and the relationships it produces. In *The Condition of the Working Class in England* (1844, 1892), a detailed document of nineteenth-century London and the state of its poor, Engels was "among the first to see the modern city as a social and physical consequence of capitalism: built and living in its modes." In the *Communist Manifesto*, Marx and Engels observe "the bourgeoisie had subjected the country to the rule of the towns…has created enormous cities."[40] Although these comments apply to the nineteenth-century city, Williams indicates that London, from the seventeenth century, manifests signs of a proto-capitalist city, divided internally.[41] Dutt's reading of *Hamlet* in the context of contemporary urban-class struggle, reflects this view that is echoed in the relocation of the play in a class-riven Kolkata in Basu's *Kolkatar Hamlet*.

More recently, writing about the contemporary political relevance of his production of *Hamlet* in 2011, in the aftermath of a regime change in West Bengal, Bibhash Chakraborty mentions the lines "Denmark is a prison" (quoted in *Kolkatar Hamlet*) and "the toe of the peasant comes so near the heel of the courtier" (cited in "*Hamlet* and Popularity") as embodying the central theme of class struggle. These lines, emphasized by earlier Bengali readings and productions of *Hamlet* to underline the political content of the play, locates Chakraborty's production firmly within that trajectory. Chakraborty justifies his choice of a city pub for the setting of his play by quoting from Dutt's essay, "*Hamlet* and Popularity" to reiterate that Shakespeare was not an ivory tower poet; he was to be found frequently, as Thomas Fuller mentions, at the Mermaid Tavern in London, mixing with the common people.[42] This characterization of Shakespeare lies on an intertextual continuum connecting Dutt's essay with Basu's and Chakraborty's *Hamlet* productions. These texts project an image of the city, whether sixteenth-century London or the Kolkata of the 1940s, 1970s or the twenty-first century, as a melting pot of the classes. This image becomes inseparable from the vernacular Marxist tradition of reading the play politically, as a document of class strife. This could be seen as a rationale for the urbanization of the vernacular *Hamlet*s.

Hemlat: The Prince of Garanhata (2006)

Bratya Basu's *Hemlat: The Prince of Garanhata* (2006) also draws from the vernacular tradition of deploying Shakespeare's *Hamlet* for a Marxist socio-political critique established by Dutt. However, staged 34 years after *Kolkatar Hamlet*, *Hemlat* is about the failure of revolution. More specifically it registers a disappointment with Left politics in Bengal that has manifested itself through an entrenched and often undemocratic single-party rule for over three decades.[43] Bratya's play also articulates a very different Kolkata of the twenty-first century and its crises. His protagonist, Hemlat, is not only identified with, but constituted by the city and its landmarks. In an interview to Ravishankar Bal, Bratya describes Hemlat as:

> He is not Hamlet dressed in a cloak…I have seen him, chatted with him, spent time in the coffee-house with him…in Khalasitolla…in the local train…in the neighbourhood tea shop. With him, a rough youth of the third front politics, I have spent time on the footpaths of College Street.[44]

Hemlat is no prince, nor is he a revolutionary. Bratya describes him: "His father may have once owned a house…But he has become marginal in today's Kolkata";[45]

> He smokes bidis, loves his girlfriend, reads pornography, masturbates, again goes to attend the neighbourhood puja but cannot quite communicate… he thinks he should join a science club, or he feels such an anarchy within him that he feels he must fight against the institution called father, the institution called society, the institution called imposture through which we live our lives.[46]

Hemlat's very name, as Ananda Lal observes, dislocates Shakespeare's Hamlet: "The vowel dyslexia gives Hamlet's name the right downwardly mobile Bengali inflection."[47]

Hemlat represents a lumpenized, lower-middle-class protagonist from Garanhata, a neighbourhood in the older, northern fringes of the city that is rapidly, unevenly and even grotesquely transforming through the development boom unleashed by economic liberalization. Pankaj, one of the night guards who open the play remarks: "And this bloody North Kolkata of ours. Madmen everywhere. Every three houses you will get a madman and a Pepsi shop."[48]

Madness, displaced from Ophelia and Hamlet and manifested instead in Hamlet's catatonic father who is killed by his uncle, Kadu (Claudius), for refusing to sign away his claim on the ancestral home, becomes the trope of both protest and impotence. A collector of tram tickets, a regular at the Mitra Café where he ate brain chops before catching a matinee at Mitra or Radha,[49] Hamlet's father's traits appear as eccentricities because they cling to a lost North Kolkata world. His ineffectual attempt to hold on to his house is an aspect of this madness that he has to die for.

Bratya's play takes an unforgiving look at a colonial city in decline, brokering away its own history and its old buildings to a criminal land mafia, hand in glove with the government. This is a Kolkata which is fast disappearing under the inscriptions of development. In the previously mentioned interview, Ravishankar points out to Bratya: "We don't see Hemlat's Kolkata in the Kolkata that we move around in. Each city bears a hidden city within it." And later in the same interview, Ravishankar notes that *Hemlat* reminded him of Orhan Pamuk's novel, *Istanbul*, which is the author's autobiography but also what Pamuk has called the "memoirs of a city."[50]

Satrajit Sarkar, sound designer of the play observes:

> Reading the play inevitably conjured up the sound of conch shells, dogs barking, pigeons calling, mosquitoes and flies, trains, the raucous cheerfulness of the burning Ghats—this was an ancient, mossy smelling dinosaur like city; its ribs, nails, loves, torn kites turning in the skyline—Garanhata, Nimtolla, Chitpur railyard."[51]

It is this hidden Kolkata of crumbling mansions and decaying families that the play tries to visualize through the ghost-haunted neighbourhood of Garanhata, unable to keep pace with a fast changing, modernizing city.

There is no place for Garanhata's disaffected, unemployed youth in the new Kolkata of malls and multiplexes being constructed on the ruins of its past. Struggling for a foothold in the new city, Pankaj, Bimal, Lachhu and their friends try their hand at odd jobs. Rendered redundant in the new city, Garanhata's youth do not rebel but keep themselves busy conciliating the local councilor to keep on the right side of the ruling Left party or distracting themselves by planning celebrations at the local club. The city's once illustrious cultural legacy is now reduced to tokenistic observations of Tagore's and Nazrul's birthdays while people only wish to listen to Bollywood songs.[52]

Popular Hindi film songs work as a leitmotif in the play. Their anodyne effect paralyses other aesthetic or even political expressions. "Kajra re"[53] is used as the new anthem of this world. Some scenes end with this music accompanied by a surreal procession of six dwarfs in a band party, raising slogans that evoke familiar Left government policies like abolishing English in primary school or censoring "*apasanskriti*" (anti-culture) that was once ironically represented by the very Bollywood music that has now become the pervasive cultural expression.

Music and dialogues from the 1970s and 1980s Bollywood films provide Hemlat's father's ghost with a vehicle through which he expresses himself and his passion for cinema. These histrionic, oft-quoted lines convey the ambience of a universe determined and mediated by Hindi films, in which language has broken down and it is impossible to speak except through dated, clichéd and kitschy dialogues. These lines also create an ironic distance between the world of Garanhata and Shakespeare's *Hamlet* in a spirit of post-modern pastiche. Bratya explains that he attempts a "deconstruction" of *Hamlet* in which the Prince of Denmark finds a parodic incarnation in Hemlat the prince of Garanhata, a puny hero of dwarfish times who lives in the shadow of a past glory in a decaying house and a dying city.[54]

Hemlat reads a cheap Bengali translation of "The great bard Shakespeare's creation *Hamlet*—edited and translated by Sri Bidhubhushan BA BL. The correct version." Although the neighbourhood boys initially mistake this book to be pornography, they later use it to stage the mousetrap play. Harish (Horatio) opens the performance by saying "Today we present to you, the great bard's creation, *Hamlet*…if this incident were to happen in our times and in our lane." The play is then hurriedly stopped by Kadu who recognizes the narrative as his own story. Sukhen, the local Left councilor warns: "I will stop it all…. I will finish you silently. I won't touch your body, hit or beat you up—but I will annihilate you through silence." Earlier in the play, Sukhen warns Hemlat not to try his humour on him: "If we win [the elections], then I will make sure that we stick cello tape on your mouth for the coming 50 years."[55]

These lines indicate the distance between Dutt's and Basu's readings of *Hamlet* and the political environment of *Hemlat* in which the protagonist feels "protest or revenge…are merely elements of recreation…the middle class's masturbation." In a world emptied of meaningful political action, Hemlat can only avenge himself through self-slaughter. There are no possibilities of rebellion or of dying in a fatal "encounter" with a hostile state power. Bratya says: "[W]e have seen a different politics in the 70's…now they will kill you at home…the most modern form of killing—the definition of the politics of silencing…this is what Sukhen wanted to say."[56]

Hemlat and his world is reminiscent of T.S. Eliot's Prufrock who is not Prince Hamlet, nor was meant to be.[57] Although the poetic voice denies the identification, the poem powerfully establishes Hamlet within a context of a modern, urban sensibility, of the *flâneur*, the disengaged and politically alienated persona that Prufrock represents. This could be seen as an alternative tradition connecting Hamlet with the city that seeps into *Hemlat*.

In the politically paralysed world of Garanhata haunted by the muffled groans of a dog in pain,[58] self-slaughter, which Shakespeare's Hamlet contemplates and abandons, seems to be the only possible destiny. While for his father, discovered with valium pills in his pocket, even suicide is aborted, Hemlat at least successfully kills himself. In the face of this bleakness, his posthumous assertion that his unborn child will undo the failures of his ancestors seems like an imposed ending. In *Hamlet*, the old king represents the possibilities of a lost world of heroism, while Fortinbras who takes over the kingdom promises order and freedom from a usurper's rule. But in Bratya's play an unbroken line of impotence and ineffectuality connects the generations. There is little to justify Hemlat's hope that his heir will have a different life. Like the musty, mossy Kolkata collapsing under the new city, he too will go under.

Much more powerful than this forced cheerfulness of the resolution is the flashback image of the young Hemlat with Shefali (Ophelia) in the closing moments of the play as they sit by the Ganges, watching ships sail by. The scene is charged with nostalgia for an idyll suffused with the innocence and promise of early romance. The semi-urban riverscape has a pastoral feel even as it evokes the memories of an older Kolkata, the old port city frequented by big ships, connected to the wide world through its international trading links. The young Hemlat dreams of becoming a sailor and standing on the deck of one of these sailing ships, in the midst of a typhoon. This was a city that once allowed these visions of growth and adventure. A longer vista opens up, taking the play out of the confines of a ghost-haunted, claustrophobic Garanhata that turns cannibalistically, incestuously and suicidally upon itself as it is besieged by an emerging global metropolis. This visual release is much more effective in dispelling the gloom of Hemlat's suicide than the unconvincing, redemptive possibilities presented by his unborn son.

The river scene also uncovers the pastoral fantasy underlying Shakespeare's play. Hamlet's anxiety of the unweeded garden that Denmark has become[59] evokes the image of a lost Eden, represented by the orchard where Hamlet's father was poisoned.[60] Just beyond the prison that is Elsinore is a flowery idyll and an old world memorialized in Ophelia's ballads, proverbs and flower-giving rituals.[61] Gertrude's elegy describing Ophelia's watery death as she sat under willows making floral garlands,[62] dislocates the play of intrigue and male revenge and shows us an alternative universe. The subterranean pastoral dream in *Hamlet* makes it particularly difficult to understand why the Bengali theatrical tradition repeatedly locates the play in and identifies with the city.

Gail Kern Paster observes how both Biblical and classical myths about the founding of cities refer to an originary moment of fratricide. The Old Testament speaks of the establishment of the first city by Cain who killed his brother Abel, took his wife as his own and had a son with her. He called the city Enoch after his son. The classical myth of Romulus' murder of his brother Remus and the establishment of Rome underlines the connection between fratricide and the city.[63] Could the moment of fratricide in Shakespeare's *Hamlet* be thought of as the moment of the city? The betrayal of old Hamlet by Claudius and Gertrude signifies the loss of a pastoral world of innocence and integrity. Does the loss of Eden facilitate the movement into the anonymous, artificial, and uncaring space of the city? In both Dutt's and Basu's reading of *Hamlet*, the nightmarish and indifferent Kolkata represents a city fatally divided by civil strife, turning against its own and devouring its young like Chronos. Yet there is also hope of renewal and change through the sacrifices of the young. But Hemlat's city fails to gesture towards any hope and the tone of the play is primarily elegiac, not revolutionary.

Afterword: Shakespeare Films and the City

It is significant to remember that the urbanizing of *Hamlet* is not peculiar to Bengali theatre. Michael Almereyda's film, *Hamlet 2000*, situates the play in the ruthless yet dazzling corporate world of Manhattan, New York.

Claudius is the CEO of "Denmark Corporation," which is based in the plush Hotel Elsinore where battles are replaced by corporate takeovers. The film is suffused in the ambience of New York—the lights of Times Square, the neon signs and glass panes of street shops, and the skyscraper-lined horizon.

Although there are no urban *Hamlets*, Indian cinematic negotiations with Shakespeare's *Macbeth* and *King Lear* have helped to forge a sense of the urban—a heightened consciousness of the layered history, feel and politics of specific Indian cities. In Bharadwaj's *Maqbool* (*Macbeth*), for instance, contemporary Mumbai with its street wars, *dargahs* and crime-torn coastline emerges as a central protagonist.

The Kolkata setting defines the very mode of Shakespearean negotiation in two English-language Indian films based on *King Lear*. In both films, the city, the erstwhile capital of the empire, becomes the site of memorializing the colonial legacy of the Bard. In Aparna Sen's *36 Chowringhee Lane*, a paean to the disappearing Anglo Indian community of Kolkata, the elderly protagonist, a Lear surrogate, recites lines from the play as she sits facing the Victoria Memorial, the symbol of the Raj.

Rituparno Ghosh's *The Last Lear* pays an elegiac tribute to the dying English theatre (and its Shakespearean repertory) of Calcutta through the reminiscences of Harry, an ageing actor who lives in the past and dreams of playing King Lear. Ghosh also pays a tribute to Utpal Dutt whose 1985 Bengali play *Aajker Shahjahan* (today's Shahjahan) provides the plot of *Last Lear*. But Ghosh's nostalgic bardolatry is at odds with Dutt's Marxist indigenizations of Shakespeare that inspired the Bengali tradition of politicized and urbanized *Hamlets*.

In Ghosh's film, Kolkata is viewed from a distance, on a CCTV screen in Harry's secluded room in an elegant mansion. A recluse, Harry and his protégé, observe the moving city, like "God's spies,"[64] reminding us of the opening sequence of Satyajit Ray's iconic film *Charulata*[65] where the bored nineteenth-century housewife looks down through opera glasses at the city streets and the passers-by, a life she cannot be a part of. Ghosh's *Last Lear evokes* a relationship with both Shakespeare and Kolkata that is framed by colonial nostalgia. Ensconced in his colonial mansion, Harry refuses to acknowledge the humdrum rhythms of contemporary Kolkata as an aspect of his own life or of his passion for Shakespeare. This relationship is very different from the one established in the Bengali theatrical tradition previously discussed. Although cinema is more able to capture the sights and smells of the urbanscape, it is in Dutt's evocation of

Dharmatolla, or Basu's bloodied city streets, or Bratya's Garanhata that Kolkata comes alive in its everyday reality and its layered histories rather than in the distant and alienating recreation of the city in *The Last Lear*; inflected by Harry's contempt for modern Kolkata and the philistinism of its busy crowds who fail to recognize Shakespearean lines. While *Hamlet* is relocated in contemporary Kolkata in Dutt's essays and Basu's and Bratya's plays, within a continuum of the history of social revolutions or their failures, Ghosh, despite the homage he pays to the theatre and to Dutt, fails to imagine Shakespeare beyond his location in an imperialist archive, preserved in the memory of an ageing actor in a colonial house, shunning the contamination by the presence and the present of the city.

Notes

1. The colonial name of the city of Calcutta was changed by the government in 2001 to Kolkata to approximate more closely with the original vernacular name of one of the villages that constituted the city, Kolikaataa.
2. Utpal Dutt (1929–93), was one of India's greatest Shakespeareans who had extensively translated Shakespeare's plays into Bengali, produced, directed and acted in Shakespearean drama and authored critical essays on Shakespeare.
3. Utpal Dutt, "*Dharmatollar* Hamlet," in *Gadya Sangraha* (Collected Prose), vol.1, ed. Samik Bandyopadhyay (Kolkata: Dey's Publishing, 2004), 129–38. (Henceforth referred to as *DH*). First published in 1971 as part of the collection of essays called "*Japen da Japenjaa*" (What Japenda chants).
4. The Naxal Movement in Bengal derives its name from Naxalbari, the place where a section of the Communist Party of India (Marxist) initiated an armed uprising in 1967 to redistribute land to the landless. The Mao Zedong-inspired radical movement soon spread among the urban youth of Kolkata who undertook a violent struggle to overthrow the bourgeois government. The young naxalites "annihilated" authority figures and fought pitched battles with the police on the streets of Kolkata. The government retaliated with repressive measures that included widespread arrests, torture and killings of undertrials in staged "encounters." By 1972, the movement had been fragmented and severely suppressed.
5. An uprising of the Royal Indian Navy started in February 1946 off the Bombay port in response to the trial of the Indian National Army (INA) officers who had fought against the British during the Second World War under the leadership of Subhash Chandra Bose. Accused of "waging war against the King Emperor," these officers were seen as revolutionaries by their countrymen. Their stories incited a mutiny in the Royal Indian Navy off Bombay that became a full-fledged anti-British movement and spread to other ports like Karachi and Kolkata. The two main nationalist political parties, The Muslim League and the Congress, disowned, opposed and even helped to quell this popular and spontaneous rebellion since their leadership was not part of its planning or execution.

However, the Communist Party of India supported it since they saw it as a revolt of the masses, led by ordinary naval ratings, dispensing with the leadership of bourgeois political parties, against imperialist powers. Dutt's play, *Kallol* (1965), celebrates the naval revolt.

6. *DH*, 137. Surya Sen was a Bengali freedom fighter who led the Chittagong armoury raid in 1930. Subhash Bose, a nationalist leader who quit the moderate line of the Congress to wage war against the British by joining the Axis powers in World War II. With Japanese support he organized the INA to fight for Indian independence. These names of nationalist revolutionaries underline the connection that Dutt is trying to make between them and the naxalites.

7. *DH*, 135.

8. As early as 1860, Ivan Turgenev, in his essay "Hamlet and Don Quixote" had criticized the "Hamletism" or blind self-absorption of the Russian intelligentsia. In post-revolutionary Russia it became synonymous with a narcissistic posturing of politically alienated individuals antagonistic to the needs of collectivization and action in the new social order. See Spencer Golub, "Between the Curtain and the Grave: The Taganka in the *Hamlet* Gulag," in *Foreign Shakespeare: Contemporary Performance*, ed. Dennis Kennedy (Cambridge: Cambridge University Press, 1993), 158–179.

9. See Arthur Mendel, "Hamlet and Soviet Humanism," *Slavic Review* 30, no. 4, (December 1971): 734.

10. In his novel, *Bend Sinister*, written after he arrived in the USA in 1940, Nabokov recounts the struggles of a freethinking philosopher in a dictatorial state. The novel contains a chapter describing the trials of a translator who must produce a state sponsored version of *Hamlet* under a totalitarian regime.

11. Mendel, "Hamlet and Soviet Humanism," 734.

12. Okhlopkov, "Producer's Exposition of *Hamlet*" quoted in Golub, "Between the Curtain and the Grave," 158.

13. Quoted in Mendel, "Hamlet and Soviet Humanism," 736.

14. Quoted by Mendel from Kozintsev's collection of essays called *William Shakespeare: Our Contemporary*, 735. In his essay, "*Hamlet* of the Mid-century" on the 1956 production of the play in Cracow, weeks after the XXth Congress of the Soviet Communist Party, Jan Kott notes the emphasis on surveillance. See *Shakespeare Our Contemporary* (London: Methuen, 1965), 49.

15. Kott quotes from Brecht's analysis of *Hamlet* in his *Little Organum* and concludes: "Brecht was writing his *Little Organum* in the years of the Second World War…Brecht was sensitive to the politics in *Hamlet*. He was more interested in the sequences of historical conflict than in the depths of the Prince of Denmarks' soul." See *Shakespeare Our Contemporary*, 54.

16. See Golub, "Between the Curtain and the Grave," 172–73.

17. See Golub, "Between the Curtain and the Grave," 162.

18. The interlocutor in "*Dharmatollar Hamlet*," in response to Japenda's Marxist reading of the play, mockingly calls Hamlet "Comrade Hamlet."

19. Dutt, "Dharmatollar *Hamlet*," 138.

20. Asit Basu, *Kolkatar Hamlet* (Kolkata: *Jaatiyo Sahitya Parishad*, 1989), 70. The text will henceforth be referred to as *KH*.

21. The interlocutor in "*Dharmatollar Hamlet*," in response to Japenda's Marxist reading of the play, mockingly calls Hamlet "Comrade Hamlet."

22. The interlocutor in *"Dharmatollar Hamlet,"* in response to Japenda's Marxist reading of the play, mockingly calls Hamlet "Comrade Hamlet."

23. According to the Hindu epic, Mahabharata, Abhimanyu was the son of Arjuna, the greatest warrior among the Pandavas, one of the central protagonists of the epic. Abhimanyu was Krishna's nephew and was married to Uttara. Having inherited his father's fighting abilities he posed a major threat to the enemy in the battle of Kurukshetra. Only 16 years old, he was brutally and unjustly killed on the 13th day of the battle through a conspiracy of the war elders who trapped him in a labyrinth from which he could not escape. Abhimanyu's son Parikshit, born after his father's death was the sole heir to the Pandava Empire and succeeded Yudhishthira to the throne.

24. *KH*, 93.

25. *KH*, 97.

26. The interlocutor in *"Dharmatollar Hamlet,"* in response to Japenda's Marxist reading of the play, mockingly calls Hamlet "Comrade Hamlet."

27. *Hamlet* 4.4. 65–88. See *Hamlet*, ed. Harold Jenkins, The Arden Shakespeare (London and New York: Routledge, 1992; first published in 1982 by Methuen). These lines are cited in "Dharmatollar *Hamlet*" as marking Hamlet's battle cry, his challenge to the old and corrupt aristocracy to what in effect may be seen as a class war. *DH*, 131.

28. *KH*, 142.

29. *Hamlet*, 2.2.192 and 2.2.581 (*Arden*, ed. Harold Jenkins).

30. Kott notes the centrality of Hamlet's comment on Denmark as a prison in Left political readings of the play. He describes the 1956 Cracow production: "It was a political drama par excellence. 'Something is rotten in the state of Denmark'—was the first chord of Hamlet's new meaning. And then the dead sound of the words, 'Denmark's a prison', three times repeated." See *Shakespeare Our Contemporary*, 48.

31. *"Shakespeare Our Contemporary,"* 101.

32. The interlocutor in *"Dharmatollar Hamlet,"* in response to Japenda's Marxist reading of the play, mockingly calls Hamlet "Comrade Hamlet."

33. The interlocutor in *"Dharmatollar Hamlet,"* in response to Japenda's Marxist reading of the play, mockingly calls Hamlet "Comrade Hamlet."

34. Jatra, a folk theatre form popular in rural Bengal and Orissa from the sixteenth century originally presented mythological tales through a melodramatic, bombastic and didactic mode. These open-air often all-night performances would be watched by large audiences. Realizing the reach of the Jatra form, Utpal Dutt deployed it for his revolutionary theatre of the masses. After 1968 when Dutt's group moved out of the Minerva theatre, he started staging street plays and poster plays in public spaces. He also started working on political plays written as Jatra and produced and acted in them, forming his own Jatra troupe. He also produced Shakespearean plays like *Romeo and Juliet* (*Bhuli Nai Priya*) in the Jatra mode for a rural audience.

35. Badal Sircar (1925–2011) was a noted experimental dramatist and director known for his politically radical plays in the 1970s. His best known play, "Ebong Indrajit" written in 1963 portrayed the angst of post-independence urban youth. His theatre company, Shatabdi, set up in 1976, marked a break with the commercial theatre, taking up the experimental techniques of alternative or "third theatre" to take plays out of the proscenium stage into public spaces like streets and parks or courtyards (Anganmanch). Sircar's plays used minimal props, lighting and costumes and improvized dialogue to communicate directly with their audience. He wrote over 50

plays that include well known plays like "Ebong Indrajit," "Baasi Khabor" "Bhoma" and others.

36. *KH*, 144.

37. *KH*, 102.

38. *"Hamlet o Janapriyota,"* first published in 1964 in a collection of essays entitled "Smoking Teacup." See Utpal Dutt, *"Dharmatollar Hamlet,"* in *Gadya Sangraha* (Collected Prose), vol.1, ed. Samik Bandyopadhyay (Kolkata: Dey's Publishing, 2004; first edition, 1998), 61–67.

39. *Hamlet*, 5.1. 134–37.

40. Raymond Williams, *The Country and the City* (New York: Oxford University Press, 1973), 303.

41. Williams, *The Country and the City*, 220–21.

42. Bibhash Chakraborty, "Paanshaalaay *Hamlet*" (*Hamlet* in a Pub), in *Hamlet: A Collection of Articles on Anya Theatre Production of Hamlet* (Kolkata: Karigar, 2011), 21.

43. Here it is perhaps pertinent to point out that Bratya Basu, an academic and playwright, has been a vociferous critic of the Left government during its final years. Bratya joined the Trinamul Congress Party that replaced the 34 year long rule of the Left in West Bengal. He became minister of culture when Trinamul came to power in 2011 defeating the Left.

44. Bratya Basu, *Hemlat* (Kolkata: Patralekha, 2007), 107. The play will henceforth be referred as *HL*. The quote refers to familiar city landmarks—Khalasitola is an old Kolkata bar made famous by its association with prominent artists and poets in the 1950s; College Street is the North Calcutta road lined with book shops and academic institutions frequented by students, booksellers and intellectuals.

45. *HL*, 105.

46. *HL*, 108.

47. *HL*, 98.

48. *HL*, 13.

49. Founded in 1920 by Shushil Roy, Mitra Café in Shovabazar is an old North Kolkata eatery known for its chops and cutlets. Mitra and Radha are old cinema theatres located near Shyambazar in North Kolkata.

50. *HL*, 111.

51. *HL*, 94. Sarkar mentions the names of old North Kolkata neighbourhoods. Nimtolla is known for its cremation grounds and Chitpur for being the nerve centre of Kolkata Jatras.

52. Rabindranath Tagore (1861–1941) and Kazi Nazrul Islam (1899–1976) are iconic literary figures of Bengal whose birthdays are observed as festive occasions. Both were prolific writers of songs that are synonymous with respectable middleclass Bengali culture. Bollywood songs refer to music from popular Hindi films, considered vulgar.

53. The song is a sensual "item number" from the popular Hindi film, "Bunty aur Babli" (dir. Shaad Ali, 2005).

54. *HL*, 105.

55. *HL*, 41.

56. *HL*, 110.

57. T.S. Eliot, "The Love Song of J. Alfred Prufrock."

58. *HL*, 110.

59. 1.2. 135–37.

60. 1.5. 35–36.

61. 4.5. 22–73; 164–97.
62. 4.7. 165–89.
63. Gail, Kern Paster, *The Idea of the City in the Age of Shakespeare* (Athens: University of Georgia Press, 1985), 9–10.
64. 5.2. 8–17; William Shakespeare, *The Norton Shakespeare*, eds. Stephen Greenblatt et al (New York and London: W.W. Norton, 1986).
65. Released in 1964 Satyajit Ray's *Charulata,* the story of the life of a nineteenth-century housewife with an unfulfilling marriage was based on a Tagore short story, *Nashto Need* (The Broken Nest). The film examines Charu's brief relationship with her brother-in-law who encourages her to explore herself and start writing.

4

Shakespeare and the Re/Vision of Indian Heritage in the Postcolonial British Context

Claire Cochrane

In the summer of 2012 New Delhi came to Stratford-upon-Avon. In what is known as the Courtyard Theatre positioned barely half a mile in one direction from where Shakespeare was allegedly born, and in the other direction from where he more certainly lies buried, the audience coming to see an Indian *Much Ado About Nothing* entered foyers lavishly decorated with baskets, stalls, fabrics, bicycles and so on, all designed to evoke the sights and especially the sounds of a tourist dream of a colourful, noisy and bustling Delhi. Their ears were assailed with contemporary popular Indian music, there was the typical cacophony of vehicle horns and the occasional patron would be accosted by an exotically-garbed individual offering to find them a good hotel for the night. The front of house announcements and warnings about mobile phones were delivered in a heavily-accented Indian voice that turned out to belong to the British Asian actor, Simon Nagra, playing Dogberry.[1]

Audience members with long enough memories might have recalled another Indian Dogberry in the 1976 Royal Shakespeare Company production of *Much Ado* that the director John Barton set in a North Indian garrison town under the nineteenth-century British Raj. Then, however, in what was a much-praised production, Dogberry was played by the distinguished white English actor John Woodvine wearing brown makeup and a turban. All the members of Dogberry's watch were played by browned-up white actors. Overall, the production derived much of its emotional depth from a focus on the sense of dislocation suffered by a community of colonizers isolated in an alien setting. But as Sylvia Morris recalled in her *Shakespeare blog*, the rationale that was given for Dogberry's Indianization was that "his linguistic errors were caused by his trying to follow the alien procedures of the British Raj" and he provided a "plausible analogue to the procedural confusion of Elizabethan policemen."[2] The rationale for not casting a naturally brown Indian-heritage actor, however, was that none of sufficient acting talent could be found.[3] That voice, however, then and indeed now, also evokes other allusions to British popular culture. Again during the second half of the 1970s, a BBC Television series called *It Ain't Arf Hot Mum*, which was about a hapless group of Second World War concert party soldiers marooned in Burma, featured a comic Indian bearer, Rangi Ram. Yet again the role was played by a browned-up white actor, Simon Bates, who was admittedly Anglo-Indian by birth. Yet again the excuse for not casting an Asian actor was that no one good enough could be found.[4] More recently, however, some British Asian actors have more powerfully taken ownership of the voice for satiric effect, dangerously but effectively creating comedy out of perceived Asian stereotypes settled within British communities.

The television series *The Kumars at No 42*, set in a north London suburb, poked fun at a family of nouveau riche Asians anxiously and blatantly enquiring about the social status of their white celebrity guests while trying to deflect the embarrassment caused by "Ummi," the comedy grandmother played by Meera Syal as the incorrigible and definitely unassimilated Indian elder. Syal was one of the writers of the other series *Goodness Gracious Me*, a radio and television sketch show that explored the conflict and integration between traditional Indian culture and modern British life and successfully parodied the British from an Indian perspective—the empire laughing back if you like.[5] The British parody of Asian speech, the "Goodness Gracious Me" cod Indian accent derives in yet more popular memory from a hit song originally sung by the comic, and yet again, browned-up actor, Peter Sellers, who played an Indian doctor in the 1960 film *The Millionairess*. When, last summer, that voice reverberated round the foyers and auditorium of a Royal Shakespeare Company (RSC) theatre the sound was a multi-layered composite of both historic and insufferable patronage and subordination and, depending on your perspective, defiant reclamation. Certainly the popular appeal of Meera Syal who played Beatrice in this latest Indian *Much Ado* has in part derived from the capacity to reclaim and then exploit the cultural stereotype. Her high profile was beyond doubt the principal selling point of the production.[6]

In many respects this production, which featured an all British-Asian cast, could be regarded as a major symbolic event in the history of mainstream British theatre. The children, or many times over great grandchildren, of the empire that for so long were admitted only sporadically to the physical heart of the British Shakespeare industry had finally been invited to share in some of the spoils of the global domination of the sixteenth-century Stratford-upon-Avon playwright that had been imposed on their forefathers and foremothers two centuries earlier. On the face of it (literally) the empire was given the opportunity to play back. Moreover, unlike the African-heritage all black production of *Julius Caesar* that had been staged earlier in the season by Gregory Doran, now the new artistic director of the RSC,[7] this *Much Ado* was directed not by a white member of the male theatre establishment, but by the British Pakistani Iqbal Khan. The music was composed by the London-based, British Indian-heritage Niraj Chag whose work weaves together Indian classical influences with rhythmically complex contemporary sounds, all of which could be heard in the production.

The nomenclature I am using in relation to the groups and individuals I have been describing tends to shift rather uneasily, veering between Indian, Asian, British Asian and Indian heritage or African heritage. Iqbal Khan, I have described as British Pakistani, Niraj Chag as of Indian heritage. The reason is that the term "Asian" is immensely problematic, a fact emphasized in Poonam Trivedi's introduction to the collection of essays in *Re-playing Shakespeare in Asia*: "Asia as an entity or concept is more than a shorthand; it embodies a complex and intricate network of contiguities and distinctions, of correspondences and pluralities."[8] I do not know if it is true that the term was a bureaucratic invention of British officials in colonial East Africa in 1948 as they attempted to categorize the incoming migrants or descendants of migrants under their control.[9] But the end result in the UK context has certainly been to treat an extraordinarily diverse number of British citizens as one homogenous lump—a phrase that Meera Syal herself used in an interview not long before she played Beatrice.[10]

Let us focus briefly on Iqbal Khan and Niraj Chagis to become aware of the very different journeys that brought them to Stratford. Iqbal Khan was born in Birmingham, the industrial city in the English midlands that is also my home and birth place. His father migrated from Pakistan in the 1960s and, if the standard pattern prevailed, his mother arrived after his father had found a job. Khan has gone on record as saying his mother was illiterate that was not uncommon in those first generation migrants who came from rural areas.[11] Many who came to the heavily industrialized Birmingham in the 1960s came from the Mirpur district of Azad Kashmir and were displaced because of the building of the Mangla Dam.[12] Chag was born in Southampton, the port on the south coast of England. He has said that his parents came from India but more specifically has dedicated a composition to his grandmother who made the migration to the UK from India via Africa.[13] The chances are then that his Indian heritage has been mediated through the mass exodus imposed on East African Asians when they came to England following expulsion from Uganda and Kenya in the late 1960s—a moment of extraordinary postcolonial complexity: formerly colonized, newly-independent Black Africans pushing out of "their" countries, the descendants of the Indian indentured labourers who had been uprooted in the late nineteenth century to leave their homeland to service the needs of Empire in colonial East Africa. While in the UK, the former colonizers were increasingly appalled by the prospect of the human products of what in the rhetoric of the time appeared to be an invasion in reverse.

If I turn to the other actors in *Much Ado* it becomes clear that they too have a complex relationship with "home." Relatively few of them were born in India. Paul Bhattacharjee played Benedict and was a distinguished stage and film actor who had previously played leading roles in RSC productions including Shakespeare's disputed play *Edward III*. He was born in southern England, the son of an Indian Hindu migrant father and a Russian Jewish-heritage mother.[14] The other two older actors, Madhav Sharma who played Leonato and Ernest Ignatius who played Leonato's brother, Antonio, may be regarded as British-Asian veterans who migrated from South India—in the case of Sharma, from a Hindu Brahmin family fifty years ago to be trained at the Royal Academy of Dramatic Art.[15] Indeed I suspect Sharma would have been happy to audition for the 1976 RSC Dogberry. Meera Syal's Hindu and Sikh Punjabi parents married in Delhi but her father, who came to England to further his education, had already endured an enforced migration from Lahore following the creation of the new state of Pakistan. His daughter, however, was brought up in a mining village not far from Birmingham in what's known as the Black Country and has written about the experience of being the only brown girl amongst a white community—of living between two cultures.[16] Her natural voice is unambiguously that of an English Midlander. The same can be said for Bharti Patel who played both Margaret and Dogberry's put-upon side-kick Verges who grew up in another Midlands city, Coventry, although her actor's CV includes the ability to speak Gujarati, Punjabi and Urdu.[17]

The actress Amara Karan who played Hero is completely different. She was born in London of Sri Lankan parents who came to England from Zambia where they had been almost certainly drawn to what, under British rule, had been Northern Rhodesia and that post-independence welcomed Sri Lankan professional expertise.[18] Robert Mountford, an unlikely name for a British Asian, was brought up by adoptive parents in Birmingham but is the product of Kashmiri/Irish parentage. To play Friar Francis who became Panditji for the Hinduization of *Much Ado* he had as he put it to "work on an 'authentic' Indian voice" something that satisfied his need not to resort to that cod comic accent.[19] All the actors represented the wide spectrum of British Asianness which, as the report into the future of multi-ethnic Britain published by Lord Bhikhu Parekh in 2000 points out, ranges from Bangladeshis, Gujaratis, Pakistanis and Punjabis; between South Asians, East Asians and Chinese; and between Hindus, Muslims and Sikhs.[20] I have not begun to expand on the complications of the Asian presence in the former Caribbean colonies and how that has added to the UK demographic mix.[21]

It could be argued that Shakespeare creates his imagined cities of Venice, Vienna, Rome, Paris and so on, and modern directors often make much of the conceptual possibilities of that imaginative relocation especially through the specific periodization that introduces thematic parallels. So *Measure for Measure* is set in the Vienna of Freud, or Julius Caesar's Rome is set in the era of Mussolini or Shylock's Venice is updated to the 1930s in a grim anticipation of the Holocaust.[22] So why should not the Messina of *Much Ado About Nothing* become Delhi? As Jyotsna G. Singh pointed out in her essay "Wooing and Wedding," written for the 2012 RSC *Much Ado* programme, the directorial decision to set the production in modern-day India made perfect sense for households where servants are commonplace, arranged marriages still standard practice and a preoccupation with male honour predicated on female chastity and fidelity is still a societal norm.[23] And, of course, if this is to be an all-Asian production where better to set it than Delhi? The problem for me was that this imposed yet another cultural homogeneity on actors for whom, as I've tried to suggest, the relationship with both the city and indeed the country as "home" territory is so complex. As the effect of individual histories was smoothed out so too were other theatre histories that have been relegated to the margins. Unlike, in theory, the "real" and, thus, appropriately exotic Indians that the RSC director Tim Supple brought to the UK in 2006 to play in his celebrated multilingual production of *A Midsummer Night's Dream* that Poonam Trivedi has sharply interrogated,[24] the *Much*

Ado company seemed to me to retain their subaltern status.[25] Despite one horrifying picture in the production programme of a facially mutilated woman in Jaipur, the production lost the opportunity to probe deeper into the darkness at the heart of *Much Ado*. Indeed, press reviews commented on the excess of physical comedy designed to create the overall feel-good effect that also unnecessarily prolonged the evening in the theatre.[26]

It is really only in the last six years or so that substantial efforts have been made to research and document the history of British Asian theatre initiatives.[27] What has been marginalized in practice has also been marginalized in the historical record. So when I say that on the whole British Asian theatre-makers have steered clear of engaging with Shakespeare, more research in grass roots regional activity in particular might ultimately tell a somewhat more nuanced story. Also, of course, all British Asians who train in British drama schools are introduced to classical acting through the Western canon. However, I think I can say that for all the strength of re-visioned Shakespeare in India, which the 2013 "Revisiting Shakespeare in Indian Literature and Culture," conference was designed to celebrate, the experience of exclusion from mainstream British theatre has inevitably contributed to the tendency of British Asian theatre companies to focus on issues of contemporary political or social relevance to British Asian communities within a multicultural Britain or, where classical texts have been inscribed or adapted, they have been mainly drawn from the Indian-heritage canon. While, as postcolonials, British Asian theatre-makers still combat the lingering effects of colonial disdain or actual racism, it is understandable that Shakespeare, the British playwright most associated with the dissemination and imposition of imperial power through literary culture, might be the most obvious one to avoid. Also more positively, well-established companies such as Tamasha and Kali Theatre Company, which were both founded by women, devote a lot of their energies to the development of new British Asian playwrights and, especially in the case of Kali, of women playwrights.[28] The exception to this is Tara Arts under their long-serving artistic director Jatinder Verma.

Tara Arts was the earliest, and remains the longest-surviving British Asian theatre company. It was set up initially in response to deep trauma: the murder of a Sikh teenager, Gurdeep Singh Chaggar, in South London in June 1976—in a horrible irony a crime perpetrated just as that first Indian *Much Ado About Nothing* was playing in Stratford. The first amateur Tara production was an adaptation of Rabindranath Tagore's *Sacrifice* (*Visargan*) in Tagore's own English translation. The production was intended to offer a humanist, allegorical or symbolic response to futile violence taken from the most dignified name in modern South Asian dramatic literature and one that was already well known in Britain and, importantly, acceptable to the largely conservative Asian audiences in the community centres where the work was first shown.[29] What was to evolve over the next twenty years was an approach to theatre that very consciously engaged with the personal, ideological and aesthetic outcomes of the complexity of the British Asian migratory experience. Jatinder Verma describes himself as an East African Hindu Punjabi who was born in Dar es Salaam and arrived in Britain with his family in 1968, a matter of weeks before a new British Immigration Act effectively slammed the door on more East African Asian migrants claiming automatic rights of British citizenship. In 1996 in an essay called "Cultural Transformations," Verma pointed out just how much migration from former British colonies had transformed Britain. "Transformation," he wrote, "is for me an existential fact, rather than an objective reading of post-war British realities." Reflecting on the etymology of the word "to translate" as meaning "to bear across," he is a "translated man" literally borne across from Africa to Britain and through his parents from India to Africa. Furthermore there is the sense that he chooses to "bear across" his ideas and sensibility of theatre to another dominant sensibility. His "culture" therefore is a rag-bag mixture of Indian, African and British mixture of in contemporary Britain.[30]

The rag bag was to be translated yet again into the fully-formed concept of a distinctive theatre language dubbed "Binglish" that aimed to create a British theatre company which, and I am quoting Verma again, "is not quite British."[31] One major influence was the study of the *Natya Shastra* that offered a model of total theatre integrating music, song, non-naturalistic makeup and costume, and, in particular, the privileging of the physicality of the actor to set against the dominance of contemporary naturalism in Western theatre. Another vital component in Binglish was the inclusion of fragments of Asian languages not imposed artificially on the Binglish performance text but arising naturally from the production process. Because of the diversity of the migrant heritage, each actor had her or his own individual histories of the acquisition of English that could result in negotiations in several different languages in rehearsal—little of which were heard (usually) onstage in the final production. Moreover the Asian, English speaker will also naturally integrate native English expressions particular to the area where she or he was born and brought up.[32] As a way of thinking about the British Asian linguistic experience, Binglish responded to what the postcolonial theorist Bill Ashcroft has identified as "the syncretic and hybridised nature of post-colonial experience."[33]

It was 15 years before Tara took on Shakespeare with two relatively modest experiments in cultural fusion with *Heer and Romeo* in 1992 that united elements of *Romeo and Juliet* with Varis Shah's eighteenth-century poem "Heer and Ranjha," and then in 1994, a retelling of *The Tempest* with just two actors working with Bunraku puppets. In between, however, Verma's ambitious, intercultural and intertextually allusive adaptation of *Troilus and Cressida* with a cast of seven cross-dressed South Asian, French and Anglo-Chinese actors referenced the horrors of both the war in Bosnia and racism in East London. The simple tunic costumes blended Chinese and South Asian traditions and the Greek characters, depicted as arrogant "Western" pragmatists laying siege to the "Eastern" Trojans, wore half-masks. The Indian influence extended to music, dance, martial arts and stamping sticks and, in the narration, the *sutradhar* from Sanskrit drama who weaves the threads of the story together.[34] Despite conceding, twenty years on, that the production was "overloaded with ideas," the belief in the value of cultural difference—the loss of which appeared to be represented by the defeat of Troy—continues to be a guiding principle in Verma's approach to Shakespeare.

Arguably, the most radical Binglish inscription of Shakespeare emerged in the 1997 production of *A Midsummer Night's* Dream, the play that has "translation" in the transformative sense at its heart. Produced in collaboration with the large west London theatre, the Lyric, Hammersmith, it subsequently toured and then was revived the following year with some cast changes. The first directorial "visions of the dream" recorded in a rehearsal journal Verma published in the production programme were of "an immaculate English lawn, complete with a small rock garden trod upon by a diverse company of 'Asian, African, Caribbean, Arab and English' performers." Athens was like a modern Western city "'airy', aloof, sans music, 'tight' in emotional expression, with a rigid code of conduct and social hierarchy." The forest, however, suggested "the 'other home' that most migrants and their descendants carry in their heads; a potpourri of Africa, Asia and the Caribbean, as well as 'olde Englande'. Earthy, full of colour...carrying emotions on its sleeve."[35] The final result, scenographically, was what the theatre critic Michael Billington described as a "wild adventure playground, with climbing frames, long green pipes and funnels to indicate mossy banks, and upended, vertical floorboards to betoken trees."[36] As has been standard practice in Tara productions, the ensemble of actors was small—just nine actors each doubling and even tripling roles. The South African-born actor Vincent Ebrahim, partnered in 1997 by the black singer-actor Pauline Black, and then in 1998 by the

Anglo-Indian Shelley King, undertook what is now the conventional doubling of Theseus/Oberon and Hippolyta/Titania. Much less usually, the Egeus, Hermia–Lysander/Helena–Demetrius cluster reappeared as the "mechanicals," and all at some points played fairies. The exceptions were Puck (David Baker in 1997/Antony Bunsee in 1998) who as a trickster "messenger of the gods" operated outside the core characters, and Bottom (Nizwar Karanj throughout) whose "dream" began and ended the play. The contemporary verbal diversity of Binglish became an audible and virtuosic performance reality as the "street language" spoken by the Athenian workmen.

It was a strategy that at its best reinforced Shakespeare's dramaturgy of separate worlds united by imagination. Certainly the imaginative capacity of the audience was challenged producing, especially in 1997, a sharply-divided critical response. For those that engaged positively with the concept, however, the atmosphere of airy playfulness was both enjoyable and appropriate for the comic heart of the play. What the reviewers singled out included Oberon and Puck painting magic flowers on Titania's feet and Lysander's eyelids. They sat disdainfully blowing bubbles while the lovers were fighting and in one extraordinary moment Bottom in an ass's head of stylized ears and cords appeared on roller skates. Musically there were classical Indian rhythms, Japanese dance and New York rap.[37]

When in 2005 Verma turned his attention to *The Merchant of Venice* what one reviewer described as the pick and mix approach to cultural references in *A Midsummer Night's Dream*,[38] was set aside in favour of very specific cultural parallels with Indian history before the British colonial rule. This time the starting point was a reimagining of Venice that now became sixteenth-century Cochin in Kerala. As Verma explained in the production programme: "Not unlike Shakespeare's London, the port-city of Cochin was also a thriving trading place with dynamic communities of Christians and Jews together with the cross cultural influences that inevitably bring together East and West."[39] The production programme printed two parallel time lines comparing the history of the Jews in England with the historic relationship between Jews and Christians in South India and in particular what happened under Portuguese rule between 1502 and 1663 when the Portuguese colonizers were virulently anti-Jewish, Hindu, Muslim and non-Catholic Christians. In 1560, under the newly-established Inquisition, all were burned alive if they refused to convert.

The Tara Company of just five actors became a troupe of Indian performers converted to Christianity and presenting the play accompanied by music composed by the Keralan classically-trained V. Chandran played live on a variety of traditional instruments plus a saxophone. The costumes blended together Indian dress but with recognizable sixteenth-century Western elements. This decision was drawn from research that suggested that as a mark of Portuguese favour Indian converts could wear European dress that subsequently and with much-modification evolved into some of the key characteristics of Kathakali costume.[40] For the acting ensemble, the doubling and, in the case of Robert Mountford who played Bassanio, Arragon, Morocco and Laucelot Gobbo, and Elena Pavli who played Jessica, Solanio, Nerissa *and* the Duke of Venice, quadrupling, was a way of pointing up apparent oppositions: "opportunistic Venice versus idyllic Belmont, Christian versus Jew, Mercy versus Revenge, Thrift versus Profligacy, Light versus Darkness."[41] Antony Bunsee played Shylock and Gratiano. Shylock the Jew loves his daughter Jessica; Gratiano the Christian loves Nerissa but both are equally intolerant of each other. The actors embodied the contradictions as they switched characters. A simple empty picture frame enabled the physical opposition of different values within a kind of liminal space and became symbolically the "ring" in which the actors all had a vested interest (Figure 4.1).

The other major theme was of conversion. Shylock is forced into conversion and ruin although at least in the Cochin context he would remain unburnt. Jessica converts herself for love but remained disturbed and always the "infidel" outsider within the "idyllic" Belmont of the play world As the troupe of actor-converts reached the "happy" ending, the "reality" of what was being played out brought breakdown and distress. It was this further reality that brought the permanent state of outsiderness that is the lot of the migrant theatre-maker.

With the rise of militant Islam post 9/11 and, in the UK context in particular, after the July 2007 London bombings the translated Asian-outsider has become, if anything, more vulnerable. *The Merchant of Venice* looked at historical parallels between cultures. In 2008, Verma's production of *The Tempest*, the play which in Ania Loomba's view is the "most widely and controversially linked to issues of colonialism and race,"[42] went very bravely (and controversially) for absolutely contemporary relevance. Claudia Mayer's design set the play in a broadly Muslim-Mediterranean world with Muslim-referenced music and costuming. Most strikingly, Miranda wore a hijab with a light face veil. It was "a world of nomads and settlers, where Caliban is a settler, while Prospero and the rest remain migrants, on the move."[43] Verma took the reading of *The Tempest* as a revenge play to focus on Prospero as essentially a man obsessed with vengeance: "a man who commits

Figure 4.1

The Merchant of Venice (2005)

Source: Tara Arts.
Notes: The actors pictured are Robert Mountford and (holding the frame) Paul Rumbelow.

Figure 4.2

The Tempest (2008)

Source: Tara Arts.
Notes: The actors are Chris Jack as Ferdinand and Jessica Manley as Miranda.

terror, literally unleashes a storm." As Verma explained in his programme note, in Shakespeare's own time the prototype magician was Marlowe's Dr Faustus. But in 2008 there were other examples of "intelligent men and women who will create and support terrible ends to revenge perceived hurt." Prospero was analogous to Ayman al-Zawahiri, the surgeon who became Osama Bin Laden's right hand man, or Bilal Abdulla, the Iraqi-trained doctor who tried to blow up a London club and drove a burning jeep into Glasgow airport.[44] Hard-won knowledge put to evil ends. Robert Mountford's Prospero described in *The Sunday Times* review as a "hollow-eyed resentful magician,"[45] was impatient, irritable and controlling of his daughter in the standard manner of the stereotypical Muslim male. When Miranda declared her love for Ferdinand pulling aside her veil became a highly significant action (Figure 4.2).

The design concept focused on the physical constraints on the island—that everyone is confined: from the exiled Prospero and Miranda, to the enslaved Caliban and Ariel, and the captured ship's passengers. As Claudia Mayer put it: "No one is at home in The Tempest: the island is a place of passage where each character yearns for freedom and a life beyond."[46] The set created a cell-like, boarded-up bunker of sloping walls dominated by six suspended ropes that served a variety of purposes—the physical effect of a tempest-tossed ship, bondage, rigging tents, look-out posts and so on. Large screens enabled projected images of faces—especially of the invisible Ariel and Prospero during his soliloquies.

As usual the cast doubled roles: Mountford played Trinculo as well as Prospero using his "native" Birmingham accent for comic effect that was in sharp contrast to the impeccable "standard" English voice of Prospero; the black African-heritage actor Chris Jack played Ferdinand and Sebastian to the white Miranda and Alonzo of Jessica Manley. In what was probably the most interesting double, the black actor Keith Thorne who played Caliban, also played Gonzalo giving an unusually rich intercultural resonance to Gonzalo's utopian vision of the commonwealth[47] that Shakespeare took from Montaigne's essay "On the Cannibals."[48] In the words of John Peter's review in *The Sunday Times,* this was: "a mixed-race, cross-gender production that brings out the play's political point—oppression, cruelty and greed are not the privilege of one race."[49] Caroline Kilpatrick, the one actor who did not double, played Ariel as moody and strong banging her head on the wall and weeping at the pain inflicted by Prospero's actions. A thoughtful review in the journal *Shakespeare* commented that,

> [T]he whiteness of Caroline Kilpatrick's skin and costume visually contrasts with Mountford's in an inversion of the normalized racial identities of colonizer and colonized, highlighting Ariel's vulnerability as a woman in a complex exploration of the structures of colonial and sexual power relations at work in the production.[50]

Inevitably the Islamic signifiers created controversy and at least one group of spectators took offence at what appeared to be a reductive appropriation of superficial features of Islamic culture that could reinforce Western negative perspectives.[51] Mountford's Prospero may have begun the play as the standard "heavy" Muslim father and vengeful militant, albeit one whose voice belied the aural caricature I explored at the beginning of this essay. By the end of the production, however, the political analogy had shifted to the renunciation of violence in the example of another doctor, al-Zawahiri's close associate, Said Iman al-Sharif, for whom imprisonment led to recantation of terror as a means of salvation. As Verma points out, it is the not-human Ariel who "offers a glimpse into what it means to be human."[52] While Michael Billington in his review observed that Prospero's acceptance of Caliban, "this thing of darkness I acknowledge mine," suddenly rings out in recognition both of the hero's colonialism and self-examination."[53] For Verma, *The Tempest*'s "humane exploration of the most inhuman experience...offers a profound comment and hope for today."[54]

In an interview with Christiane Schote recorded in 2003 at the height of the Iraq crisis, Verma addressed "the reality of cross-culturalism" and his own position as a migrant who is both an outsider and an insider within the dominant European culture:

> We can't paper over these differences. These are differences in outlook, of how the mind works, which go deep and which are not just a question of diplomacy. That's the domain we exist in. I don't think there is such a thing as a universal. I think there are only particularities which are based on where you are born, which kind of language you speak, which give you a certain outlook on the world...And that's what to me is exciting about the work; it is based on these differences. So the starting point, I think, is to see difference squarely in the face and then see, is there a connection with someone else's. That is all we can offer.[55]

Where Verma's journey with Shakespeare will take Tara Arts next is by no means certain although in June 2013 there was talk of a *Measure for Measure* where Isabella's veil becomes a metaphor for a whole society that is to be unveiled. The veil, which in Christian and Muslim culture can serve both as a means of female restraint *and* female self-determination, is yet another powerful signifier of difference. Shakespeare's famously problematic play may yet accommodate those differences to make the connections to creative and therapeutic effect.[56]

Notes

1. *Much Ado About Nothing* produced by the Royal Shakespeare Company and directed by Iqbal Khan played at the Courtyard Theatre in Stratford-upon-Avon from 26 July until 15 September 2012 before a short season at the Noel Coward Theatre in London from 24 September until 27 October.
2. Sylvia Morris, "Round the globe with Much Ado About Nothing" *Shakespeare blog* (blog). 6 August 2012, accessed 30 July 2015. http://theshakespeareblog.com/2012/08/crossing-the-globe-with-much-ado-about-nothing/
3. For an account of the 1976 RSC production see Pamela Mason, *Much Ado About Nothing* (London: Macmillan Education, 1992); also William Shakespeare. *Much Ado About Nothing*. ed. John F. Cox (Cambridge: Cambridge University Press, 1998).
4. *It Ain't Half Hot Mum (1974–81),* accessed 17 July 2013, http://www.imdb.com/title/tt0081878/
5. *The Kumars at No. 42 (2001–06),* accessed 17 July 2013, http://www.imdb.com/title/tt0081878/http://www.imdb.com/title/tt0300792/
   BBC Home Page, Comedy, "Goodness Gracious Me," accessed 17 July 2013, http://www.imdb.com/title/tt0081878/http://www.imdb.com/title/tt0300792/http://www.bbc.co.uk/comedy/goodnessgraciousme/

6. Meera Syal went to play Shakespeare in Stratford at the invitation of Michael Boyd, the then artistic director of the RSC. It was she who suggested Iqbal Khan as the director of *Much Ado About Nothing*. Meera Syal in a public interview with Claire Cochrane, Old Birmingham Repertory Theatre, 24 March 2013.

7. *Julius Caesar* produced by the Royal Shakespeare Company and directed by Gregory Doran played at the Royal Shakespeare Theatre, Stratford-upon-Avon from 28 May to 7 July 2012 before a UK tour.

8. Poonam Trivedi, "Replaying Shakespeare in Asia An Introduction," in *Replaying Shakespeare in Asia*, ed. Poonam Trivedi and Minami Ryuta (New York: Routledge, 2010), 1–18.

9. Claire Cochrane, *Twentieth Century British Theatre Industry, Art and Empire* (Cambridge: Cambridge University Press, 2011), 224.

10. Jonathan Owen, "Meera Syal 'I Didn't Want to Reach 50 and be full of Regrets'," *Independent* 6 May 2012, accessed 3 March 2013, http://www.independent.co.uk

11. Terry Grimley, "Iqbal Khan back at Birmingham Rep for East is East." *Birmingham Post* 23 September 2009, accessed 11 November 2012, http://www.birminghampost.net

12. Claire Cochrane, "Engaging the Audience: A Comparative Analysis of Developmental Strategies in Birmingham and Leicester since the 1990s," in *Critical Essays on British South Asian Theatre*, ed. Graham Ley and Sarah Dadswell (Exeter: Exeter University Press, 2012), 100–18.

13. Chag, Niraj, *Niraj Chag Composer and Musician*, accessed 1 March 2013, http://nirajchag.com/

14. Tragically Paul Bhattacharjee was found dead on 12 July 2013 following a formal declaration of bankruptcy. His obituary was published in the *Guardian* newspaper on 19 July 2013.

15. Sharma Madhav, *Madhav Sharma Blog*, accessed 28 July 2013, http://www.madhavsharma.com/

16. Owen, 2012.

17. Bharti Patel, *Bharti Patel*, accessed 28 July 2013, http://www.castingcallpro.com

18. Richard Godwin, "That's Amara! Meet Amara Karam, Simon Pegg's Latest Leading Lady." *London Evening Standard* 27 April 2012, accessed 14 August 2013, http://www.standard.co.uk

19. Andrew Davies, "Culture: Rob's Career off to a Flying Start; Rob Mountford has Already Starred in a top Television Drama and Trod the Boards with the RSC—and he's barely been out of Drama School Two Years. Andrew Davies Caught up with the Birmingham-born Actor En Route to Beijing." *Birmingham Post* 11 June 2002, accessed 1 August 2013, http://www.birminghampost.net

20. B. C. Parekh, *The Future of Multi-Ethnic Britain Report of the Commission on the Future of Multi-Ethnic Britain* (London: Profile Books, 2000), 30–31.

21. Cochrane, *Twentieth Century British Theatre*, 226.

22. For example Orson Welles' 1937 Mercury Theatre modern-dress production of *Julius Caesar* referenced Mussolini's Rome; In 1975 at the Greenwich Theatre in London Jonathan Miller set *Measure for Measure* in Freud's Vienna; In 1999 Trevor Nunn's National Theatre production of *The Merchant of Venice* set the play in 1930s' Venice.

23. Jyotsna G. Singh, "Wooing and Wedding," in programme for *Much Ado About Nothing* (Royal Shakespeare Company, 2012).

24. Poonam Trivedi, "Shakespeare and the Indian Image(nary): Embod(y)ment in versions of *A Midsummer Night's Dream*," in *Replaying Shakespeare in Asia*, ed. Poonam Trivedi and Minami Ryuta (New York: Routledge, 2010), 54–75.

25. As Iqbal Khan, himself said at a keynote speech given at the BBA Shakespeare symposium held at Warwick University on 2 July 2013, about twelve of the *Much Ado About Nothing* cast were regarded as "difficult" Asian actors, i.e., their previous work had been associated with radical political theatre and there were some tensions about working within the RSC company structure.

26. Michael Billington, "Much Ado About Nothing-Review," Rev. of *Much Ado About Nothing* directed by Iqbal Khan for the Royal Shakespeare Company, Courtyard Theatre, Stratford-on-Avon *Guardian* 2 August 2012, accessed 3 March 2013, http://www.guardian.co.uk

27. Since 2006 there have been a number of publications addressing the history of Black British and British Asian theatre. These include Dimple Godiwala, ed. *Alternatives Within the Mainstream: British Black and Asian Theatre* (Newcastle: Cambridge Scholars Press, 2006); Graham Ley and Sarah Dadswelleds. *British South Asian Theatre A Documented History* (Exeter: Exeter University Press, 2011); Graham Ley and Sarah Dadswell, eds. *Critical Essays on British South Asian Theatre* (Exeter: Exeter University Press, 2012) and Dominic Hingorani. *British Asian Theatre: Dramaturgy, Process and Performance* (Basingstoke: Palgrave Macmillan, 2010).

28. Ley and Dadswell, eds. *British South Asian Theatre*, 104–30; 131–62.

29. Ley and Dadswell, eds. *British South Asian Theatre*, 13–56.

30. Jatinder Verma, "Cultural Transformations," in *Contemporary British Theatre,* ed. Theodore Shank (Basingstoke: Macmillan, 1996), 55–61.

31. Jatinder Verma, "The Shape of a Heart," in *Alternatives within the Mainstream: British Black and Asian Theatre*, ed. Dimple Godiwala (Newcastle: Cambridge Scholars Press, 2006), 383–389.

32. Additional comments from Jatinder Verma are based on two personal interviews conducted by the author at the Tara Arts Centre in Earlsfield, London on 20 February and 24 June 2013. Much of the detailed description of the Tara Arts Shakespeare productions selected for this essay is drawn from archival research. As an audience member I saw only the 1998 revival of *A Midsummer Night's Dream* and the 2005 production of *The Merchant of Venice*.

33. Bill Ashcroft, Gareth Griffiths and Helen Tiffin, eds. *The Empire Writes Back: Theory and Practice in Post-Colonial Literature* (London: Routledge, 1989), 41.

34. Details of the production of *Troilus and Cressida* come from clippings of reviews held in dated archival production boxes held in the Tara Arts Centre.

35. Jatinder Verma, "A Chronology for Shakespeare's *Dream*—Our First Production in Tara's 20th Year." Programme for *A Midsummer Night's Dream*, Tara Arts and Lyric Theatre Hammersmith, 1997.

36. Michael Billington, "Cuts to the heart," Rev. of *A Midsummer Night's Dream*, directed by Jatinder Verma for Tara Arts, Lyric Theatre, Hammersmith, London *Guardian* 3 February 1997.

37. Billington, "Cuts to the heart"; Meera Syal. "Global Vision's Good Medicine," Rev. of *A Midsummer Night's Dream* by Jatinder Verma. Tara Arts, Lyric Theatre, Hammersmith, London, *The Express* 31 January 1997.

38. Hardeep Kohli, "A Midsummer Night's Dream, Lyric Hammersmith, London," Rev. of *A Midsummer Night's Dream*, directed by Jatinder Verma for Tara Arts, Lyric Theatre, Hammersmith, London, *Herald* 5 February 1997.

39. Ania Loomba's chapter "Religion, Money and Race in The Merchant of Venice" begins with Salman Rushdie's novel *The Moor's Last Sigh* that tells the story of the marriage between a Christian girl and a Jewish man of Cochin. Ania Loomba,

Shakespeare, Race and Colonialism (Oxford: Oxford University Press, 2002), 135–160.

40. Jatinder Verma, interview with the author 20 February 2013.
41. Jatinder Verma, "The Merchant of Venice." Programme for *The Merchant of Venice*, Tara Arts 2005.
42. Loomba, *Shakespeare*, 135.
43. Claudia Mayer, "Notes on Design." Programme for *The Tempest*, Tara Arts, 2008.
44. Jatinder Verma, "Director's Vision." Programme for *The Tempest*, Tara Arts, 2008.
45. John Peter, "The Tempest—Review," Rev. of *The Tempest* directed by Jatinder Verma for Tara Arts, Arts Theatre, London *Sunday Times* 20 January 2008.
46. Claudia Mayer, "Notes on Design." Programme for *The Tempest*, Tara Arts, 2008.
47. *Tempest* 2.1 148–165.
48. Michel de Montaigne, "On the Cannibals," trans. and ed. M.A. Screech, *The Complete Essays* (Harmondsworth: Penguin, 1993), 228–41.
49. Peter, "The Tempest–Review."
50. Shelly Baker, Katherine Evans, Lauren K. Monaghan-Pisano, Karwir Nam, and Rachael Williams, "Review of Shakespeare's *The Tempest* (directed by Jatinder Verma for Tara Arts) at the Arts Theatre, London, January 2008," *Shakespeare* 4 no. 1–4 (2008): 320–23.
51. As reported by Jyotsna G. Singh in the general discussion that followed the keynote lecture given at the "Revisiting Shakespeare in Indian Literature and Culture" on 8 March 2013 that forms the basis of this essay.
52. Verma, "Director's Vision."
53. Michael Billington, "The Tempest, Arts Theatre," Rev. of *The Tempest*, directed by Jatinder Verma for Tara Arts, Arts Theatre, London, *Guardian,* 12 January 2008.
54. Verma, "Director's Vision."
55. Christine Schlote, "'Finding our Own Voice' An Interview with Jatinder Verma" in *Staging New Britain Aspects of Black and South Asian British Theatre Practice*, ed. Geoffrey V. Davis and Anne Fuchs (Brussels: Peter Lang, 2006), 317.
56. As this essay goes to press in 2015 there has been another Tara Arts Shakespeare: *Macbeth* directed by Jatinder Verma and with Robert Mountford in the title role. Verma set the play in a modern-day British-Asian extended family arguing as he took family as "one of the stereotypical perceived virtues of Asians" that the murder of Duncan, "has more resonance as patricide rather than regicide." Most radically the witches were represented as all singing and dancing Indian hijras, 'Third Gender', transsexuals and transgenders legally recognized only in India and Germany. Jatinder Verma, "Director's Note" Programme for *Macbeth*, Tara Arts, 2015.

5

Indian Shakespeare in the World Shakespeare Festival

Thea Buckley

This essay looks at Indian Shakespeare productions in the World Shakespeare Festival held in the United Kingdom in 2012. I aim to give an intercultural perspective, using both first-hand and secondary accounts of three different Shakespeare plays that were translated into Indian contexts and/or languages and performed for the global festival: *Twelfth Night, All's Well That Ends Well* and *Much Ado About Nothing*. In examining these Indian Shakespeare productions, the essay problematizes the idea of a continuing "global" dialogue between the UK and India, between the cultures of the land of Shakespeare's birth and one that has adopted Shakespeare. The essay argues that the term "global" is a simplistic representation of a historic, intercultural relationship that involves interaction and negotiation on multiple levels. The variables involved here include not only geographical and historical distance, and time and space, but also those cultural and linguistic distinctions between individuals, states and nations. The question remains whether these three Indian Shakespeare productions, in Hindi, Gujarati or English, successfully fused not only languages and literature but also cultures, unifying their audiences under a shared appreciation of Shakespeare.

The World Shakespeare Festival (WSF) ran from April through November 2012. The festival was a major part of the four-year Cultural Olympiad that accompanied the London Olympic Games and it comprised multiple celebrations that culminated during the 2012 Olympics. The WSF took place at venues throughout the UK. The festival foregrounded foreign and intercultural Shakespeare including: international touring productions, collaborations between international and UK theatres, and UK theatre productions set in other cultures. The Arts Council England website terms the festival "the biggest celebration of Shakespeare ever staged."[1] The website states that the WSF was produced by the Royal Shakespeare Company (RSC) in collaboration with Shakespeare's Globe Theatre and eminent UK and international arts organizations. The site gives figures that indicate global participation in the festival, with nearly 60 partners and "thousands of artists from around the world" that took part in "almost 70 productions, plus supporting events and exhibitions, right across the UK, including London, Stratford-upon-Avon, Newcastle/Gateshead, Birmingham, Wales and Scotland and online."[2] The festival was widely publicized by methods that varied from electronic media to local London flyers. The success of this can be gauged by audience testimony in recordings and in reviews on websites such as *Year of Shakespeare*,[3] all of which indicate that on the whole the WSF plays were attended by both national and international audiences, including the Indian diaspora. The Globe Theatre alone, which had targeted its multicultural London diaspora, recorded 75 per cent new audiences.[4] In 2012 over one million tickets went on sale for the WSF on 23 April, traditionally celebrated as Shakespeare's birthday, a symbolic date that simultaneously marked the festival's official beginning.

As part of the WSF, major Shakespearean theatres in the UK joined forces with theatre companies from around the world including two from India—Arpana and Company Theatres. Shakespeare's Globe Theatre in London held the 2012 "Globe to Globe" festival, staging 37 of Shakespeare's works as presented by troupes from different countries in their native languages and interpretations. The RSC held productions in Stratford-Upon-Avon in collaboration with Mexican, American and Russian theatres, alongside its own season titled "What Country Friends Is This?" that showcased selected Shakespeare plays highlighting global exploration and sea voyages. In addition to these, the RSC held its own commissioned Shakespearean adaptations set in India and South Africa, and also hosted visiting companies from Brazil and Iraq to perform productions set in their native countries, all of which also later toured to London.

Of the three Indian Shakespeare WSF productions under discussion here, two were performed at the Globe Theatre by visiting Mumbai theatre troupes: Company Theatre, with *Twelfth Night* (*Piya Behrupiya*) and Arpana, with *All's Well That Ends Well* (*Maro Piyo Gayo Rangoon*). *Twelfth Night* was performed on 27 and 28 April and *All's Well* on 23 and 24 May. The third of these productions, the Delhi-set *Much Ado About Nothing*, was performed by an Indo-UK cast at the Royal Shakespeare Company's Courtyard Theatre in Stratford-Upon Avon from 26 July–15 September; it then toured at London's Noel Coward Theatre from 24 September–27 October.[5] In comparing and contrasting the approaches taken by these three Indian Shakespeare productions, this discussion draws on first-person evidence, including recorded accounts of attendance at the plays as well as accounts of those involved and director interviews.

In their preface to the 2012 *Much Ado* programme, the RSC's outgoing Artistic Director Michael Boyd and Executive Director Vikki Heywood declared, "Shakespeare is no longer English property. He is the favourite playwright and artist of the whole world."[6] During the WSF, the RSC and Globe Theatres were both similarly careful to situate the relationship between India and Shakespeare in a global context. Complicating this shared intercultural appreciation of Shakespeare is the fact that India's relationship with the playwright has arguably moved beyond the postcolonial; it is no longer mediated through Britain. In an article published in the *Guardian* as part of its special WSF series, entitled "Why Shakespeare is…Indian," Poonam Trivedi mused, "Though colonialism brought him to the subcontinent, Shakespeare has been utterly absorbed into the Indian imagination."[7] In other words, in India, Shakespeare is no longer an inheritance so much as a birthright.

Shakespeare has long been assimilated culturally by India's major artists. An example is the opening narration of the Hindi film *Angoor*,[8] a 1982 adaptation of *The Comedy of Errors* by the noted lyricist and film director Gulzar. At the film's beginning, introducing Shakespeare as a famous playwright, Gulzar not only elides any mention of the poet's nationality but even represents him in live portrait form, posed by an actor of unambiguously native Indian ethnicity. The portrait reappears at the closing and winks, as if in a sly nod to this inside joke. This same naturalization of the formerly English Bard was at work when I interviewed *Twelfth Night* director and National Award winning actor Atul Kumar at the Globe Theatre before the evening performance. When asked, "Why Shakespeare?" he animatedly responded, "Shakespeare has been done ever since the English came into our country. It's nothing new—he's our playwright as much as he is anyone else's in the world [because]…he talks to us *here* and *now*."[9] For Kumar, Shakespeare's contemporary relevance clearly means as much to him as the playwright's several-hundred-year presence in his native theatre heritage.

While the plot of Kumar's *Twelfth Night* generally stuck to the play's original Shakespearean storyline, the Hindi translation, prepared by Amitosh Nagpal (Sebastian), was reset in an Indian context with folk song and dance. As in the rest of the Globe to Globe plays, there were English subtitles, which were consigned to intermittently summarizing the plot action. "We haven't changed names,"[10] Kumar told reviewer Aradhna Wal. "The place is still Illyria; the characters are Orsino, Viola and Olivia. But the language and the setting have to blend. Cesario becomes 'Cejario.'"[11] Wal termed the resulting mix "glocal"[12] Shakespeare. *Times of India*'s Purvaja Sawant felt that the actors made the most of the latent possibilities in different local dialects to portray their own individuality, writing that among "a mix of Hindi and occasional English words thrown in for poetic and comical effect, what elevates the show are the various Indian accents by the characters."[13] Kumar himself expressed to Shai Hussain that it was "great to do Shakespeare in an Indian accent, and show that there's actually an enormous muscularity, clarity and musicality in doing it that way."[14] Actor Geetanjali Kulkarni (Viola) echoed Kumar's emphasis on language, explaining to Saumya Ancheri, "We've maintained the Shakespearean atmosphere, but we've used colloquial words. Amitosh [the translator] belongs to Punjab, so the flavour of *truckwaali bhasha* [truck-driver's language] is there."[15] This colloquial translation was arguably meant to encourage audience enjoyment and participation in what reviewer Peter Smith called "populist Shakespeare,"[16] recalling "I was assured by the Hindi-speaking woman sitting next to me that the translation 'is a modern prose version which is accessible for people who wouldn't normally come to the theatre.'"[17] Thus, Duke Orsino (Sagar Deshmukh) opened the play with "*Ishq ke khurak hai agar gana—bajana to bajate raho*" (If music be the food of love, play on [1.1.1]).[18] Literal translation was a Globe condition; intending to enhance the global flavour of its offerings, the theatre had mandated that these visiting productions remain straight translations rather than adaptations.[19]

Kumar's play negotiated this distinction loosely; Wal noted, "as the mannerisms and costumes echo Indian heartlands, one wonders how fine the line is between translation and adaptation."[20] When I asked Kumar himself what happens when Shakespeare's plays are adapted into another culture, he offered a frank view that transcended such quibbles: "He doesn't feel like [we are] doing an adaptation."[21] Such subcontinental straightforwardness towards Shakespeare is a contemporary attitude, posits Poonam Trivedi:

> From the nineties onwards [...] Indians have felt freer to approach Shakespeare. There is no longer the need to "adapt," rather they can make bold to "play" around with Shakespeare's text, with what was once the colonial book, and deconstruct it for their own needs.[22]

This boldness was visible as Kumar explained that he had chosen *Twelfth Night* simply as it had been the most appealing play of several that the Globe had suggested, in an uncomplicated decision: "I didn't want to pick up a tragedy—I'd just done *Othello*. Simple."[23] He added with a wry grin, "I've never done a musical before,"[24] indicating the irony of a situation once unimaginable when musicals dominated popular Indian Shakespeare. Comparisons to Bollywood became inevitable. Kumar elaborated on his inspiration behind the play's Indian context, telling *Guardian* reviewer Andrew Dickson,

> [W]e felt there had to be a lot of singing and dancing and music. The play is full of sex and love, fights, high passion and high drama, so we have to respond to that [...] We've come up with a kind of musical. Almost like Bollywood.[25]

Kumar's resulting *Piya Behrupiya* exploited the rich seams of India's musical heritage, featuring 18 songs. Composer Gagan Dev Riar (who also played Sir Toby Belch) described the process, telling Wal: "We've taken music from different regions in India. We've changed lyrics to explain situations, and for some scenes we composed our own songs."[26] Actor Mantra Mugdh (Sir Andrew Aguecheek) added that "for one song everyone in The Globe raised their hands and swayed to the music. We felt like rockstars!"[27] This production privileged comedy, heightening this by playing down the play's more sober aspects; for example, it over-exaggerated Olivia's (Mansi Multani) songs of lament and omitted Malvolio's (Saurabh Nayyar) suffering. With its emphasis on dance, the production also lent itself to physical comedy that blurred the original boundaries, as reviewer Deepa Punjani wrote: "Unmindful of the class hierarchies in the original, here almost all characters appear at par in their social standing as they quite literally jostle their shoulders with each other."[28] This subversive comic trend was perhaps best epitomized by the show's finale: while the newlyweds tenderly bestowed plastic wedding garlands on each other in the best Bollywood-comic-resolution style, Malvolio exaggeratedly searched the audience for a life partner and, finding none his equal, cheerfully garlanded himself.[29] He succeeded in bringing down the house, including both its *desi* audience and guest spectators.

Such humorous moments needed no translation. However, defining the "Indian" aspect of these productions was arguably complicated, especially in the case of those that were tailored for international touring; the concept of "India" itself is already sufficiently nebulous. The addition here of a mixed native-foreign-diasporic audience, and even a diasporic cast and director in the case of *Much Ado*, not only complicated an intercultural relationship but also risked creating an exoticized and artificialized representation of the same. For example, in the case of the Globe to Globe productions, visiting companies were given particular guidelines, as Globe to Globe director Tom Bird explained.[30] These guidelines set out the Globe Theatre's preferred staging practices, including natural sound and lighting; companies were specifically requested not to use English and not to rewrite the original Shakespearean plots. In attempting to set his production in the context of a modern, heterogeneously polyglot India, *Twelfth Night* director Atul Kumar expressed to Andrew Dickson at the time that "the one thing that is making him worry is the Globe's stipulation that no English should be used"[31]—a simplistic guideline, Dickson pointed out, "that takes little account of how in India language itself has become globalized, along with so much else."[32] *All's Well* director Shanbag told Draupadi Rohera that in reworking the play for both India and the UK he had to prepare two different versions, not because of the cultural differences but "because in terms of sets, sound etc. the demands of the Globe are the complete opposite of the demands of traditional Gujarati theatre."[33] Therefore, in some cases the Globe's regulations actually detracted from the cultural authenticity of inherently intercultural global productions.

In discussing the intercultural nature of Indian Shakespeare, Mark Thornton Burnett observes that "Shakespeare sits easily alongside Indian representations [of legends] and forms."[34] This argument could be extended to further suggest that the relationship involves Shakespeare sitting easily *within* Indian forms. Some may view such subsuming as a usurpation rather than an absorption—a cultural substitution that goes beyond linguistic translation. Alexa Huang, for example, termed it "textual resistance"[35] when Nayyar's yellow spandex tights replaced Malvolio's original cross-garters. This permeability is arguably the trend for twenty-first-century Indian productions that revisit Shakespeare—beyond an adaptation or appropriation, they are an internalization or an intercultural fusion. An even more apt metaphor for this amalgam might be, as Poonam Trivedi puts it (paraphrasing literary critic Mário de Andrade's translation metaphor), a *cannibalization*, one where,

> Shakespeare is no longer the other, but exists as absorbed into the cultural imaginary of the nation, the result of a process where [...] the original has to be "devoured" for the colonized to break free, and where the act of devouring is both a violation and an homage.[36]

Nayyar's self-garlanding, again, was a prime example of this cannibalization, in being both a violation of and an homage to the original, and it was a highlight of the production.

In digesting and reconstituting Shakespeare, thus, the ultimate creative product often transcends an easy external categorization. Discussing festival productions of intercultural Shakespeare, in her essay "What Country, Friends, is This?" Huang critiques the term "binary," frequently applied to guest versus host cultures, as a simplistic marketing ploy.[37] Huang points out that directors of touring Asian Shakespeare productions "often emphasize their own cultural contexts rather than the binary modes of the local and the foreign [...] favored by [...] the marketing language of festivals."[38] This concept of one's "own" Shakespeare was expressed by Kumar, "I don't think it is possible for me to ever do a straight up translation of Shakespeare—ever!"[39] he confessed to Ancheri. "We have taken it out of its context and played around with it and made it our own."[40] The same concept of naturalizing Shakespeare was reiterated by Sunil Shanbag, *All's Well* director and Indian national theatre award winner, who told Dickson, "We'll be performing in the spirit of the play, but we've made it our own. That's where your critics may be a bit surprised—how many people have made Shakespeare their own."[41] Although the Globe to Globe's printed materials displayed the tagline "Shakespeare's Coming Home,"[42] Shanbag's comment singled out the local amongst the global, while simultaneously dismissing any assumptions of the Bard's continued Anglo-centricity.

Like *Twelfth Night*, Shanbag's production of *All's Well* employed live Indian song and dance as narrative devices, in the style of the indigenous Bhangwadi theatre, or as the Globe programme described it, one that "originally catered for an audience of daily wage labourers in the 19th century."[43] The director told reviewer Zafri Nofil that the play was not originally his first choice, but that "although *All's Well* is often referred to as being one of Shakespeare's problem plays I found it had interesting layers and was easily adaptable to an Indian context."[44] Translated by Mihir

Bhuta and presented by Arpana Theatre, this *All's Well* was supposedly "the first Shakespeare completely in Gujarati to ever play in the UK."[45] Shanbag added that Globe to Globe Festival Director Tom Bird had originally invited him to direct a play in the Gujarati language "because of the large Gujarati-speaking population in and around London."[46] Bird had explained during the Intercultural Symposium that the Globe to Globe festival was primarily designed to involve local diasporic audiences in London, of which the Indian community is one of the largest.[47] Ironically therefore, like Kumar's first Hindi Shakespeare offering (which cheekily had also incorporated Punjabi, Urdu and Hinglish), this production abroad was apparently also Shanbag's first time to work in Shakespeare in a specific Indian language, namely, Gujarati.[48]

Shanbag's version privileged the world of class status and business, resetting Shakespeare's problem play neatly into the world of mercantile India and reframing the original war as one of international trade. As Shanbag described this cultural transposition to Nofil, "We've set it in small town Saurashtra, which then moves to Mumbai in 1900, and then Rangoon. The nobility of the original has been replaced with the mercantile class in Mumbai in 1900."[49] The director elaborated to Rohera, "From the outset, I knew I did not want to make a play for the so-called 'global theatre market' minus any cultural roots or local politics [...] My play had to reflect the dreams, passions, anxieties of a clearly defined Gujarati community."[50] In Shanbag's version, Heli/Helena (Mansi Parekh) is awarded the higher-caste Bharatram's/Betram's (Chirag Vora) hand in marriage after curing merchant prince Gokuldas (Utkarsh Mazumdar) of tuberculosis. "This same character, we have been told to sizeable laughs from the crowd, didn't think much of English medicine"[51] UK reviewer Matt Wolf noted wryly, observing the intercultural in-jokes lost in translation. While the heroine Heli showed off impressive vocals, Wolf was also struck by this *All's Well*'s indigenous "musical soundscape accompanying her every vibrant step of the way,"[52] one that included three musicians on the harmonium, *tabla* and *dholak*. The significance of this soundscape was noted by the audience, including Sarah Olive: "What was markedly different and regional about this performance was the way in which song, dance and gesture punctuated the action [...] to do much of the storytelling work [...] as a fusion of Eastern and Western traditions."[53] In lieu of a universally comprehensible text, Shanbag's production thus successfully showcased theatre arts to tell its intercultural story.

This cultural fusion was most evident in the RSC's 2012 adaptation of *Much Ado About Nothing*, set in modern Delhi by its Birmingham-born director Iqbal Khan and performed by an Asian heritage cast that was mostly second generation British. The RSC had not put on an "Indian" *Much Ado* since John Barton's 1976 production, set in a more remote nineteenth-century Indian garrison town under the British Raj, with few Indian heritage actors, according to the programme notes.[54] In a pre-show talk, Khan detailed the background behind his production's contemporary "Indianization," explaining that the former RSC Artistic Director Michael Boyd "had also seen my work and thought I was a good fit. None of that was about us being Asian—it was for the World Shakespeare Festival, and as soon as Michael mentioned setting it in India, my heart sank."[55] He elaborated, "The exotic is anathema…Shakespeare should be contemporary, […] urgent. I thought the modern was much more relevant for India."[56] Part of the challenge in defining "modern India," let alone setting Shakespeare here, is arguably that the country is actually multicultural; this challenge is in turn symptomatic of many centres that produce Asian Shakespeare, as the region is by nature intracultural as well as intercultural.

Each of the directors defines contemporary India in his or her own way: award-winning actor-director Kumar, whose recent Indian-origin play *Hamlet, the Clown Prince* was written and performed in multiple languages and countries, spoke to Dickson of "the reality of today's contemporary Indian theatre—influences from all sorts of places, traditional as well as modern, and now internationally too."[57] Huang attributes these multi-geographical influences to the freeing of Asian Shakespeares from artificial regional strictures, a "deterritorializing, an effect […] that unmarks the cultural origins of intercultural productions because they work against assumptions about politically defined geographies […] artificial constraints that no longer speak to the realities of theatre making."[58] *Much Ado*'s supposedly "Indian" culture was left undefined even in a glowing tribute uttered by British Asian TV comedy star and leading lady Meera Syal (Beatrice): "Being able to explore this amazing play through our own cultural lens has been so rewarding and illuminating, and, we hope, made the story sing with new relevance."[59] In order to elaborate on to whom or to what Shakespeare's plays should be newly relevant, it has perhaps become too complicated to disentangle each cultural strand of the production.

In examining what is "Indian" in the intercultural, it is relevant to quote Jyotsna Singh's piece in the RSC programme, titled "Wooing and

Wedding."[60] She writes that in the production, "early modern Messina is transposed to contemporary Delhi in a way that richly illuminates and transforms the idioms of *both* worlds. Contemporary India, like early modern England, is a society in transition, with shifting realignments within social hierarchies and norms."[61] This intercontinental parallel was echoed by Khan when he told *Guardian* reviewer Nosheen Iqbal, explaining his choice of the Delhi setting:

> The more seriously I thought about the themes of the play—chastity and pure blood lines, the rituals of courtship, the arrangements of marriage—I realised all of those things are incredibly vital in India.[…] Delhi is about as Elizabethan a place as you could find in the modern-day world.[62]

In his pre-show talk, Khan shared Singh's emphasis on the transitional nature of Indian society, stressing that his play must be set in "authentic"[63] India, itself authentically complex in that "the ancient and modern sit side by side, spirituality and technology, gender roles are complicated. Even women who challenge these have codes of hundreds of years of tradition."[64] While Khan's production portrayed typical "traditional" power structures, whether between servants and masters or fathers and daughters, it also emphasised the poignancy latent in each moment that an outdated code resulted in a necessary challenge and a more equal renegotiation.

In setting the play in a largely English-speaking modern Delhi society, the Shakespearean (largely prose) text could be left largely untampered with and still sound realistic. The main textual deviations were substitutes such as "Delhi" for "Messina" and "temple" instead of "church," in several instances. Among the Indian WSF productions, *Much Ado* most resembled modern-day India in all its infinite variety, the cutting edge juxtaposed with the conservative. Here one saw many more familiar signifiers of India's ongoing globalization than in the Globe to Globe productions. Indian-accented English traded places with Hinglish; while the ubiquitous television was missing, mobile phones were used for Beatrice's overhearing scene; Nirag Chag's haunting music and dance compositions fused classical and contemporary instruments and rhythms. The cultural merger was seamless. Conversely in *All's Well*, India and the UK had still uneasily coexisted in places: "a (largely gentle) collision of East meets West may have been evoked by […] the way Bharatram's outfit became increasingly and symbolically Anglicized," wrote Olive.[65] Here, however, Beatrice moved gracefully and naturally between Eastern and Western outfits and signifiers—saris, T-shirts, bathrobes and hair-removal cream. While much was made of the distinguished peacekeeping fatigues of the suave, newly returned expat Benedick (played with sensitive distinction by the late Paul Bhattacharjee), an equally memorable joke revolved around the lover's plastic home-grown comfort Bata chappal-type sandals, at one point jokingly slapped by his friends in the direction of his lovesick head.

Despite the authenticity of its Delhi setting, artificially heightened exoticization was still involved in the *Much Ado* production. For example, the set, complete with a grandfather tree and an ornate haveli that withdrew to reveal a cremation ground and monsoon rain, was devoid of the usual city-street extras such as stray animals or peeling posters. The foyer, papered with Hindi magazines, was hung with lights and bicycles and sported a gleaming central tuk-tuk, draped with plastic garlands. The entering audience was further treated to the smell of freshly-made *samosa*s for sale, the sight of rows of glittering bangles (also ready for purchase) and the sound of a Delhi wedding-music procession against a backdrop of blaring traffic horns so genuine they induced homesickness. An online trailer for the production featured clips of the show and its opening music intercut with scenes from the city of Delhi, apparently to lend further authenticity.[66] This attention to cultural detail was not apparent for other "intercultural" RSC adaptations of the decade, such as Artistic Director Gregory Doran's recent South African *Julius Caesar* or the "Chinese *Hamlet*," *The Orphan of Zhao*. This *Much Ado*'s "Indianness" was possibly a marketing strategy aimed at the larger UK population of Indian diasporic audiences, such as one memorable self-described Punjabi men's club on an excited outing, who lit up the theatre foyer en masse with multicoloured turbans.

Several reviewers critiqued the production's content and choices as too simplistic, as opening the subject but then leaving them wanting more. Kate Rumbold felt that while this *Much Ado* richly featured elements of Indian society and culture, it stopped short of exploring the deeper issues regarding the intercultural mingling of these elements including what they might have told us "about Shakespeare's play and about Indian culture."[67] Rumbold also argued in favour of complicating the nature of this shared Indo-UK heritage, hinting at latent controversy in the choice of second-generation British Asian actors to represent postcolonial Indian culture and concluding that it was likely that in the "hyper-global context of the World Shakespeare Festival [...] the internationalism of the play came under new scrutiny."[68] Perhaps in comparison the "native" Indian cast of the Globe plays seemed more "authentic," yet the actors and directors of the three plays that I met backstage seemed equally sure of their own authentic cultures, whether global or local. To sum up, Indian Shakespeare resists easy definition. Kumar pinpointed this situation when he cited his invisible, subtle Indian influences:

> Everyone kept saying, "You just spent three years in Kerala; we didn't see anything [in your work] to do with Kathakali or Kalari [Keralan art forms]?" The essence of what I'd learned from my gurus had already gone into me; obviously the essence went into my *Hamlet* [...] It was a Western clown, yet there is hardly anything I as an actor will do that does not have Kathakali or Kalari in it.[69]

Similarly, our cultures resist surface-level evaluation: nowadays, should an Indian Beatrice wearing a T-shirt be judged as any less valid of a cultural representation than a *desi* Beatrice dressed in a sari?

These UK-India festive Shakespeares left an immediate intercultural legacy. After the WSF, Atul Kumar had remarked to Ancheri, "We cannot stop humming the songs of the play—including my 6-year-old daughter who is now in the play—and hope we can leave our audiences filled with our music for days to come."[70] Atul Kumar might have brought his show back home to India, but something of the Globe and its audiences had been indefinably and reciprocally woven into the production. As he told Ancheri, he recalled

> the smell of beer in the yard, the groundlings [audience in the pit] waving screaming laughing clapping dancing along with the songs of the play, standing ovation, backstage warmth of heaters and freezing cold of London, and rain pouring down on actors as their teeth chattered and they still sang full throttle![71]

Geetanjali Kulkarni similarly revealed that she had renewed a pre-existing, longstanding relationship with the Globe space and its presiding playwright. She said that she had told her husband as they watched a play at the theatre seven years previously "that this is an actor's stage and I want to perform here,"[72] averring "I feel Shakespeare baba listened to my wish and it came true."[73] For my own part, as an audience member, cultures merged when I was able to share the WSF productions, while briefly available online as full recordings, all the way from the UK with my American family living in India. The website was simply called *The Space*,[74] a truly global site transcending time zones and geography, in a locale where the only compass bearing is a shared love of Shakespeare. If the 2012 Olympics were intended to unite the world's people in a shared love of sport, the concurrent Cultural Olympiad succeeded through the WSF in bringing Shakespeare lovers old and new closer together, in an experience transcending linguistic and cultural distinctions. In our shrinking world this love of Shakespeare could be argued to grow with each revisitation of his genius and through each creative mind that gives to his works a new and glocal habitation.

Notes

1. "2012 marks the World Shakespeare Festival and a new RSC artistic director," *Arts Council England*, accessed 5 July 2013, https://web.archive.org/web/20130609181248/http://www.artscouncil.org.uk/news/arts-council-news/2012-marks-world-shakespeare-festival-and-new-rsc-/
2. "2012 marks the World Shakespeare Festival."
3. *Year of Shakespeare*, accessed 18 April 2012, http://yearofshakespeare.com/
4. Tom Bird, presentation at the Intercultural Symposium, London, 18–19 May 2012.
5. At this time, the RSC also had an ongoing amateur "Open Stages" festival that included a one night performance in July of *Baba Shakespeare*, a remake of the film *Shakespeare Wallah*, directed by Emmeline Winterbotham with an Anglo-Indian cast. This production is omitted in the discussion here since it is an adaptation of a film, rather than of a Shakespearean work.
6. Michael Boyd and Vikki Heywood, "Introduction," *Much Ado About Nothing* RSC programme brochure, 2012.
7. Poonam Trivedi, "Why Shakespeare is...Indian," *Guardian*, 4 May 2012, accessed 5 May 2012, http://www.theguardian.com/stage/2012/may/04/why-shakespeare-is-indian
8. *Angoor*, directed by Gulzar (1982; Mumbai: A.R. Movies, 2008), DVD.
9. Atul Kumar in discussion with the author, April 2012.
10. Aradhna Wal, "The Bard Goes Glocal," *Tehelka—India's Independent Weekly News Magazine*, 1 September 2012, accessed 30 July 2013, www.tehelka.com/2012/08/the-bard-goes-glocal/
11. Wal, "The Bard Goes Glocal."
12. Wal, "The Bard Goes Glocal."
13. Purvaja Sawant, "Theatre Review: Piya Behrupiya," *Times of India*, 5 April 2013, accessed 30 July 2013, http://timesofindia.indiatimes.com/entertainment/hindi/bollywood/news/Theatre-Review-Piya-Behrupiya/articleshow/19378329.cms
14. Shai Hussain, "Much Ado About A Lot Of Things," *The Non Resident Indian*, 22 July 2012, accessed 30 July 2013, www.the-nri.com/life/arts/much-ado-about-a-lot-of-things
15. Saumya Ancheri, "Five Things About Atul Kumar's Hindi Version of Twelfth Night," *Time Out Mumbai*, 22 June 2012, last modified 2013.
16. Peter J. Smith, "*Twelfth Night*," *A Year of Shakespeare: Reliving the World Shakespeare Festival 2012*, eds. Paul Edmondson, Paul Prescott and Erin Sullivan (London: Arden, 2013), 221.
17. Smith, "*Twelfth Night*," 221.

18. These lines are quoted in Shrabani Basu, "The Play's the Thing," *The Telegraph India*, 13 May 2012, accessed 30 July 2013, www.telegraphindia.com/1120513/jsp/7days/story_15482800.jsp#.Vd3nC-E4Hko

19. Tom Bird (presentation, Intercultural Symposium, London, 18–19 May).

20. Wal, "The Bard Goes Glocal."

21. Wal, "The Bard Goes Glocal."

22. Poonam Trivedi, "Shakespeare In India," *MIT Global Shakespeares*, accessed 18 April 2012, http://globalshakespeares.mit.edu/blog/2010/03/20/india/

23. Atul Kumar in discussion with the author, April 2012.

24. Atul Kumar, April 2012.

25. Andrew Dickson, "World Shakespeare Festival: Around the Globe in 37 Plays," *The Guardian*, 20 April 2012, accessed 24 April 2012, www.theguardian.com/stage/2012/apr/20/world-shakespeare-festival-globe-theatre-rsc

26. Wal, "The Bard Goes Glocal."

27. Wal, "The Bard Goes Glocal."

28. Deepa Punjani, "Piya Behrupiya Play Review," *Mumbai Theatre Guide*, 17 August 2012, accessed July 30, 2013, www.mumbaitheatreguide.com/dramas/reviews/19-piya-behrupya-hindi-play-review.asp#.dpuf

29. A clip of the play can be seen on YouTube here: http://youtu.be/d2kOErGjw0I

30. The press release can be seen here: www.shakespearesglobe.com/uploads/ffiles/2012/05/131178.pdf

31. Dickson, "World Shakespeare Festival."

32. Dickson, "World Shakespeare Festival."

33. Draupadi Rohera, "Gujarati at the Globe," *Hindustan Times*, 20 May 2012, accessed 30 July 2013, www.hindustantimes.com/entertainment/gujarati-at-the-globe/article1-858462.aspx

34. Mark Thornton Burnett, *Shakespeare and World Cinema* (Cambridge: Cambridge University Press, 2013), 72.

35. Alexa Huang, ""What Country, Friends, Is This?": Touring Shakespeares, Agency, and Efficacy in Theatre Historiography," *Theatre Survey* 54.1 (2013), 72.

36. Poonam Trivedi, "'Filmi' Shakespeare," *Narratives of Indian Cinema*, ed. Manju Jain (Delhi: Primus Books, 2009), 245.

37. Huang, "What Country, Friends, Is This?" 79.

38. Huang, "What Country, Friends, Is This?" 79.

39. Ancheri, "Five Things."

40. Ancheri, "Five Things."

41. Dickson, "World Shakespeare Festival."

42. See page 1 here: www.shakespearesglobe.com/uploads/ffiles/2011/10/326025.pdf

43. See page 11 here: www.shakespearesglobe.com/uploads/ffiles/2011/10/326025.pdf

44. Zafri Mudasser Nofil, "Hindi, Gujarati Adaptations Set to Wow World Shakespeare Fest," *Dna India*, 21 March 2012, accessed 30 July 2013, www.dnaindia.com/entertainment/report-hindi-gujarati-adaptations-set-to-wow-world-shakespeare-fest-1665344

45. Bird announced this during the symposium. Also, see page 2 of the printed copy here, http://issuu.com/bedeabza/docs/121743

46. Nofil, "Hindi, Gujarati Adaptations."

47. Bird, "Intercultural Symposium."

48. According to *theartsdesk* reviewer Matt Wolf, who was thus informed in an "informal post-show confab in the Globe's forecourt."

49. Nofil, "Hindi, Gujarati Adaptations."
50. Rohera, "Gujarati at the Globe."
51. Matt Wolf, "Globe to Globe: All's Well That Ends Well, Shakespeare's Globe," *theartsdesk*, 25 May 2012, accessed 2 September 2012, www.theartsdesk.com/theatre/globe-globe-alls-well-ends-well-shakespeares-globe-0
52. Wolf, "Globe to Globe."
53. Sarah Olive, "A Year of Shakespeare: All's Well That Ends Well," (London: Arden, 2013), 35.
54. *Much Ado About Nothing* brochure, 2012.
55. Iqbal Khan, interview by Nicky Cox, 31 July 2012, "The Director Talks."
56. Khan, "The Director Talks."
57. Dickson, "World Shakespeare Festival."
58. Huang, "What Country, Friends, Is This?" 78.
59. Jyotsna Singh, "Wooing and Wedding," *Much Ado About Nothing* brochure, 2012.
60. Singh, "Wooing and Wedding."
61. Meera Syal, *Much Ado About Nothing* brochure, 2012.
62. Nosheen Iqbal, "Much Ado About Delhi: RSC's Indian Shakespeare," *The Guardian*, 1 August 2012, accessed 2 September 2012, www.theguardian.com/culture/2012/aug/01/much-ado-rsc-indian-shakespeare
63. Khan, "The Director Talks."
64. Khan, "The Director Talks."
65. Olive, "All's Well That Ends Well," 35.
66. The trailer can be seen here: www.youtube.com/watch?v=09M7QiA3Pa8&feature=youtu.be
67. Kate Rumbold, "A Year of Shakespeare: Much Ado About Nothing," (London: Arden, 2013), 150.
68. Rumbold, "Much Ado About Nothing," 151.
69. Atul Kumar, *Hamlet the Clown Prince*, directed by Rajat Kapoor, Warwick Arts Centre, Warwick, 19 March 2011.
70. Ancheri, "Five Things."
71. Ancheri, "Five Things."
72. Ancheri, "Five Things."
73. Ancheri, "Five Things."
74. "The Space," BBC and Arts Council England, www.thespace.org

Shakespeare and Indian Films

6

The Othello-figure in Three Indian Films
Kaliyattam, Omkara and Saptapadi

Trisha Mitra

I who am poisoned by the blood of both,
Where shall I turn, divided to the vein?

—Derek Walcott, "A Far Cry from Africa"

In the manner of flirtatious behavior, having frowned, she spoke:
For me, affection with Muslims is impossible;
I smell blood coming from the legends of this race
Why should anyone be content that they are good and pious
[When] they still have in their veins the influence of the blood of jihad?

—Akbar Allahabadi, "Lightning of the Church"[1]
(Translated by Miriam Murtuza)

The performance of Shakespeare's plays can be interpreted as sites of negotiation between the colonizer and the colonized whenever they have been performed in a colonial set-up. The performative bodies of the participants onstage have as special an import in postcolonial locations as they have had in colonial times. Adaptations and appropriations of the play *Othello* continue to attest and revisit the histories of racial struggles around the world. It is suspected that even if Shakespeare had never intended *Othello* to be a play strictly about racial issues, the political history of the world has heightened this aspect. The introduction of Shakespeare's plays into a colonial location, for example in India under the British, had hardly ever been innocent. It is not unusual to consider Shakespeare's plays in the light of the colonial project of "civilizing" the natives by "improving" their familiarity with elevated Western literature. It is evident from academic as well as non-academic literature that *Othello* still plays a significant role with respect to discourses of race.

Othello's racial inheritance has been questioned and challenged, with critics claiming that he was perhaps not really a "Moor" but a "mestizo," a racial affiliation that would make him into a "hybrid" figure who relatively might have had more agency than a "black" person.[2] Hybridity does not always necessarily transfer the person under consideration to a more powerful or emancipated position. Bearing in mind that under a colonial framework Othello would have nevertheless be positioned in opposition to the "white" characters in the play, one might proceed to conclude, however reductive it might seem, that Othello was quite simply of a non-Caucasian racial heritage. This dissolves what one might regard as the radical potential of isolating and understanding what might have been Othello's cultural inheritance or his "hybridity" that might give the contemporary audience/readers an access to the "interstitial-space" he occupies.[3]

In this essay, I explore the cinematic appropriation of the figure of Othello in three Indian films located in different sociological backgrounds. Focusing on *Omkara*, *Kaliyattam* and *Saptapadi*, I intend to examine the characteristics that have been adapted by directors and scriptwriters from the original text and the variations that have been introduced to add additional layers of meaning. *Omkara* is situated, not in some urban location that might remotely resemble Venice but in the heartlands of Uttar Pradesh where the fight for power aligns goons and politicians. *Kaliyattam*, too, is located far away from any metropolitan space in the villages of Kerala. *Saptapadi* is based primarily in the city, but several incidents including the one that culminates in the estranged couple's reunion takes place far away from any urban location. Each of these locations has its individual cultural legacy that makes it interesting to note how an English literary text has been used as a source to project its romances and anxieties.

As Shakespeare's play progresses, one eventually recognizes that Othello takes pride in his contribution to the Venetian state by defending it against the Turks. His racial heritage is hardly ever mentioned and the descriptions given of his physical appearance in the text highlight him as a quintessential outsider. The tales that enamour Desdemona and draw her emotionally to Othello are about the battles he had won, the people he had helped the authorities to conquer and the distant lands he had visited in the process. There are never stories about his youth or a childhood spent with parents. The only object he has inherited is a handkerchief from his mother that he passed onto Desdemona. The disappearance or misplacement of the handkerchief seems to be of paramount significance since it can be viewed as a condensed symbol of nuptial sheets. As Neely points out, the handkerchief becomes a sign of sexual fidelity in a marriage that becomes questionable after its disappearance.[4]

Othello is a play that exposes the fears and apprehensions of not only the playwright but also that of the audiences of the Elizabethan age and the ones that followed. The unmistakable dread of miscegenation can be traced throughout the text. It is seen as something unnatural or an incredulous act that betrays some invisible code that regulates society. The fact that a moor might be bold enough to consider asking a "white" European lady to marry him seems to be as alarming a prospect as the lady agreeing to enter into a state of matrimony with him. *Othello* might have been quite stimulating for the Elizabethan cultural imagination already disposed to the horror of the predatory, physically, powerful, black man "forcefully" claiming a white woman as his companion. The Othello we are introduced to in the play hardly fits this role. He is seen primarily in terms of the function he performs and his unwavering allegiance to Venice. Well recommended for his services and appreciated as a potentially wonderful husband, he is exempted from undergoing the trial that his father-in-law wants. Othello is duly warned to be distrustful of the woman who had betrayed her own kith and kin by marrying the "black Moor."

Omkara is more or less a direct adaptation of the Shakespearean play. Omkara, or Omi, the Othello figure here is a local goon who is awarded an electoral nomination and who in turn nominates Keshuv (Cassio), instead of Langda Tyagi (Iago) as the *bahubali*. This creates a friction and Langda, seeking vengeance, plants seeds of suspicion in Omkara's mind about his bride-to-be, Dolly. Omi smothers her to death and later, realizing how he had been manipulated by Tyagi, kills himself. In this adaptation there is a slight alteration in the scheme of events. It is the Emilia figure, Indu, who kills her husband out of disgust for his manipulative actions.

This film has been seen as an adept representation of the socio-political conditions in Uttar Pradesh where there are gangs that assist political parties in their quest for gaining and consolidating power. Omkara is a dreaded figure among his political opponents because of his ruthlessness, but at the same time he is well loved by the people in the area where the political party he is affiliated to dominates. Langda Tyagi is named so because of his limp (*langda* meaning "lame" in Hindi). Quite like the character he has been drawn from, Tyagi ensnares unsuspecting individuals like Keshuv and Omi (Omkara) in order to serve his purpose. Tyagi becomes vengeful after being bypassed for a much sought after and lucrative electoral nomination. Unable to resist the temptation of ruining the life of the one person who could have made his dream come true, he plants seeds of suspicion in his mind, which ultimately destroys Omi's domestic bliss.

One is led to suspect that the marriage between Omi and Dolly (Desdemona) had been sanctioned and supported by the leader of this political party, Bhai Saab, for the same reason that the Duke had granted his blessings to Othello in Shakespeare's play. Omkara is indispensable to the implementation of Bhai Saab's political manoeuvrings. In a society steeped in class, caste and feudalism, it is the don, "bahubali," who is given the task of easing the process for the politicians. As the film progresses, it is made quite apparent that Omi does not enjoy the same social status as a lot of the other characters in the film. His father was a Brahmin who had cohabited with a woman from a lower "jati" (which may be loosely translated as caste), which meant that Omi was an illegitimate child of mixed-caste parentage. He is never allowed to forget that. Despite that, because of his outstanding performance as a muscleman, he is given the coveted position in the hierarchy that exists within the predominantly and acutely caste-conscious Hindu gang where Omkara also becomes a lower-caste individual giving orders to upper-caste party-workers. His elevation, thus, triggers eddies of resentment. These elements play a major role in the garb of democratic politics.

Omkara is reassured by Dolly's confidence in his qualities. Aware of the social conditions under which they had come together, their marriage is celebrated by Omi's friends and acquaintances. However, everyone immediately notices the stark difference in the skin-colour of the couple and the old woman in Omi's village declares as much. There is the traditional admiration for fair skin, speculation but not accusation or criticism. Dolly's skin colour, lighter than most of the women in the film, is meant to be an indicator of her caste purity and virginal beauty. Indu (Emilia) does not however hesitate before calling Omi names because of his visibly darker skin. He is teased and called a crow and other names, but is eventually accepted by her and euphemistically, described as Krishna, an incarnation of Lord Vishnu, which would perhaps position Dolly as his non-conjugal consort, Radha. The origin of the name "Krishna" is the Sanskrit word *Krsna*, which means "black" or "dark."

In *Kaliyattam*, Othello, or Perumalayan, is a *Theyyam* dancer, the leader of a group of artistes. It also follows the Shakespearean narrative closely. Significant layers of meaning are added primarily by the religious context of the movie. Theyyam, a practice indigenous to northern Kerala, is a ritual where the specialists wear elaborate costumes seeking to portray a deity, male or female, and then virtually become embodiments of the deity or spirit. In this altered state, the performer is revered as a god and is believed to possess the immense power to prophesize, bless and heal. The dancer is from a lower-caste community and as an embodiment of the deity, he becomes more powerful than the Brahmins and the Nayyars who form the upper crust of the society stratified by caste. Perumalayan invites the wrath of the Iago-figure, Paniyan, because he promotes Cassio as the next in line to the coveted position of the lead dancer and Iago remains relegated to the position of a clown. Perumalayan is seduced into believing his wife's infidelity and he suffocates her to death. He subsequently immolates himself in the ritual fire of the Theyyam.

Theyyam is a ritual that has been recently renewed and revived. This trend has been perceived in some circles as that society's urge to reassert itself in an age of globalization. This attempt to revitalize the consciousness of the people has met with severe opposition because of the perception that these performances are steeped in the caste politics of the times. At the very same time there is a counter impulse that is more celebratory when it comes to Theyyam. There have been protests marking the performances of Theyyam at several institutions under the conviction that it renews the older caste prejudices that democratic India has always attempted to do away with.[5]

Another variation of the ritualized *kaliyattam* has been found circulating in the lore of the land where the Theyyam represents the embodiment of the goddess who has the power to heal people afflicted with small pox. Perumalayan in the film *Kaliyattam* bears pockmarks that indicate that he had once suffered from the disease. He considers himself blessed because he thinks that it was the goddess who had healed him and helped him survive when he had been left in the forest to die. Having dedicated most of his life towards the training that one requires to undergo in order to become a Theyyam dancer, Perumalayan's talents make him into a much sought after dancer.

Theyyam dancers are scripturally required to belong to the subaltern groups of society. It is a ritual that found mainly in North Malabar and is performed in sacred groves, temples or in the households of the economically privileged. In *Kaliyattam*, Perumalayan, the Theyyam dancer, is from a lower caste and is given the privilege of momentarily transcending traditional caste hierarchies by embodying a god. This offers him fleeting immunity against upper-caste wrath but does not empower him at all times. He does represent an incarnation of a god and carries much respect within the performative space but outside it he is as disenfranchised as the rest of his community. Despite his talents he is still regarded as a social inferior who cannot easily gain access into the social space reserved for the members of the upper castes let alone marry an upper caste woman. One might be led to believe that Perumalayan transcends caste barriers by marrying Thamara. Like Omkara, he too is defended on the grounds that he was an indispensable and talented dancer who had always been respectful of the unwritten codes of social behaviour and had no known traits that might indicate that he was less of a gentleman/an upper caste.

Jayaraaj, the director of *Kaliyattam*, has explained in an interview that the process of embodiment had been used as a backdrop to explore what he sees as a "split-personality" in a "black" Othello who willingly or unwillingly wears the mask of a "white man." It is significant to note that despite the intentions of the director, Perumalayan does not wear the mask of a "white man," but neither does he wear one of the upper castes. He wears the mask of a god. The performer constantly oscillates between the position of being a lower-caste individual and a god. Perumalayan does not really develop a "split-personality" but his dilemma is most definitely heightened by the role he plays during the performances. He has the power to bless people from all walks of life when he embodies a Theyyam but always has to finally moult out of his costume and all that is left of him is the material reality of his body. His very physicality remains forever as a marker of his liminal position in the stratified social structure in Northern Malabar. He is perpetually caught between the role his occupation demands him to perform and his personal subjectivity, and is powerless in his social status. His transformation is always temporary; constantly slipping between the two roles, he is fully aware of the fact that he cannot ever expect to improve his lot.

Perumalayan never attempts to align himself with the upper castes on a material plane. He willingly participates in self-surveillance realizing that his only association with the upper castes is because of his marital relationship with Thamara. Like Othello, his insecurities regarding his socio-physical characteristics contribute to his victimization. Paniyan (Iago) feels betrayed when Perumalayan gives his own performative role of Theechamundi to Kanthan (Cassio). Paniyan is unforgiving because of this oversight and proceeds to wreck Perumalayan's precarious marriage. For Perumalayan it might have been quite a challenge to have been able to marry the upper-caste and socially superior Thamara, the daughter of the village head. Having done so, Perumalayan's sensitivity to this issue and the "ocular proof" that Paniyan provides him with is enough to unsettle him and doubt his wife's fidelity.

In the Bengali film *Saptapadi*, *Othello* is deployed in the course of the film to promote the larger agenda of secularism, defined in India as the equality of all regions before the Constitution and the law. It is primarily a romance where a snobbish "English" girl, Rina Brown (played by Suchitra Sen), initially looks down upon the Bengali student, Krishnendu (whose name can be literally translated as "dark moon"). She calls him "blackie" but eventually falls in love with him after his remarkable performance as Othello in a production of the play by university students. He reciprocates her love but is coerced by her English father to convert to Christianity. His own father, a rigid Hindu patriarch is unable to come to terms with it and disowns his son. Krishnendu's father persuades Rina to let go of his son and she reproaches Krishnendu and breaks up with him. Krishnendu then enters the fold of evangelical Christianity. Rina, in a moment of dramatic recognition, is made aware of the fact that she was a product of an episode of sexual violence. Her English father had sexually abused his Indian domestic help and the woman waiting upon her was actually her biological mother. The film concludes on a seemingly optimistic note with the once estranged couple reunited and reigniting their lost romance. We should, however, not take this optimism at its face value because the film is fraught with tensions of caste, class, race and nation-building couched in romance.

Paromita Chakravarti notes that while adaptations of Shakespeare's plays might give the impression of providing "a 'secular' space outside the fold of traditional religion and caste," they are "neither secular nor neutral."[6] Neither is the film *Saptapadi*, which ostensibly appears to be a promoting a new secular nation where interracial or inter-caste romantic unions are celebrated, not condemned. The staging of the play *Othello* within the film signals the relationship it bears with the dilemmas of the characters of the Shakespearean and the actors who have played the role of Othello through the ages. Released in 1961, the film is set in pre-independent India of the 1940s. The romance in the film might appeal to its viewers as a representation of liberal modernity but a closer look might reveal that the modernity is fraught with several problems.

The film begins with a drunken Rina Brown being carried into a missionary's improvised military hospital. The missionary doctor is, of course, none other than Krishnendu (played by Uttam Kumar). He does not recognize her at once and he sprinkles water on her, hoping that she wakes out of her drunken slumber. This might remind one of ritualistic immersion that is a part of the rite of baptism. In a flashback the audience is given the details of their romance. Krishnendu had been an exceptional medical student and a footballer who had been able to compete with and challenge the European students at his college. Rina Brown, an Anglophiliac, had always jeered at him for his racial inferiority. The dynamic between the duo changes after their parts in the performance of *Othello*. Rina, who had initially harboured feelings for the English student Clayton (who does not quite reciprocate her sentiments), gradually falls in love with Krishnendu.

Krishnendu had been called on to do an impromptu performance because Clayton was found to have fallen ill. It is also ironic in this particular case that the European man seems to have a weaker constitution than the "Indian native" the colonial masters had once condescendingly declared as "weak" and "effeminate" subjects. Pitted against him, Krishnendu in contrast is not only of robust health but an ideal multifaceted Indian student who is able to straddle the demand of the age that requires him to respect traditions as well as modernity. Quite the Renaissance man, he is a medical student who is well-versed in Shakespeare. Ever ready to rise to any occasion, Krishnendu performs the role of Othello with ease. This might be taken as an indicator of how the Favonian colonial subject has been produced through an a historical study of Shakespeare. As far as the movie goes, Krishnendu has only a little while to prepare for his part when Clayton fails to appear.

In *Saptapadi*, before the performance of the play Othello, Krishnendu's face is well-blackened by the make-up artist in order to racialize him with respect to the "white Desdemona." Krishnendu is not a "real unpainted Nigger."[7] He is neither the "Moor" he represents on stage nor the Englishman he has replaced onstage. Before the performance when Rina is made aware of Clayton's condition, she refuses to participate. Later she agrees, putting forward the condition that Krishnendu would not touch her during the performance. The performative stage, as seen within this film, is a space where social anxieties are played out. Rina Brown, the daughter of an Englishman, cannot bear to be touched by a "blackie." Sudipto Chatterjee and Jyotsna G. Singh have suggested that in colonial times the presence of a "native" on stage and his proximity to a white Desdemona might have been an unusual and highly controversial sight. While Rina Brown had racially aligned herself to the English, her later realization that her mother was an Indian woman shatters her socio-ideological moorings. As Paromita Chakravarti has suggested, Rina Brown represents the New Woman who is a "perfect combination of the spiritedness of a European heroine" and the submissiveness of a traditional Hindu woman. Krishnendu enters the fold of Christianity in order to be allowed to marry Rina while Rina succumbs to the persuasions of Krishnendu's father to let him go since he would never have place in society if they were to get married.

It is pertinent to mention that the director, Ajoy Kar, had employed other artists to perform the voice-overs for the actors in the play scenes because the actors' voices were heavily accented. Desdemona's part was done by the British actress Jennifer Kapoor and Othello's by the notable Bengali actor and theatre artiste Utpal Dutt. Suchitra Sen is elsewhere reasonably anglicized and capable of fluently peppering her Bengali dialogues with English words like "bastard." At the end of *Saptapadi*, we come to realize that Rina Brown, the Anglo-Indian Desdemona, a product of "sin" as her English father had spitefully declared, is the truly hybrid, liminal figure who is "divided to the vein." The movie concludes with the reunion of the lovers and Krishnendu carries Rina in his arms, away from the gaze of the audience, in the direction of a church that can be seen in the light of a breaking dawn.

The Othellos we witness in these films are talented individuals who are restrained and circumscribed by issues related to caste and faith. It is improbable that Perumalayan would have gained any social mobility by marrying the upper-caste Thamara. Omkara's caste might have at times helped him gain political mileage, but he would perhaps never been as respected as the Bhai Saab of the party. Here it is important to address the question of adaptation. How is adaptation distinct from other modes of intertextuality? Julia Sanders suggests,

> An adaptation signals a relationship with an informing source-text or original... On the other hand, appropriation frequently affects a more decisive journey away from the informing text into a wholly new cultural product and domain. This may or may not involve a generic shift, and it may still require the intellectual juxtapositioning of at[ ]least one text against another.... But the appropriated text or texts are not always as clearly signaled or acknowledged as in the adaptive process. They may occur in a far less straightforward context than is evident in making a film version of a canonical play.[8]

Here, an adaptation is seen as a text that is in constant dialogue with the source-text, a site where meaning is constantly negotiated. I shall venture on to say that there are unpredictable anxieties of influence here as well. The term "to adapt" means to layer the structure or function of an entity so that it is better fitted to survive and to multiply in its new environment. Adaptation can therefore also be thought of as being exclusively intermedial, involving the transfer of narrative elements from one medium to another. There might eventually be a significant modification or a radical mutation in the text that seeks to accommodate itself in a new environment by creating a new entity that might simultaneously indulge in a strange relationship with the source and yet be intelligible independently. What we need to do is isolate and study the transmedial myths or cultural ideas that make the Othello figure popular in our postcolonial location.

The films *Kaliyattam* and *Omkara* claim to be "adaptations" of *Othello*. The directors have acknowledged their debt to Shakespeare and have claimed to have interpreted the play within their ideological co-ordinates. I would like to argue that such an adaptation of Othello in the postcolonial location is without doubt an appropriation because the very act of transferring filtered-down narrative elements from a Shakespearean context into an Indian one involves an act of appropriation.[9] We cannot, by the virtue of our location, ignore the fact that the Othello-figure is dislocated in order to assist us in our interrogation of caste issues. When one considers *Saptapadi*, it is the racial as well as the religious factor that comes into play. The interaction between the characters Rina and Krishnendu onstage had an intensity that was carried forward by their offstage romance. The religious differences as well as their different racial moorings create impediments for Rina and Krishnendu's romance. The film might hint at their reunion but their marriage is never shown onscreen.

When it comes to Perumalayan and Omkara we see the "epidermalization of [caste]," to adopt Fanon's concept of the "epidermalization of race." The physical attributes of the Othello-figures become markers of their caste inferiority while the "whiteness" of the Desdemonas indicates caste purity and superiority. In the Indian context, with respect to *Kaliyattam* and *Omkara*, it is the transgressive nature of the inter-caste romance of star-crossed lovers that appeals to the audience. In *Kaliyattam*, cosmetics had been used to heighten the actor's skin tone to make him look exceptionally dark and pock-marked. His ugliness is attributed to the fact that he had been afflicted with smallpox as a child and had once accidentally burnt himself in the Theyyam fire. His ugliness is seen not just as a marker of his inferior caste but also as a result of the tribulations he undergoes because of his poverty. Thamara, on the other hand, is exceptionally fair. Omkara's dark skin (and by extension his relative ugliness) can be attributed to his caste affiliation since his sister too is of a similar complexion. In her essay on Bhardwaj's *Omkara*, Florence Cabaret has suggested that "[by] resorting to colour-blindness (as the cast is an all-Indian cast), it contests the orientalist pattern of the black man's violence against the white woman."[10] Thus, Bhardwaj's film is neither colour-blind nor does it do away with tensions regarding the skin-colours of the various characters in the film.[11] Iago/LangdaTyagi (played by Saif Ali Khan) is of a lighter complexion than Omkara and so is Keshuv (Vivek Oberoi). Omkara's sister, Indu/Emilia (played by Konkona Sen Sharma) married to Langda, is of a darker complexion than both her husband and Dolly (Desdemona). While the film might not be replicating the "orientalist pattern," racial/caste differences are not only visually highlighted in this film, the cast too appears to have been picked with a certain degree of awareness of the actors' complexions.

Fair-skin fixation is not uncommon in the Indian context where in a startling parallel dark-skinned people are considered less attractive. There has been a promotion of "dusky-skinned beauties" in recent times but the prejudice exists in popular imagination. Bipasha Basu plays the role of an entertainer (Chamanbahar "Billo") in *Omkara*, or to put it more coarsely a contemporary equivalent of the courtesan Bianca, while Kareena Kapoor (who has a fairer complexion than both Sharma and Bipasha Basu) plays the role of Dolly. Both Dolly and Thamara are beautiful but more importantly, it might seem, they are light-skinned, like Rina Brown. This seems to be no mere coincidence. Their complexion is repeatedly compared to that of the Othello-figures'. The difference in complexion heightens the transgressive element in such romances. "Romance" is often employed as a literary tool to transcend the problems developed by the plot, but in these films it is the very root of complications that cannot be resolved.

Othello has secured a cult-like status in this cultural situation owing to what Umberto Eco has termed as an "archetypical appeal" of a cult object that can be reduced and dislocated so that one only remembers parts of it. What we have inherited are primal anxieties related to miscegenation. Celia R. Daileader has coined the term "Othellophilia," which she defines as "the critical and cultural fixation on Shakespeare's tragedy of inter-racial marriage to the exclusion of broader definitions and more positive visions of inter-racial eroticism."[12] Caste, not race, in the Indian context is a vital yet an unstable and fragile maker of social difference. *Othello* can be perceived as a domestic drama where a husband is falsely convinced that he is being cuckolded, a theme that appeals across predominantly patriarchal cultures including in India, caste anxieties of lineage. The films express a hybridity where the Othello-figure becomes a socio-political symbol for the victims of hegemonic structures. It holds special appeal because the character is not an outsider nor is he completely dispossessed; he is talented and has heroic elements but is unable to negotiate with the intercommunal or caste dynamics. While *Saptapadi* edges towards the ideal situation, the redemptive quality of the film is diluted because Krishnendu slowly metamorphizes into the "white man but with black skin," a surrogate Clayton. Despite the attempts to present Krishnendu as a secular figure, the allure of the white and Christian in the film are apparent. He crosses over, but it does not mark a moment of transcendence from his position as the "other" in a colonial state because he is assimilated into the status of the ideal colonized subject. In an Indian situation these films inadvertently flag "the other" within the national boundaries. While the tragic narratives in *Omkara* and *Kaliyattam* do not overtly recommend intercaste conjugality, the reunion of the inter-religious lovers in *Saptapadi*, which is primarily a romantic film, suggests that such a romance, if not a marriage, might after all be possible.

Notes

1. Miriam Murtuza. Poems by Akbar Allahabadi, 4 January 2013, http://www.columbia. edu/itc/mealac/pritchett/00urduhindilinks/txt_akbarallahabadi_miriammurtuza.pdf. Syed Akbar Hussain of Allahabad, more popularly known as "Akbar" Allahabadi, had written several satirical shers or poems indicating the sentiments of people of his class under the British rule. He repetitively refers to a certain "Miss" in his works who might have been a European woman but keeping in mind his the satirical strains in his work we might consider that she might have been a rather anglicized woman of Indian origins. Here, she expresses her doubts about his allegiances.

2. Ania Loomba, "Local-manufacture Made-in-India Othello fellows." In *Issues of Race, Hybridity and Location in Post-colonial Shakespeares*, ed. Tom Hoenselaars (London: Arden Shakespeare, 2004). For a more detailed discussion of this point in the context of the essay one may look at Ania Loomba's paper.

3. Here I intend to draw from Homi Bhabha's conceptualization of "hybridity" and "interstitial spaces." In his well-known essay "The Location of Culture" he has explained and elaborated upon these two terms in detail.

4. Carol Thomas Neely, "Women and Men in Othello," in *William Shakespeare's Othello*, ed. Harold Bloom (New York: Chelsea House Publishers, 1987). Carol Thomas Neely

in her remarkable work "Women and Men in Othello" has discussed the importance of the handkerchief and the significance Othello endows it with after he discovers that Desdemona no longer has it.

5. Theodore P.C. Gabriel, *Playing God: Belief and Ritual in the Muttappan Cult of North Malabar* (Indiana University: Equinox Publishing Limited, 2010). I found Theodore P.C. Gabriel's extensive research has been invaluable since he has described the origins and the contemporary relevance of theyyam in great detail. According to him, the festival had suffered a backlash when Communism in Kerala was very much in vogue and sought to eliminate vestiges of what could have been perceived as oppressive religious practices. The ritual, however, has now once again been revived and is very often performed at educational institutions.

6. Aebischer, Pascale, Edward J. Esche and Nigel Wheale, ed. *Remaking Shakespeare: Performance Across Media, Genres and Cultures* (United Kingdom: Palgrave Macmillan, 2003), 50.

7. Loomba, "Local-manufacture." Ania Loomba in her essay explains the dilemma that the English adaptations of Othello in the India context were faced with. There were doubts not only about the color of the "natives" but also of their ability to perform the role.

8. Julia Sanders, "What is Appropriation?," in *Adaptation and Appropriation* (London: Routledge, 2007), 46.

9. Florence Cabaret, "*Indianizing* Othello: Vishal Bhardwaj's *Omkara*," in *Shakespeare on Screen: Othello.* (United Kingdom: Cambridge University P, 2015). Cabaret has put forward an interesting suggestion claiming that, "*Omkara* is representative of a post-independence way for approaching Shakespeare rather than a postcolonial reclaiming of Shakespeare" with its exploration of rural political landscapes and contemporary apprehensions regarding caste-consciousness and intercaste marriages (Cabaret "Indianizing Othello," 109).

10. Cabaret, "Indianizing Othello," 107–21.

11. Celia R. Daileader, *Racism, Misogyny, and the Othello Myth: Inter-racial Couples from Shakespeare to Spike Lee* (Cambridge, UK: Cambridge University Press, 2005). Daileader has aptly noted how, "Anglo-American culture generally 'casts' black men as Othellos" (Daileader, 7). The Indian film industry appears to be no different in this aspect whether it is Omkara in *Omkara* or Perumalayan in *Kaliyattam.*

12. Daileader, *Racism, Misogyny.* In this book Celia R. Daileader has used this term, "Othellophilia." In her study she has traced the roots of the fascination that inter-racial unions have held in Western societies.

7
Shakespeareana to *Shakespeare Wallah*
Selling or Doing Shakespeare in India

Paramita Dutta

Shakespeare Wallah, the second film from Merchant Ivory Productions (the collaborative enterprise of producer Ismail Merchant and director James Ivory), was released in 1965, a year after the quadricentennial birth celebrations of Shakespeare.[1] This film showcased the events in the life of a British theatrical troupe (that also had a few Indian actors in it) and its myriad experiences while touring and performing Shakespeare in various regions in post-independence India. The theatre company was called The Buckingham Players and was run by the actor–manager Tony Buckingham whose wife Carla and daughter Lizzie were principal actors of the same troupe.

What is most interesting about this film is that its central roles were played by none other than the members of an actual British theatrical troupe, Geoffrey Kendal's Shakespeareana (that consisted mainly of British and some Irish actors and later incorporated some Indians and Americans as well), that had actually toured India with their Shakespearean productions from the 1940s up to the mid-1980s with a break from 1948 to 1953.[2] Over a mere period of two and a half years, between June 1953 and December 1956, Kendal and his troupe gave a total of 879 performances to audience/spectators ranging from royalty to school children, and urban middle classes to semi-urban masses.[3] The actor–manager of Shakespeareana, Geoffrey Kendal, played his counterpart Tony Buckingham in the film, his wife Laura Liddel enacted the role of Carla, Buckingham's wife, and their younger daughter Felicity Kendal acted as the Buckinghams' daughter Lizzie, and it would not be far-fetched to assume that they were simply playing versions of themselves on reel. The Kendals' elder daughter, Jennifer, not only did the costumes for the film but also played the bit role of the British Mrs Bowen, the owner of the Hotel Gleneagles in Kalikhet, one of the places where the players stay during their tour. Jennifer's husband, the soon to be famous Indian film idol Shashi Kapoor, performed the role of the wealthy Indian playboy Sanju Rai, a character described by the director as "shallow but exuberant,"[4] but who is nonetheless an attractive man with whom Lizzie falls head over heels and quite hopelessly in love with. As Geoffrey Kendal fondly and rightly reminisces in his autobiography published in 1986, also called *The Shakespeare Wallah*, "All our family had roles in the film."[5]

Geoffrey Kendal's passion for Shakespeare was deep and profound as was his affinity for India, as asserted by him and his family time and again. The Second World War and the Entertainment National Service Association (ENSA) where Kendal was recruited as an actor brought him to India for the first time. In Bombay he met Peter Meriton, the man with whom he had previously arranged theatrical shows in Lancashire schools. It was Meriton's brainchild that they open a little touring company that would play in schools and colleges in India, especially after the end of the war, a suggestion that would redirect the course of Kendal's life. The idea was not forgotten and was rekindled at a chance meeting after they were both back in England and by the end of 1946 the Shakespeareana Company was conceptualized. Soon they sailed to India "armed with Shakespeare," whose plays in Kendal's perception "were so much appreciated in India."[6] Thus began the Kendals' tryst with India, an association that would last a lifetime.[7] In an early diary entry written in Ootacamund on Christmas Day in 1956, Kendal had gone into raptures over the varied Indian climate, was warmly appreciative of the different creeds living in harmony in India and had ended by pronouncing that "India is my home."[8] Although the exact kind and nature of his professed love for India would merit general scrutiny, it can be definitely said that he forever upheld the peripatetic life he led in India and would choose coming back to this country if he could, rather than live permanently in England where his roots lay. It was because of his love for India that his youngest daughter Felicity Kendal came all the way to this country and scattered his ashes in the Indian Ocean after he had breathed his last in a hospital in England after a prolonged period of illness.[9]

Geoffrey Kendal's first meeting with the producer–director duo of Ismail Merchant and James Ivory took place in 1963. Since they wanted to make a film about a life similar to his, of an English actor-manager touring in India with a company performing Shakespeare, he graciously lent them his diary written during his early days when India became independent. This became the starting point of the screenplay of the film *Shakespeare Wallah* co-written by the novelist Ruth Prawer Jhabvala and the director James Ivory, although the diary was not drawn directly upon.[10]

The neologism "Shakespeare Wallah" was neither coined by Ismail Merchant, James Ivory nor Ruth Prawer Jhabvala, as Geoffrey Kendal himself used to be called so.[11] Nonetheless, during a *Conversation with the Filmmakers*, the producer Ismail Merchant explicates that the "Wallah" in the title of the film means a tradesman or one who sells something, here Shakespeare, whereas the director James Ivory wishes to stress that it actually implies one who is associated with something, and here, one who "does" Shakespeare.[12]

This chapter proposes to trace how the troupe Shakespeareana and the film *Shakespeare Wallah* either sell or do Shakespeare in India, and what the implications entail. It argues that if the real life troupe Shakespeareana had mostly succeeded in "selling" Shakespeare to the educated Indians and students of schools and colleges, which accounted for its fame and continuing run in that circuit, the troupe The Buckingham Players in the film only manage to "do" Shakespeare as they are able to and in the only way they know how to, clinging to their colonial attitudes and keeping all their "Englishness" intact, incapable of moulding themselves to the changing times and the changing India after independence. Consequently, they are shown to fail miserably, not only in connecting with the Indian audience that is breaking free from its colonial past but also in "selling" Shakespeare in a manner that would bring in more business for them and ensure their growth and popularity. The aim of this chapter is also to look at how the film through its portrayal of the decline and commercial failure of the Shakespearean troupe argues against the hegemony of canonical Shakespeare, sounding the death knell of antiquated performances that overlook the historical location and multifaceted nature of the spectators. It further suggests that the meteoric rise and popularity of commercial Hindi cinema as a powerful alternative meant that the time for "different

Shakespeares"[13] had come, as opposed to a universal, timeless and transcendental Shakespeare. It can be said that the film *Shakespeare Wallah* puts forward popular mass culture as a powerful force that needs to be addressed and suggests that to be a commercially successful "Shakespeare *Wallah*" in India, one needs to come down from the colonial ivory tower, feel the pulse of the common masses and tap their diverse desires in order to effectively reach out to them.

Poetically and visually alive, *Shakespeare Wallah* is an extraordinary film, in spite of its shoestring budget of 80,000 dollars. The money was acquired by the makers from the sale of the world distribution rights of their film *The Householder* (1963) to Columbia Pictures. The real reason *Shakespeare Wallah* was shot in black and white was that there was no money to shoot in colour. This proved to be aesthetically fortunate and enhanced the film by creating evocative chiaroscuro effects. As the makers were unable to afford the steep expenses of studio sets everything was shot on location, in the hill station of Kasauli, in Punjab, in Simla, in Alwar in Rajasthan and in Lucknow.[14] Satyajit Ray scored the lilting music of this film and his photographer Subrata Mitra worked as cameraman. Ivory calls himself the "lucky recipient" of their profound talents.[15] The film's merits were enough to qualify it for entry to the Berlin Film Festival in 1965 and Madhur Jaffrey, the actress who played the Hindi film heroine Manjula in the film, was awarded the Silver Bear Award for Best Actress.[16]

The film is about the waning fortunes of The Buckingham Players who tour all over India, providing classic Shakespearean theatre—with all its Englishness intact—to anybody who is willing to pay for it, from an Indian maharaja of declining fortunes who is a great Shakespeare aficionado (played by Utpal Dutt), one who can randomly and effortlessly quote from Shakespeare's plays at the dinner table, to Indian school audiences who are bound to study the works of the English Bard as an integral part of their educational curriculum. The troupe's doing or performing Shakespeare stems from their boundless passion for the Bard and blends with their economic necessity of earning a livelihood (hence, selling Shakespeare), and is the only way of life known to them or available to them in the film.

One may pause at this point to consider what India actually means or how it is portrayed in the film that chronicles the life of a travelling company of players doing and selling Shakespeare in that country for its people. Although we get beautiful glimpses of the scenic variety and beauty of India as the players travel through the deserts of Rajasthan by car or go up to the hilly regions of Kalikhet, we never get a taste of what performances of Shakespeare in the different regions of India among its diverse people may imply, especially as the players perform from Shakespearean plays only in their classic English style, regardless of the locale they visit. Their performance of Shakespeare is neither mediated nor sifted through the various social, cultural, historical, political, ideological filters of the target culture and audience. The troupe traverses various territorial spaces but does not make any inroads into the diverse cultures. As a result, although we get to see different geographical locations of India as we travel with the troupe, the difference is not reflected in the cultural domain of the performance, does not display any localization and adaptation, and we do not get a vivid and vibrant portrayal of the pluralities that constitute the distinctive nature of India as a cohesive whole. This is especially so as all the places and people shown are seen through the eyes of the players of the British troupe, and the vista through their in-built colonial lens is nothing if not limited, one-dimensional and often discordant. The charming diversity in unity that is the uniqueness of India, which is hinted in Kendal's diary entry mentioned earlier, does not find place in the representation of India in this film as India is viewed from the myopic lens of the British Tony Buckingham who has a marked colonial attitude towards all things Indian and an innate sense of smug superiority.

It may be noted here that although Geoffrey Kendal moved with his troupe in India systematically from region to region, occasionally cutting across classes, his personal autobiographical reflections in *The Shakespeare Wallah* were not anchored in India's historical and political situation. The turbulent political realities of the independence of India do not seem to mould his perceptions regarding the country or significantly affect him. His strong statement regarding the Partition of India, calling it a '*great* mistake' (emphasis mine) that caused "immense suffering,"[17] is a lone one and at other times he blithely glosses over such historic events such as Mahatma Gandhi's assassination in 1948, only recounting its effect on his personal itinerary and not recording it as a momentous event in India's history.[18] Shormishtha Panja astutely observes that Kendal's merely referring to the Partition as a 'great *mistake*' underplays its life-changing impact on the common people of India. To top it all, Kendal's approach to the father of the nation's untimely demise is more than casual, to the point of getting the date of his assassination wrong.[19] In this way, according to Panja, Kendal appears to be "numbing his mind against the impact of history and to shield theatre from it" and does not seek to explore "the connection between theatre and the people, the power of theatre to implement change, the close link between theatre and politics."[20] In this sense the director's portrayal of Tony Buckingham as aloof and untouched by any political, social and cultural realities of the country he has adopted finds resonances in Kendal's own ahistoricity. In this film, Tony Buckingham aspires to give to Indian audiences a sort of universal, timeless and transcendental Shakespeare, whether they require him or not. Yet again, he can be said to have been modelled on the real life Kendal, especially if we recall and accept Felicity Kendal's appraisal of her father in her introduction to his autobiography *The Shakespeare Wallah* where she asserts that,

> My father's passion was more to do with giving than gaining, and what he wanted to give was Shakespeare...to hundreds of thousands of people, in fact, who would meet the plays often for the first time, and remember them forever. In this he succeeded, and that is his achievement.[21]

The difference that can be perceived is that Buckingham succeeded in communicating, but not selling, Shakespeare as an idea; he gives the classic English Shakespeare but fails to create connoisseurship in his intended audience. Perhaps it entertains, but there is no appreciation of what he so passionately offers.

The reasons may not be too far to seek. The British troupe presents Shakespeare as it always has and its dramatic style in post-independence India in the film appears to be archaic and entirely outmoded. The players are shown performing scenes from *Antony and Cleopatra, Hamlet, Twelfth Night, Othello* and *Romeo and Juliet* at various locations in the film but, owing to their training or their ingrained colonial attitudes, they are never shown trying to mix with local traditions or adopt any other traditional or folk theatre form as a vehicle to make Shakespeare more accessible and enjoyable to the target Indian audience. As a result, an unbridgeable distance and lack of connect develops between the theatre performers and their audience. They never feel nor understand that Shakespeare needs to be Indianized at all, or that their kind of English theatre ought to be adapted, even if not recast, to cater to the Indian temper and audiences for increased viewership and appeal. The transition that India undergoes from colonial to postcolonial times seems to be lost on The Buckingham Players who seem to be perpetually living on the stage and never descend from it on the terra firma of reality. The Buckinghams fail to realize the metamorphosis in the mindset of the common Indian viewer after the country's independence as one who was neither attracted nor compelled to watch the English fare of the erstwhile rulers. Quite unfortunately, they keep on churning out performances that would perhaps only be popular with the educated Indian steeped in a typically English education.

Felicity Kendal in her BBC documentary *Indian Shakespeare Quest* had said,

> The rise of nationalism in the twenties and thirties returned the spotlight to Indian culture. As Independence approached, Shakespeare's days in the Indian sun looked numbered. My parents couldn't have picked a worse time to launch their company Shakespeareana. Shakespeareana was launched in January 1947, just seven months before Independence.

In the *Conversation with the Filmmakers*, James Ivory asserts that in the last days of the British Raj there was a great interest all around in Shakespeare's plays. However, between 1947 and 1964, the period in which the film is based, the audience dried up and just a handful of people were interested in seeing Shakespeare performances. He goes on to say that while writing the script Ruth Prawer Jhabwala thought that she could work on this and it would be a metaphor of the disappearance of English and Western culture. However, as John Pym has aptly assessed, the film was not so much "a reflection of the end of the Raj, as of the fate of its individual idiosyncratic camp followers."[22] Merchant Ivory's 1969 film *The Guru* too dealt with the failure of the West to connect with Indian culture, but with a marked difference. In *The Guru* the West is more inclined to take from India what it can in terms of culture and spiritual enlightenment, whereas in *Shakespeare Wallah* the West feels that it has a lot to give the Indians in the form of the riches of its civilization that is embodied in Shakespeare.[23] One may note here that the diminishing interest in Shakespeare that both Felicity Kendal and James Ivory mention could more suitably be termed as the diminishing interest in Shakespeare as presented in the classic English style, as did the Kendals in real life or the Buckinghams in the film. It does not refer to the tradition of adapting and appropriating Shakespeare as various Indian languages and cultures did and continue to do, through translation and performance, since the end of the nineteenth century, much after the foreign playwright was imported into India in the last quarter of the eighteenth century.[24]

Apropos this essay's proposition, it is not that the British or the colonial manner in which Shakespeare is performed by the players in *Shakespeare Wallah* has no takers at all. The way Shakespeare is received by the characters in the film tells a lot. There appears to be a clear demarcation in the film between the Indian people who have not yet freed themselves from the shackles of their colonial past, are suffering from a strong colonial hangover and who idolize Shakespeare (such as the Indian maharaja and Sanju Rai), and those representing the new emerging independent India (such as the officer-in-charge of the school, Manjula and the audiences), who neither have much knowledge of nor an unqualified fascination for Shakespeare presented in characteristic English style. Buckingham's performances are a hit with the former section of the Indian educated elite who are oriented towards Shakespeare, but fail to impress or attract the latter, or the majority of the Indian people in the film.

Buckingham is piqued beyond measure when he fails to sell his kind of Shakespeare, an instance being when he cannot secure the desired number of performances in the school at Kalikhet. He rues mournfully to his wife Carla at night in a scene in *Shakespeare Wallah*:

> I just can't get it out of my mind. We've been here year after year. Five, six, seven performances. They couldn't see enough of us. But it's such a rejection—a rejection of me. Of everything I am, everything I've done. Nowadays...why should they care?.... It's not appreciation I am talking about. Carla, it's—Why are we here...instead of in Sheffield or in Bristol or in—at least somewhere like that. Did I have to come all the way to India because I wasn't good enough for those places?.... No, it wasn't that. We were idealists, you and I. Both of us.

The Buckinghams were not only self-proclaimed "idealists" but, with their regular performances at schools in British India, had been more than assured of their role, in John Pym's words, as "dispensers of truth, the truth of literature," their medium being Shakespeare. However, they slowly realize that much has changed and India after independence has turned into a place of impermanence for them. They sense they have lost their stronghold and should have gone back after India became independent in August 1947.[25] They experience a nostalgic yearning for those glorious days of the past, when India was a British colony, and find it difficult to accept with equanimity the transformation in the Indian audience which, according to Tony Buckingham in the film, was the most wonderful audience in the world, more so possibly because it was uncritically appreciative and inevitably applauded their performances. He is a character unable to accept criticism and rejection, unable to move on and adapt with the times and cannot advance any "Indian Shakespeare" that may attract a new viewership. Buckingham remains entrenched in his colonial beliefs. His desperate offer to sell Shakespeare in an attractive, "package performance of comedy, tragedy and *Hamlet*," hardly generates any enthusiasm in the officer-in-charge of the school who is more pre-occupied with the two demands of NCC and cricket, and dismissively declares that there is no time for the Shakespeare performances of The Buckingham Players. One is immediately reminded of the incident at the beginning of the film where the troupe is shown driving through the vast landscape of Rajasthan. Their car breaks down and while they wait, hoping fervently some help would arrive, a *madari* gets his performing monkey to entertain them with tricks. At the end of the performance, he unhappily declares that his art was no longer valued by anybody, in an exercise in introspection heavily flavoured with truth and pathos, which prompts the most senior member of the troupe, Bobby to wryly observe, "Our story exactly!" The truth and wisdom of this comment comes home to the audience watching the film at the point when the interaction between the officer-in-charge of the school and Tony Buckingham takes place. It has been rightly said that in this film "the action unfolds with melancholy regret and melancholy inevitability against the panorama of India."[26] In the film, the people who do not suffer from colonial hangover (who form the majority here) and who do not have a colonial education cannot value the Shakespeare the Buckinghams do and want to sell and are unwilling to buy him by watching and paying for such performances, resulting in the players' dwindling fortunes.

It has been appropriately argued that the film could be read as a critique of Buckingham's imperialist mentality. Tony's inability to comprehend why his art is being rejected in favour of native Indian traditions and his extreme nostalgia for India as a pre-independence colony of the British Empire is a limitation of his understanding that is directly responsible for the failure of his troupe to adapt to a changing India. He is unsuccessful in treating Indians as equals to present a truly intercultural theatre that speaks to an Indian audience on equal terms instead of talking down to them from a higher level.[27]

When he is trying to persuade the officer-in-charge of the school in Kalikhet to allow his company more shows in the school, he pointedly remarks that Shakespeare must unquestionably be in the school curriculum and that he has been told that their performances are not only very popular in schools and colleges but also very "helpful" to the students. We may ask whether the missionary zeal of "helping" Indians so characteristic of British imperialists also lurks beneath, and is inseparable from Tony's means of earning a livelihood by performing Shakerspeare. When later the officer-in-charge makes conversation about the Founder's Day celebrations of the school that Tony had missed and where the Guest of Honour, the Minister of Mines and Fuels had delivered an excellent speech that he feels Buckingham would have liked, the latter retorts disdainfully: "Uh. Full of misquotations from Shakespeare?" The surprised officer-in-charge remarks that the Minister had only alluded to "our ancient Sanskrit writings." The superior feeling and high-handed attitude that Tony Buckingham has about all things Shakespeare and British, is blatantly laid bare in this single instance when he is unable to envisage an Indian minister quote from anything other than Shakespeare, or even quote correctly from the Bard. It is this attitude that prevents him and his troupe from connecting with his target audience, and colours his performances of Shakespeare, a playwright who was anyway viewed as "the most authoritative representative of the culture of the coloniser."[28]

It is a well-known historical fact that the British introduced the study of English literature and language in the Indian education system with the passage of the Indian Educational Act of 1835 and the study of Shakespeare's texts were given place of pride in the curriculum as they were meant to uphold and impart the humanistic ideals of the British civilization. Shakespeare was also included in the syllabi of the civil services examination and helped establish the cultural authority and supremacy of the British, and made staging the plays a popular activity in schools and colleges.[29] Ania Loomba has said that "English literature was a universal source of morality and knowledge; even Indian nationalism was attributed to the study of Shakespeare."[30] It cannot but be emphasized how colonial educationists and administrators used the canonical Shakespeare to not only celebrate the superiority of the so called "civilised races" but to reinforce cultural, gender and racial hierarchies by interpreting his plays in a conservative fashion and never questioning or destabilizing them.[31] Tony Buckingham, especially in the instance referred to previously, seems to subscribe to these imperialist views.

In this film, this division between Shakespeare and the British on the one hand and India and indigenous traditions on the other is laid directly in the open in the statements of Mrs Bowen, the owner of the Hotel Gleneagles in Kalikhet where the Buckinghams are staying. While conversing with Carla, Beryl Bowen observes, "It's not like the old days. What do these people know about *our* theatre? Shakespeare and all that" (emphasis mine). Beryl's perception that Shakespeare is always *theirs*, a uniquely superior and innately British possession that is far above in stature to Indian culture and people, which may only be given to the Indians from a pedestal but cannot amalgamate with their culture, makes the gulf between the British and Indians remain unbridgeable in her eyes, and cross-cultural assimilation or intercultural theatre, inconceivable concepts. Similarly,

Tony too does not have the affective capacity to accept that there can be any other kind of Shakespeare, any intercultural or Indian Shakespeare that would directly speak to an Indian audience and that they may fashion for the target audience and possibly reap profits from.

In the film, the only flavour of the local or any indigenous art form in India is presented in the form of Hindi cinema, and its popularity, power and vogue here is embodied in the figure of Manjula, the fashionable, flamboyant and temperamental Hindi film actress, and the mistress of the affluent Indian playboy Sanju Rai who later becomes the romantic love interest of Buckingham's daughter Lizzie. Cinema has, since its nativity, been regarded as the arch-enemy of theatre and Geoffrey Kendal too, in his autobiography, had spoken of the threat he felt after the arrival of cinema and expressed his concerns at how it might spell doom for theatre as a tradition in particular, and touring actors in general.[32] This threat of the cinema, in the film *Shakespeare Wallah*, is epitomized by Manjula.

At one point in the film, Sanju invites Manjula to a performance of *Othello* by The Buckingham Players, strategically thinking that the mere presence of a film star at a show will draw crowds and rake in money. Manjula agrees, even if out of jealousy, curiosity about and hatred of her rival Lizzie who is performing. She enters the theatre hall towards the end and her arrival causes the expected sensation and disruption. Instead of watching the critical and deeply moving scene of Desdemona's murder by Othello on the stage, the audience's attention is turned on Manjula, with many of them hankering after her autograph amidst general mayhem. The enraged Tony Buckingham loses his composure and cannot continue with the performance before he has admonished the rowdy audience. Much later, when Sanju personally tries to tender an apology for the commotion caused by his guest, Buckingham reacts to the evening's events by calling it the "victory of the motion pictures over theatre." The high priest of Shakespeare, presented in the classic English style, is seen to lose out to the popularity of the glamorous Hindi film industry and its flashy stars. The players are unable to either do or sell Shakespeare when competing with this representation of popular mass culture.

Geoffrey Kendal describes this phenomenon in his autobiography while talking about how the makers approached the film, "The actors were seen as last of the British Raj, hanging on to a dying culture in an out-of-date medium, while the cinema, representing modern India, took over with its new and vital power."[33] Although one may agree with his general outlook on the representation of cinema in this film, one cannot help but take issue with his describing theatre as an "out-of-date medium," which it has never been, in spite of age-old and stiff competition from the film industry. In my opinion, a more accurate assessment would be describing the Buckinghams' theatrical style and dramatic tradition to be "out-of-date" especially in the context of newly independent India where an upsurge of nationalistic tendencies and resistance to the British outlook would be inevitable. As John C. Tibbetts has observed, culturally, the world in the film is too impatient for Shakespearean drama per se and too preoccupied with the novelties of entertaining musical films. The travails of The Buckingham Players only exemplify the schisms opening up between old and new worlds, between classical and popular entertainments, especially as they are sluggish about changing with the times.[34] They, according to Patricia Storace, are "constrained by their theatrical calling, which has lost popularity to Indian films that represent the new, indigenous Indian culture."[35] Nandi Bhatia has also argued that the dramatic response generated by Manjula's presence, in contrast to the tepid response to the players' performance of *Othello*, only affirms the symbolic importance of commercial Hindi cinema for Indians, just as the stark loss of interest among the Indian populace signals the necessity of being attentive to the shifting historical contexts of Shakespearean performance and reception.[36]

The unruly behaviour of the audience, not only in the presence of Manjula but later during a performance of *Romeo and Juliet* (the catcalls and hooting), may also be interpreted as a show of opposition to a fading dominant culture imposed from outside and one that gradually seems foreign and incomprehensible to native traditions such as the rising Hindi film industry. The diminishing appeal of Shakespeare may also symbolize the loss of colonial authority and resistance to cultural imposition from outside.[37]

The colonial Tony Buckingham has little idea of how to sell Shakespeare in postcolonial India and Sanju Rai, his aide and faithful admirer of the values that his outmoded British theatre represents, fails to help him with his stunted vision and ineffective strategy. Tony does not even imagine inviting a Hindi film star to his show, and Sanju can only envisage inviting Manjula as his guest and not use his influence and good will with both her and the Buckinghams to bring about a collaboration between them and make her part of their theatrical production. This alone could have been an excellent promotional stratagem to sell their brand of Shakespeare better through her "star power," using her acceptability with the masses as a means to reach a wider audience. Instead, both of them obsess about the classical status of Shakespeare in their conversations with the other characters and in their general attitude.

That Shakespeare is viewed as the repository of high culture is more than evident in Sanju's perceptions and ideas and powerfully affects his relationships with the women around him. After being mesmerized by Lizzie's beautiful enactment of the role of the hapless Ophelia in a performance of *Hamlet*, he comes to his girlfriend Manjula and excitedly tells her about the philosophy and poetry to be found in Shakespeare that has touched his heart and stirred him to his innermost depths and praises Lizzie saying, "She's a very fine artist. For such people we can have some respect. Don't you get tired of your films? Always the same—singing, dancing, tears, love."

As Nandi Bhatia has perceptively observed, this positioning of Shakespeare at a level above Hindi films by an upper class Indian is indicative of elite attitudes, which reproduce the colonialist divisions of "high" and "low" culture and treat popular Hindi cinema as "low" art and also deny adequate respect to the practitioners of this art.[38] This disparagement of art forms meant for the masses and its artists is not only peculiar to colonial characters such as Sanju Rai in the film, but is also displayed by certain critics such as Parama Roy, in whose perception Manjula functions as "a *debased* example of an Indian modernity, characterized as it is by the *repetitive*, *puerile*, and *loutish* pleasures of mass culture (including Bombay cinema and cricket)" (emphases mine).[39] It seems that Roy is naturally aligning with an aristocratic and high cultural order (that the Buckinghams feel they naturally belong to and Sanju Rai is anyway part of by virtue of being descended from a feudal aristocratic family) which belittles mass culture as immature, coarse and commercial, especially as opposed to purist Shakespearean theatre. Although I do agree with Roy when she goes on to propound that the logic of the film is "quasi-Orientalist" and that Manjula is simultaneously a representative of "Indian modernity" and "Indian tradition," I find it difficult to accept that it is so in its "worst aspects."[40] That the mainstream cinema actress, the popular Manjula, would be embodying the "worst" aspects of Indian modernity and tradition is a parochial value judgement that Roy nurtures along with the colonial Buckinghams and Sanju. That is not the premise of the film, which spells doom for purist and conservative Shakespearean theatrical performances and depicts the allurement and success of popular mass culture, the mainstream Hindi cinema of emerging and liberated India, through the figure of Manjula.

In the film, Sanju gets attracted towards Lizzie because she performs Shakespeare, and considers her a finer artist than Manjula, whom he refers to as a mere "songstress." This also emanates from a particular cultural outlook that considered that, originally in India, professional actors mostly belonged to lower castes whereas Shakespearean professional actors have always been regarded very highly in dramatics per se, irrespective of their blood or birth. Thus, when Lizzie enquires about his love affair with Manjula, he protests, "What do I care for her? She's only an actress." When the innocent Lizzie reminds him that she too, is an actress, Sanju vehemently asserts, "No, you are different." The difference cannot be articulated even by the colonially educated Sanju because it is a psycho-social perceptual position, deeply ingrained in a people, present over a vast demographic entity with a long and colourful history, precisely what the Buckinghams needed to perceive and study to be a commercial success.

The aura and status that performing Shakespeare had endowed on Lizzie in Sanju's eyes is gradually dissipated when Sanju realizes that she too has as public a life as any other actress (such as Manjula) and attracts similar attention from males in the audience over which he has absolutely no control. Sanju had been more correct than aware when he had evaluated Lizzie and found her to be "different" as previously mentioned. She is unique in that scenario. She neither belongs to the old colonial world represented by her father and his troupe, the Indian maharaja, Sanju and Mrs Bowen nor is she a part of the emerging new world and sensibilities as seen reflected in the officer-in-charge of the school, Manjula and the audiences who often come to watch their performances without any capacity for discernment or appreciation, and who do not pay obeisance to the canonical Shakespeare. She occupies a curiously liminal space, somewhere in between. Although in the film she is a Shakespearean actress, she loves acting per se and not only acting Shakespeare. She is not the least perturbed, as Sanju is, of the public lives actors have to lead where they may often be forced to "dress and undress in public."

Performing Shakespeare, which had been the marker of difference between Lizzie and Manjula in Sanju's eyes, soon ceases to be so and Shakespeare is brought down from the pedestal when Sanju can no longer appreciate Lizzie's art and is unable to accept her in spite of her brave attempt to embrace the old colonial world as represented by him. She offers to give up everything, even acting, which is her life's passion, for him, in vain. At the end of the film, Lizzie leaves India for England to make her fortunes in acting in the country of her origin after facing disappointment in love. She represents the next generation and through her attempts to acclimatize to the change in her life and her situation we harbour some hopes of evolution, which was sorely lacking in the Buckinghams who had nearly frozen in time.

Lubna Chaudhry and Saba Khattak see in Lizzie's departure to England, after Sanju's failure to commit to her, a gendered and political stance privileging all things English and feel that the filmmakers have created a film that yearns for colonialism.[41] In my reading, exactly the contrary happens, as has been discussed so far.

Valerie Wayne, on the other hand, argues that the film "depicts cultural hybridity primarily through the figure of Sanju," who is shown to be caught between his Indian nationality and a mix of his love for Lizzie and wistfulness for the Raj in a manner that blurs the lines between "coloniser and colonised, oppressor and oppressed."[42] It may be opined that given her nationality Lizzie may be thought of as a colonizer or oppressor, but as a character and in her relation with Sanju she is neither. Sanju too as a character may be colonized, even post-independence, but is never oppressed. Sanju is limited by his typical orthodox Indian male sensibility and not nationality, when he rejects Lizzie's love. This is because Lizzie ultimately fails to conform to his expectations of and concept of a woman he would like to marry, given her strong female identity, one who would be the treasure house of his family "izzat" or honour and not have the kind of autonomy and choices that she exercises so naturally in her life.

For Nandi Bhatia, hybridity in this film fails completely and we are shown the general failure of the East and West to connect and merge in India when viewed from a colonial perspective. The film depicts the passing of an era. According to her, Shakespeare and the Raj are laid to rest by an emerging new India that The Buckingham Players find difficult to accept or understand.[43]

Kendal was deeply aggrieved by the premise of this film as he thought that his touring company, Shakespeareana, had been a success and had taken Shakespeare to all corners of India. Instead of affirming and celebrating that feat the film showed The Buckingham Players to not only be down on their luck and unsuccessful in procuring shows for schools, but also overshadowed by the popular and alluring Hindi movie industry. He felt that the film "was in some ways close to our experience, yet at the same time seen through a different pair of eyes. We did not recognise ourselves."[44]

It should be borne in mind that the existing reviews of some of the performances of Shakespeareana were greatly favourable and commendatory of their skills in acting and stagecraft. They performed *Hamlet, Othello, Julius Caesar, Macbeth* and scenes from *The Merchant of Venice* between October 1947 and January 1948 at St. Xavier's College Auditorium, Calcutta. R.H. Lesser reports that they had "caused a sensation" and is appreciative of the use of spectacle and their talent in acting, and finds the "actors fully deserving the great applause accorded them." Another review of their performances at the Shantiniketan open air theatre that came out in *The Statesman* of 15 January 1954 also records that Shakespeareana gave "two highly appreciated performances of *Macbeth* and *The Merchant of Venice* to capacity crowds"[45] all of which reaffirms the sense of success that Kendal had about his touring company. He records in his autobiography how only in August 1982, while watching the film on television he finally reconciled himself to its depiction of the failure of a theatrical company in India disturbingly resembling his own and how it had earlier unsettled his sense of the success that his troupe Shakespeareana enjoyed in India.[46] Kendal, who had never been at ease with the cinematic medium, says about the film *Shakespeare Wallah*, "it was ironic that in the whirligig of time it was the despised cinema that told the world of my existence and to a certain extent of my fight."[47]

However, given Kendal's personal sense of success and satisfaction with his troupe Shakespeareana's productions of Shakespeare in schools and colleges in India, the film *Shakespeare Wallah* depicts his "fight" through the portrayal of The Buckingham Players only "to a certain extent" and no more.

The Kendals, on the contrary, did receive appreciation in the English theatre circuit and schools in India and although their group ultimately disbanded and they were reduced to just husband and wife performing some scenes from Shakespeare, their sojourn in India was not entirely "short-lived" as Shormishtha Panja says,[48] since they did perform up to the mid-1980s. In 1990, Geoffrey and Laura Kendal were even honoured with the Sangeet Natak Akademi Award for bringing Shakespeare to all parts of India.[49] At the same time, it is deeply ironical that their success and contribution was recognized only in India and not in England. Ananda Lal attributes this paradox to the Indians' lack of adequate knowledge of British theatre after independence and the Second World War and their colonial hangover that led to their obeisance to and uncritical acceptance of all things British, which allowed the Kendals to fill in the vacuum during the late 1940s and early 1950s when hardly any foreign Shakespeare companies toured India.[50] There were only a few exceptions, such as Norman Marshall and Eric Eliot as we have seen earlier.[51] According to Lal,

By mid-century British Shakespearean theatre had changed completely, away from the classical elocutory and historical/pictorial style to highly radical experiments by such directors as Barry Jackson (modern-dress *Hamlet*, 1925), Fyodor Fyodorovich Komissarzhevsky/Theodore Komisarjevsky (simple realistic acting and symbolic sets in *King Lear*, 1936) and Tyrone Guthrie ("magical" *A Midsummer Night's Dream*, 1937), not to speak of the young Peter Brook (Watteau-esque *Love's Labour's Lost*, 1946; minimalistic *Romeo and Juliet*, 1947, "throwing out the scenery").[52]

The Kendals, however, had not evolved from the "classical elocutory and historical/pictorial style" as Lal mentioned and had been untouched by radicalism of any sort. They were forgotten, unlike these pioneers in Britain who are still remembered and acknowledged for their avant-garde techniques. As Lal succinctly puts it: "The Kendals had, in fact, passed their sell-by date with Shakespeareana."[53]

When Kendal was asked by Indu Saraiya in 1984 about the new trends in English theatre, he had openly professed his ignorance by remarking, "Difficult to say." He had further derided directors working with Shakespeare in Britain by calling them failed actors and ones who approach each play with one idea, whereas, "Shakespeare's plays were not written with one idea—not by any means."[54] Quite evidently, there was no love lost between Kendal's concept of Shakespearean theatre and the radical experimentation practised in Britain, and he fiercely clung to his old world approach.

Whatever may have been their position (or lack of it) in the global theatrical scene, the contribution of Shakespeareana and the Kendals to the English-theatre circuit in India could never be written off. They did leave an indelible impression especially in the minds of young Indian actors who toured with them or saw their performances at an early age. Many such actors later rose to prominence in their own right and often credited the Kendals for the craft they had learned.

A pioneering figure of modern Indian theatre and National Award winning actor, Utpal Dutt, who had been awarded the prestigious Sangeet Natak Akademi Fellowship for contribution to theatre in 1990, had worked with the Kendals in the beginning of his tryst with theatre. His association with them began the first time they had come to Calcutta in 1947, and then again in 1953 when they called him to join them at Madras for their India and Pakistan tour.[55] In an interview with Samik Bandyopadhyay, Dutt claims to have learnt all the rules and methods of a professional repertory company from the Kendals and said that their theory of carrying everything with them on their tour was the correct theory.[56] He had learnt from them that "There is no art without discipline and no discipline without sacrifice."[57] Dutt even dedicated his book *Shakespearer Samajchetana* (1972) to Geoffrey Kendal, proclaiming him to be his "guru," one who had trained him to act Shakespeare.[58]

Acclaimed actor, writer, director and producer, Madhav Sharma, who is now based in UK but worked with the Kendals at the beginning of his career from 1960–62, calls them "The Good Companions" and asserts that joining them,

transformed my life—teaching me that anything is possible in life if the tide is taken at the flood, the importance of following one's dream as long as one is prepared for the inevitable hard work in learning any craft, and confirming my belief...in the universality of art and culture.[59]

Padma Bhushan and Padma Shri Naseeruddin Shah, an actor who has also won the National Film Award thrice, recently in *The Anupam Kher Show—Kucch Bhi Ho Sakta Hai* on television, credited the inspiration behind his foray into acting to be Geoffrey Kendal, who would perform in his school every year. He was greatly impressed by his presentation of selections from Shakespeare and his seamless transformations from the characters of Macbeth to that of Hamlet or Shylock and had himself started out by imitating him. Naseeruddin calls Geoffrey Kendal his "ustad," which means "guru" or teacher, and describes their relationship to be similar to that of the disciple–teacher duo of Ekalavya–Dronacharya of *The Mahabharata*.[60] Nothing more can vouch for the success of the Kendals as theatre practitioners in India and the influence they had on budding talents. The Buckinghams of *Shakespeare Wallah*, unfortunately, foreclose that possibility by remaining fossilized in time.

Notes

1. *Shakespeare Wallah*, directed by James Ivory (1965; New York: The Criterion Collection, 2004), DVD. All future references to the film follow from this and have not been cited again.
2. See Dan Venning, "Cultural Imperialism and Intercultural Encounter in Merchant Ivory's *Shakespeare Wallah*," *Asian Theatre Journal* 28, no. 1 (2011): 155, accessed 16 October 2012, doi 10.1353/atj.2011.0000 and Nandi Bhatia, *Acts of Authority/Acts of Resistance: Theatre and Politics in Colonial and Postcolonial India* (Ann Arbor: The University of Michigan Press, 2004), 69.
3. Bhatia, *Acts of Authority/Acts of Resistance*, 57.
4. Robert Emmet Long, *James Ivory in Conversation: How Merchant Ivory Makes its Movies* (Berkeley: University of California Press, 2005), 78.
5. Geoffrey Kendal with Clare Colvin, *The Shakespeare Wallah* (London: Sidgwick and Jackson, 1986), 145.
6. Kendal, *The Shakespeare Wallah*, 12, 73–85.

7.   It must be noted here that Shakespeareana was neither the first nor the only theatrical troupe of its kind that travelled to various parts of India performing Shakespearean plays. Lewis's theatrical troupe performed Shakespearean plays at Calcutta Maidan between 1872 and 1876. Herr Bandman too visited Calcutta with his troupe in 1882. Post the suppression of native drama that had been on the rise during the Swadeshi movement after the Partition of Bengal in 1905, various troupes from London visited India such as the ones of Charles Allen (1909), Matheson Lang (1911 and 1912), Allen Weekly (1912) and Harding and Howitt (1918). The Grant Anderson Theatre Company under the management of the English actor manager Anderson arrived in India in 1930 and even employed the great Indian actor Prithviraj Kapoor who toured India with this troupe and won great acclaim for his role of Laertes in *Hamlet*. In 1948 Norman Marshall performed plays of Shakespeare in the cities of Delhi, Agra, Allahabad, Calcutta and Bombay. Eric Eliot brought his acting troupe to India in 1951 See Bhatia, *Acts of Authority/Acts of Resistance,* 55, 57, and Shashi Kapoor with Deepa Gahlot, *The Prithviwallahs* (New Delhi: Roli Books, 2004), 11.

8.   Felicity Kendal, *White Cargo* (London: Michael Joseph, 1998), 85.

9.   See Felicity Kendal, *Indian Shakespeare Quest,* directed by Patrick Mc Grady and presented by Felicity Kendal (Wavelength Films for BBC, 2012). All future references to the BBC documentary follow from this and have not been cited again.

10. John Pym, *The Wandering Company: Twenty-One Years of Merchant Ivory Films* (British Film Institute, London: BFI Publishing, 1983), 37.

11. Venning, "Cultural Imperialism and Intercultural Encounter," 162.

12. *Conversation with the Filmmakers*, performed by Ismail Merchant, James Ivory, Felicity Kendal, and Shashi Kapoor (New York: The Criterion Collection, 2004), DVD. All future references to this interview with the filmmakers follow from this and have not been cited again.

13. I borrow this term from Jyotsna Singh's article "Different Shakespeares: The Bard in Colonial/Postcolonial India," *Theatre Journal* 41, no. 4 *Theatre and Hegemony* (1989): 445–58.

14. Robert Emmet Long, *The Films of Merchant Ivory* (New York: Harry N. Abrams, Inc, 1991), 46–47.

15. Long, *James Ivory in Conversation*, 84.

16. Long, *The Films of Merchant Ivory*, 47.

17. Kendal, *The Shakespeare Wallah*, 92.

18. Kendal, *The Shakespeare Wallah*, 100.

19. Shormishtha Panja, "Lebedeff, Kendal, Dutt: Three Travelers on The Indian Stage," in *Transnational Mobilities In Early Modern Theater,* eds. Robert Henke and Eric Nicholson (London: Ashgate, 2014), 254–55.

20. Panja, "Lebedeff, Kendal, Dutt," 254, 255.

21. Felicity Kendal, introduction to *The Shakespeare Wallah*, by Geoffrey Kendal with Clare Colvin (London: Sidgwick and Jackson, 1986), viii.

22. Pym, *The Wandering Company*, 37.

23. Long, *The Films of Merchant Ivory*, 55.

24. See Vikram Singh Thakur, "Shakespeare Reception in India and The Netherlands until the Early Twentieth Century," *CLCWeb: Comparative Literature and Culture* 14, no. 2 (2012), 1–9, accessed 25 October 2013, <http://dx.doi.org/10.7771/1481-4374.1958>, and Poonam Trivedi, introduction to *India's Shakespeare: Translation, Interpretation*

and Performance, eds. Poonam Trivedi and Dennis Bartholomeusz (Delhi: Pearson Longman, 2006), 16–17.

25. Pym, *The Wandering Company,* 37.
26. Pym, *The Wandering Company,* 36.
27. Venning, "Cultural Imperialism and Intercultural Encounter," 155.
28. Nandi Bhatia, "Imperialistic Representations and Spectatorial Reception in *Shakespeare Wallah* (1)," *Modern Drama* 45, no. 1 (2002): 61+, accessed 30 December 2013, URL http://go.galegroup.com/ps/i.do?id=GALE%7CA97755086&v=2.1&u=inbhc&it=r&p=AONE&sw=w&asid=88d91f1a47ed40a7bbee4cc3f6a61293
29. Bhatia, *Acts of Authority/Acts of Resistance,* 53–54.
30. Ania Loomba, *Gender, Race, Renaissance Drama* (Manchester: Manchester University Press, 1989), 18.
31. Ania Loomba and Martin Orkin, "Introduction: Shakespeare and the Post-Colonial Question," in *Post-Colonial Shakespeares,* ed. Ania Loomba and Martin Orkin (New York: Routledge, 2004), 14, accessed 17 October 2013, E-brary.
32. Kendal, *The Shakespeare Wallah,* 144.
33. Kendal, *The Shakespeare Wallah,* 145.
34. John C. Tibbetts, "Backstage with the Bard: Or, Building a Better Mousetrap," *Literature-Film Quarterly* 29, no. 2 (April 2001): 10, accessed 31 December 2013, www.johnctibbetts.com/PDFs/Backstage%20With%20The%20Bard.pdf
35. Patricia Storace, "The Poet of Karma," The New York Review of Books (7 October 1999): 26, quoted in John C. Tibbetts, "Backstage with the Bard," 10.
36. Bhatia, "Imperialistic Representations."
37. Bhatia, *Acts of Authority/Acts of Resistance,* 72.
38. Bhatia, *Acts of Authority/Acts of Resistance,* 71.
39. Parama Roy, "Reading Communities and Culinary Communities: The Gastropoetics of the South Asian Diaspora," *Positions: East Asia Cultures Critique* 10, no. 2 (2002): 491, accessed 16 October 2012, Project Muse.
40. Roy, "Reading Communities and Culinary Communities," 492.
41. Lubna Chaudhry and Saba Khattak, "Images of White Women and Indian Nationalism: Ambivalent Representations in *Shakespeare Wallah* and *Junoon,*" in *Gender and Culture in Literature and Film East and West: Issues of Perception and Interpretation,* eds. Nitaya Masavisut, George Simon, and Larry E. Smith (Honolulu: University of Hawai 'i Press, 1994) 19–25, discussed in Venning, "Cultural Imperialism and Intercultural Encounter," 160.
42. Valerie Wayne, "*Shakespeare Wallah* and Colonial Specularity," in *Shakespeare: The Movie: Popularizing the Plays on Film, TV, and Video,* eds. Lynda E. and Richard Burt Boose (London: Routledge, 1997), 101, quoted in Venning, "Cultural Imperialism and Intercultural Encounter," 160.
43. Bhatia, *Acts of Authority/Acts of Resistance,* 68–75.
44. Kendal, *The Shakespeare Wallah,* 145.
45. Ananda Lal and Sukanta Chaudhuri eds. *Shakespeare on the Calcutta Stage: A Checklist* (Calcutta: Papyrus, 2001), 38–39, 41.
46. Kendal, *The Shakespeare Wallah,* 153.
47. Kendal, *The Shakespeare Wallah,* 144.
48. Panja, "Lebedeff, Kendal, Dutt," 256.
49. Venning, "Cultural Imperialism and Intercultural Encounter," 162.

50. Ananda Lal, e-mail message to author, 12 July 2015. My deepest gratitude to Professor Ananda Lal, Department of English, Jadavpur University, for discussing this issue with me via e-mail.
51. See note 7.
52. Ananda Lal, e-mail message to author, 12 July 2015.
53. Ananda Lal, 12 July 2015.
54. Indu Saraiya, "The Shakespearewallah's Remembrance of Things Past," *The Sunday Statesman* (Kolkata), 3 June 1984, 2.
55. See Samik Bandyopadhyay, "Utpal Dutt: An Interview by Samik Bandyopadhyay," in *Contemporary Indian Theatre: Interviews with Playwrights and Directors*, ed. Paul Jacob (New Delhi: Sangeet Natak Akademi, 1989), 12, and Arup Mukhopadhyay, *Utpal Dutt: Jeevan O Shrishti* (Kolkata: National Book Trust, 2010), 26–30.
56. Bandyopadhyay, "Utpal Dutt," 12.
57. Mukhopadhyay, *Utpal Dutt: Jeevan O Shrishti*, 31.
58. Mukhopadhyay, *Utpal Dutt: Jeevan O Shrishti*, 30.
59. Madhav Sharma, e-mail message to author, 28 September 2014. I would like to thank my dear friend Ms Thea Buckley, doctoral student of The Shakespeare Institute, England, for providing me with the contact information of Mr Madhav Sharma and enabling me to communicate with him. My sincerest gratitude to Mr Sharma for responding to my e-mails in spite of his ill health.
60. Naseeruddin Shah, interview by Anupam Kher, *The Anupam Kher Show—Kucch bhi ho sakta hai*, Colors Television, 3 August 2014.

Translation and Issues of Language and Politics in Regional Shakespeares

8

Mapping Shakespearean Translations in Indian Literatures

T.S. Satyanath

Introduction

It has been generally presumed that the early Shakespearean translations into Indian languages followed a two-phase activity, an early phase of adaptations, followed by a phase of faithful literary translations. Generalizing on a conspicuous characteristic feature of translation activity of Shakespeare in Kannada[1] and extending it to the Indian scene, scholars,[2] have pointed out that Kannada's response to Shakespeare represents two ambivalent and parallel streams of sensibilities: one corresponding to literary tradition, which could be roughly identified as sensitive to the educational and academic, and the other to the stage tradition, which could be identified with a newly emerging public sphere. However, it is worth noting that Murthyrao actually points out that stage versions preceded literary versions. Furthermore, a majority of the Shakespearean studies subsume a text-centred approach of literary analysis and consider faithful translations as superior to adaptations, which were mostly done for stage productions. Accordingly, Shakespearean translations have been studied as literary texts rather than as theatrical productions and not as studies of public sphere and its sensibilities. On the contrary, it has also been pointed that many early adaptations have been done to cater to the culture-specific needs such as divergent social sensibilities of the theatre going audience who were not exposed to English and its literary culture.[3] Above all, it is the itinerant nature of the professional theatre that constantly facilitated modifications in the textual and production aspects of early Indian drama and this led to transformations. Issues such as the plays chosen for translation, the background of the translators and the nature of the audience were highly fluid in the translation culture of nineteenth-century India, as a majority of the early plays adopted during this period were, in fact, meant for the use of professional theatre groups. Transformations in theme, locale, characterization, genre, structure, and so on keeps taking place in early Shakespearean translations and a majority of them appear to be centred around the audience's sensibility and sensitivity to culture. It is pertinent to point out that in the prefaces to their Kannada translations M.S. Puttanna and Srikantheshagowda have attempted to justify their transformations by suggesting cultural appropriateness as being the reason for the liberties that they have taken.[4]

There is a need to see theatre as a potential platform for discursive exchanges between a play, its audience, theatre artists, playwrights and the subsequent discussions. As the discussions and debates pertaining to the performance continue in print, conversations and mass media that includes scripto-centric, phono-centric and body-centric representations, the theatrical public sphere may be considered as one of the most effective public spheres for the communication and circulation of ideas. Theatre as public sphere is actually a modification of public sphere theory from a focus on the political accomplishment of a single economic class to a potential situation or an institution in which diverse aesthetic and social epistemologies are simultaneously present.

In order to understand and map the processes involved in the transformation of Shakespearean plays during the early phase of Indian translation, we need to take a look at the bibliographic information available on Shakespearean translations in Indian languages. Methodologically speaking, a database of Shakespearean translations in Indian languages that includes the name of the translator, the year of translation, the title of the translation and the publisher needs to be put together in order to get a comparative perspective. A series of comparative analyses on aspects like title transformation, background of the translators, publishers and the professional theatre companies for whom the translations were made can provide us an understanding of Shakespearean translations in a comparative perspective within the theatrical public sphere and literary culture during the late nineteenth and early twentieth centuries. However, the bibliographic information available in the bibliographies is not uniform across different Indian literatures and, hence, comparisons might not provide an actual picture of the translation activity. Elsewhere, for Shakespearian translations in Kannada, such a detailed analysis has been attempted[5] and I have avoided going into such an analysis here. Several studies such as Bhatia,[6] Gokhale,[7] Hansen,[8] Lal and Chaudhuri,[9] Loomba,[10] Mohanty,[11] Shankar,[12] Singh,[13] and Trivedi and Bartholomeusz[14] are some of the attempts to map Shakespeare in Indian languages. A majority of them take positions looking at Shakespeare either from the perspective of text or theatre (director/actor/performance). Against such a backdrop, the present study is an attempt to map Shakespearean translations from a theatrical public sphere point of view.

The early adaptations of Shakespeare into Indian languages, many of which have often been claimed as unfaithful and have been criticized, actually deserve a relook as zones of hybridity. If these early adaptations could be viewed as negotiations between the European and Indian writing cultures then we can have at least two different points of viewing the activity of translation. The first one is a Euro-centric position of mapping the correspondences between the original and the translated texts. This could be roughly designated as the influence and reception model of understanding the translation process. Alternatively, we can think of an Indian literatures-centric position from which the translation process could be mapped. Such a model not only maps the translation processes from a diametrically opposite position but also provides an opportunity to understand adaptations within the cultural context in which they were produced and consumed. Such a perspective also reverses the dominant Euro-centric view of translation theory and instead provides a view that maps the translation activity from within the translating culture. Thus, the issue of originality and unfaithfulness in translation is contested and, instead, the ways in which a recipient culture maps and negotiates the cultural differences is addressed. In fact, many early translators have pointed out that it is the cultural mismatch between the two cultures that prompted them to adapt rather than seek literal translations. In addition, the aesthetic sensibilities of the newly emerging public sphere of early modern Indian theatre during the mid-nineteenth century needs to be mapped in order to understand these translations within such a cultural context. A margino-centric perspective rightly addresses these issues. The term margino-centric refers to a diametrically opposite way of understanding a relationship in terms of a centre to margin approach, which could be a relationship of power. It also suggests that margino-centricism as perspectives from the margin are pluralistic in nature, as margins are multiple whereas centre is unitary. Furthermore, within the dominant centre and oppressed margin(s) relationship, it also suggests a counter-structure and subversion. Some scholars believe that a passive influence of Sanskrit poetics and an active influence of Sanskrit drama (and their products) have created and nurtured a theatrical aesthetic sensibility during the mid-nineteenth century.[15] On the contrary, this essay argues that consequent to the emergence of a theatrical public sphere during the nineteenth century, in which the modern Indian drama and Shakespearean translations emerged, a new hybrid aesthetic sensibility emerged that combined the Indian classical tradition, European colonial modernity and local popular and folk sensibilities.

Translations and Adaptations: The Musical Theatre

Shakespeare has been widely adapted and translated into different Indian languages, particularly for theatre during the early phase. In order to understand this process we need to map the aesthetic sensibilities of modern Indian theatre as public sphere, in which the majority of the audiences were neither familiar with the canon of their own classical theatre nor with that of the European theatre. Thus, neither dramaturgy of Sanskrit and/or vernacular theatre traditions, nor that of the European tradition was easily accessible when the modern Indian theatre as a public sphere emerged. If at all a poetics of theatre was present, it was actually an un-codified poetics of practice, from the folk and popular performing traditions that existed in different regional and vernacular traditions of India. However, this will not rule out the possibility of permeation of the elements of the previously mentioned traditions into popular and folk performing traditions in the vernacular folk theatre traditions of India. Thus, the Indian adaptations of Shakespeare during the late nineteenth and early twentieth centuries were clearly distinctive in terms of their cultural characteristics. Popularly known as Parsi theatre all over India, *Company Natak* in several Indian languages and *Sangeet Natak* in Marathi, these adaptations reproduced translations and adaptations of classical Sanskrit plays and Shakespearian plays within the context of the pictorial realism of Victorian theatre (touched up by nineteenth-century French melodramas). These adaptations were quite removed from both the stylized conventions of their Elizabethan origins on the one hand and whatever was available within the folk and popular theatre traditions in Indian vernacular performing traditions on the other. It is the emergence and development of this theatrical public sphere and its sensibilities that is going to be discussed here.

Though the Parsi theatre was not the first to become musical, it flourished mainly in the former Bombay Presidency province and its sphere of influence was confined mainly to the railway routes connecting various cities of British India. However, the productions of the Parsi theatre owe much to Shakespeare and to the Shakespearean productions from England. Interestingly, the musical components of Parsi theatre as well as other vernacular and regional theatres actually came from the indigenous classical, popular and folk traditions. At the same time, it is the stagecraft, themes and stage conventions, lighting and costumes that the Parsi theatre took from the west. Above all, Parsi theatre was quick to discover the commercial potentialities of not only the indigenous traditions but also the Shakespearean and other Western theatrical techniques. As a matter of fact, it is now presumed that the Parsi theatre borrowed little from Shakespeare beyond the general outlines of the plot, but the theatre companies ensured the biggest and most widely circulated presence of Shakespeare within the Indian theatrical scene. Many travelling theatres performed Shakespeare in various cities of British India, sometimes going as far as Rangoon and Singapore.[16] At the same time, many of these performances were made into films in the silent era and then reproduced in the early talkie era. In a sense, the Parsi theatre was not only modern India's first commercial urban theatre but consequent to its penetration into the length and breadth of the country, it was also India's first national theatre.[17] Let us take a look at the itinerary of the Parsi theatre during the latter part of the nineteenth century and the early part of the twentieth century. Figure 8.1 provides the itinerary of Parsi theatre companies.

The vernacular company theatres in Marathi, Hindi, Gujarati, Tamil, Telugu and Kannada, within their respective itinerary spheres, filled up the gaps left over by the itinerary of the Parsi theatre companies. Furthermore, the itineraries of these vernacular theatre companies acted as a complementary mode of popularizing the musical theatre and creating a new public sphere. These vernacular theatre companies moved through smaller towns performing in village fairs, *urs* and such traditional precolonial public spheres in the linguistic regions where they operated. As the geography of such itineraries also constituted long standing bilingual regions, they also acted as catalysts in the spread and popularization of the techniques of Parsi theatre and the sensibilities of its public sphere into

Figure 8.1

The Itinerary of Different Parsi Theatres

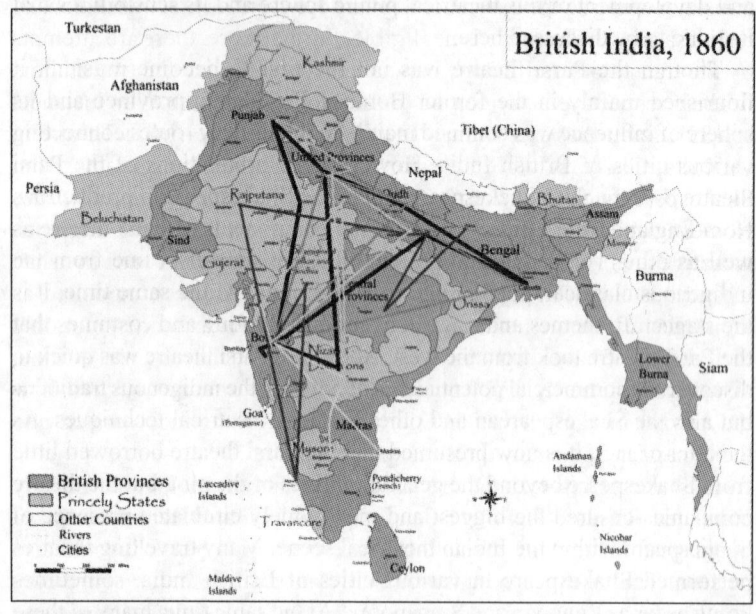

Source: Khajuria.[18]

the vernacular and regional theatre public spheres. Above all, there was a continuous exchange of ideas and components between the European proscenium theatre, the pan-Indian Parsi theatre, the regional company theatres and the local folk theatres that levelled the radical differences that could have existed among these divergent theatrical traditions and made them compatible for consumption at the national level.

If one looks at the fertile crop of Shakespearean translations in Marathi, Kannada and Tamil,[19] and notes that a majority of them done during the early phase were translations for the professional companies, then the significant role played by the musical company theatres in the early phase of Shakespearean translations becomes evident. The intention of the present study is not to map such a vast body of translations in Indian languages as the bibliographic information regarding Shakespearean translations is not uniformly available in other languages.

The interventions of the Parsi theatre in the development of a hybrid sensibility that is a composite of the European and classical Indian sensibilities could be understood not only by the fact that a single translator has translated both Kalidasa and Shakespeare in several Indian languages, but also from the fact that even in the absence of a single translator doing so the difference in years between the first translations of Kalidasa and Shakespeare is negligible. Furthermore, there are attempts by the translators and theatre companies to synthesize the two authors in their respective activities of translating and staging. For instance, in 1831, Babu Prasanna Kumar Tagore established the Hindu Theatre in Calcutta. The first night's performance consisted of extracts from Shakespeare's *Julius Caesar* and Bhavabhuti's *Uttara Rama Charita*. However, this performance was in English. Apart from such attempts, narrative poems like the Bengali *Yogesh Kabya* written in 1881 by Ishan Chandra Bandopadhyay has a protagonist who has been modelled as an intellectual of the nineteenth century with his indebtedness not only to Kalidasa, Bhavabhuti and Harsha but also to Shakespeare, Milton, Wordsworth, Shelley and Tennyson.[20] All these attempts suggest how the newly emerging hybrid sensibilities were getting incorporated into the dynamics of the new theatrical public sphere.

It is interesting to note that as eighteenth century Europe eagerly translated Kalidasa and other Sanskrit classics into different European languages, the zeal for translating Shakespeare into Sanskrit could also be seen. This zeal was so intense that a Sanskrit translation of the play *The Comedy of Errors* as *Bhranti Vilasam* by Shaila Dikshitar appeared as early as 1877 and a Sanskrit translation of *A Midsummer Night's Dream* as *Vasantikasvapnah* by Paravastu R. Krishna Rao-Acharya[21] appeared in 1895. The translator's objective, according to his introduction, was to introduce Sanskrit scholars to the poetry of Shakespeare and to show India's educated elite that Shakespeare wrote as well as Kalidasa, or vice versa. In fact, starting from William Jones, Kalidasa has been repeatedly called "the Shakespeare of Hindustan." A Sanskrit translation of *The Merchant of Venice* appeared in 1964 and a translation of *Hamlet* as *Chandrasenah: Durgadeshasya Yuvarajah* appeared in 1980.

In this connection, it is interesting to take a look at the first appearance of translations from Kalidasa and Shakespeare in Indian languages. Table 8.1 provides information regarding the first translations of Kalidasa's *Shakuntalam* and the plays of Shakespeare. While in Bengali, Marathi and Sindhi, the gap is just a year, in the case of Kannada it is two years. In Telugu, Tamil and Urdu the gap is six years. In Gujarati, Hindi and Oriya the gap ranges from 12 to 17 years. In these languages too the tendency to translate Kalidasa and Shakespeare more or less at the same time exists. The Malayalam translations, however, remain to be scrutinized. The case of Assamese deserves a special mention here, as it is a classic case of

Table 8.1

Table Showing the Details of the First Translations from Kalidasa and Shakespeare in Indian Languages

Language	Year	Title	Translator	Year	Shakespeare Work	Translator
Bengali	1854	Shakuntala	Ishvar Chandra Vidyasagar	1853	The Merchant of Venice/Bhanumati Chittabilas	Harachandra Ghosh
Gujarati	1867	Shakuntala	Jhaverilal Umiyashankar Yagnik	1852	The Taming of the Shrew/Nathari Firangioz Thakame Avi	Dinshah Aredeshir Talyarkhan
Hindi	1864	Shakutala Natak	Raja Laxman Singh	1880	The Comedy of Errors/Bhramajalaka	Ratnachandra
Kannada	1869	Shakuntala Natakavu	Churamuri Sheshagirirao	1871	The Comedy of Errors/Nagadavarannu Nagisuva Nataka	Chenna-basappa
Malayalam	1861	Bhasha Shakuntalam²³	Ayilyam Tirunal Rama Varma	1888	The Merchant of Venice/Porsya Svayamvaram	NA
Marathi	1861	Shakluntala	Krishnashastri Rajavade	1862	Hamlet	Nanasaheb Peshwa
Nepali	1889	Shakuntalam	Motiram Bhatta		NA	NA
Oriya	1898	Shakuntala	Harihar Rath	1881	Tempest/Banabala	Ramashankar Ray
Panjabi	1900	Shakuntala	Charan Singh		NA	NA
Sindhi	1898	Shakuntala-Dushyant	Gagan Singh Atmasingh Advani	1897	The Merchant of Venice/Hasna Dildar	Kalich Beg
Telugu	1870	Shakuntala Natakamu	M. Shashacharyalu	1876	Julius Caesar/Sijaru Charitramu	V. Vasudeva Shastri
Tamil	1876	Cakuntalai Vilacam	Ramachander Kavirayar	1871	The Merchant of Venice/Venis Varttakan	Vicuvanata Pillai
Urdu	1890	Shakuntala	Hafiz Muhammad Abdullah	1894	Othello	Munshi Jvala Prasad

Source: Author.

hybridity involving Shakespeare, Kalidasa and the medieval Assamese performing tradition. According to Sarma[22] in the year 1857, Gunabhiram Barua wrote the first modern Assamese play, *Ramnavami Natak* (published in the literary magazine *Arunodaya*), which is an adaptation of *Romeo and Juliet* interspersed with elements from Kalidasa's *Abhijñānaśākuntalam*. In addition, the play also incorporated medieval Assamese Vaishnavite performative elements from the Assamese Ankiya Nat. Thus, *Ramnavami Natak* epitomizes the hybridity of colonial modernity represented by the Shakespearean theme, traditionality and classicism represented by Kalidasa, and the regional performative tradition represented through elements from Ankiya Nat. However, *The Comedy of Errors*, translated into Assamese as *Bhrama Ranga* in 1888 by Lakshmi Nath Bezbarua, may also be considered as the first translation of a Shakespearian play.

The significant implication of clustering together of the translations of Kalidasa and Shakespeare in Indian languages suggests the overlapping nature of colonial modernity and Indian classicism and the hybridity that was characteristic of nineteenth-century India. As a majority of these translations were intended for the theatre companies, it further substantiates the role played by the newly emerging sensibilities of the theatre going public implying the importance of mapping translations within the nineteenth-century theatrical public sphere.

Commenting on the nature of hybridity, Chatterjee[24] observes as follows:

> Attempts in different parts of India, be it Bengal, Bombay Presidency or other places of theatre activity, were to synthesize the varied strands of available material to create a hybrid variety. The visible attempt was to syncretise Western theatre, "the major colonial paradigm," with the available traditions and aesthetics of native folk performance.

Early Modern Indian Theatre and its Public Sphere

Among the nineteenth-century critics Shakespeare definitely enjoyed a privileged position because of an inherent bias towards the West by the English-educated class that was emerging on the scene. In this regard, Das[25] draws our attention to Bankim Chandra Chatterjee's assessment of Shakespeare as "the one man in the world's literature whose works hold up a mirror to every possible pathos of man's inner life" and Hemachandra Bandopadhyay's eulogy of Shakespeare: "Kalidasa belongs to India, you to the world." There were also attempts to undertake comparative analyses of the characters Miranda, Desdemona and Shakuntala by Bankim Chandra Chatterjee and Rabindranath Tagore. The translations of such analyses appeared in Indian languages serving as ideal models for a comparative study of Western colonial modernity and Indian classicism. Furthermore, such comparisons claim that Shakespeare's heroines were timeless creations and imply that the Indian classical heroines were similar.

The early phase of Indian modernism characteristically consists of a pro-modernity position that corresponds with colonial modernity, a pro-traditionality position that corresponds with classicism and traditionality, and a third hybrid position that is a synthesis of the first two. The early modern theatre, by the very nature of its divergent audience sensibilities, represents the hybrid position. No other schematic diagram than the sketch given in Figure 8.2 could satisfactorily represent the complexity of hybridity that is being suggested here. Adya Rangacharya's (Sriranga) article *Samanyara Shekspiyar* (Shakespeare of ordinary people) in

Figure 8.2

Kalidasa and Shakespeare Hand in Hand, Suggesting the Hybridity of Indian Classicism and Colonial Modernity

Source: Balurao.[27]

Shekspiyarige Namaskara (salute to Shakespeare), edited by Balurao[26] consists of an illustrative sketch by the artist R.S. Naidu, a renowned painter and faculty member at the Jaganmohana School of Arts, Mysore, to demonstrate one of the important statements, "Kalidasa as Shakespeare of Hindustan."

A re-reading of the sketch by Satyanath[28] helps us to appreciate its significance:

> Kalidasa and Shakespeare are represented with hand in hand and dressed in appropriate attires, suitable to the worlds that they represent. While Kalidasa has a palm-leaf manuscript in his hand, Shakespeare has a scroll. Everything looks like a perfect demonstration of a harmonious East–West encounter. However, a closer look reveals that Kalidasa is represented on the right side and Shakespeare to his left. We all know that in Indian iconographic tradition, *vama* (left) conventionally suggests inferiority and insignificance with reference to its right counterpart.

Here, Kalidasa could be easily replaced by Vyasa or any other ancient Indian poet and this provides the appropriate entry point for formulating the hybridity that I have mentioned. The sketch of Naidu could serve as an ideal model of hybridity between colonial modernity and Indian classism/traditionality and the public sphere in which nineteenth-century Indian theatre needs to be mapped. At the same time, it could also serve as a margino-centric approach, that is, reading hybridity in terms of Indian sensibilities or understanding Shakespeare through theatre and the nineteenth-century public sphere.

The hybridity between colonial modernity and traditional classicism appears to be fairly deep-rooted in the nineteenth-century public sphere itself. It is not just accidental that during the period of early modern Indian drama many writers who translated Kalidasa in Indian languages have also translated Shakespeare. It has been observed that there are several such instances from different Indian languages. Both Kalidasa and Shakespeare have been translated by Lala Sitaram in Hindi, Govina Pilla in Malayalam, Atulchandra Hazarika in Assamese, Kumara Guruparar and P. Sambandha Mudaliyar in Tamil, and Basavappa Shastry, D.V. Gundappa and Masti VenkateshaIyengar in Kannada.[29] In the case of Marathi, G.B. Deval not only translated a musical version of *Mricchakatika* (1887) and *Vikramorvashiya* (1989), but also translated *Othello* as *Zunzarrav* (1890) for the Aryoddharak Dramatic Company. It is noteworthy that these translations coming from two diametrically different cultures were happening simultaneously.

The playwrights for the Parsi theatre and the company *Nataks* were translating from Kalidasa, Bhavabhuti and Shudraka from classical Sanskrit and Shakespeare from English, and were also writing independent plays in which they appear to have freely mixed themes and conventions from both the cultural sources. As a consequence, both classical Sanskrit plays and Shakespearean plays had to be not only translated by the same translator and at the same point of time as we have seen before, but the plays of the two traditions underwent changes to create hybrid thematic and structural patterns during this period. In fact, we can see the emergence of a uniform structural pattern in thematic, musical, stagecraft and audience sensibilities.

Hence, there is a need to look at early modern translations from an audience-centred perspective, in order to capture the essence of the transformations that have gone into these translations. As a case study, let us see how Kalidasa's *Shakuntalam*'s Kannada translation (Curamari Sheshagirirao, 1869) and Shakespeare's *A Midsummer Night's Dream*'s Kannada translation *Pramilarjuniyam* (Srikantheshagowda, 1886) are structured, and a significant role is played by the sensibilities of the audience and public sphere in the formulation of these translations.[30]

The verse format of Kalidasa has been translated into a corresponding verse format in Kannada, sometimes retaining the same meter while at other times experimenting with a different one but from the Sanskrit metrical system (*vritta* and *kanda*, but usually referred popularly as *padyas*). Srikantheshagowda uses the same metrical system in his adaptation (vritta and kanda).The prosaic Sanskrit dialogues of Kalidasa have been translated into a colloquial variety of speech from the North Karnataka region by Sheshagirirao. Srikantheshagowda uses the standard variety of Mysore Kannada for higher-level characters (the Mahabharata and *Rati-Manmatha* episodes) and a lower variety for the rude mechanicals (play within a play). Several songs have been written by both the translators to suit the nature of the musical theatre that was prevalent and popular around that time, which were new introductions into these translations. The songs are highly lyrical and poetic in nature. Whereas *Shakuntala's* translation contains songs based on classical *ragas* from Karnataki and Hindustani styles of music (popular tunes of Hindi, Kannada and Marathi *bhajans*) and also folk tunes (*saki* and *lavani*), *Pramilarjuniyam* has more or less a similar format, though Karnataki ragas are more frequently used (popular Telugu and Kannada *kirtan* tunes). Both translations consistently use *vilambit/gamaka* for verse (slow style of singing without the use of instruments,) ragas for songs (music with *tabla/mridangam/dholak*) and folk tunes for popular numbers.

There is a need to understand this translation strategy from the point of view of audience sensibilities, the public sphere. As pointed out earlier, the early modern theatre was itinerant in nature and professional in approach. Hence, its audience was not only heterogeneous but also had diverse regional sensibilities. It is this diversity that has gone into the construction of these adaptations. The use of the Sanskrit verse format and the vilambit/ gamaka style of music suggest that attempts were made to preserve the classical dimension of Sanskrit/Kannada literary tradition intact in the adaptations. An attempt was made to keep the ornamentation intact, both in textual and musical formats. This was done to cater to the sophisticated sensibilities of the elite section of the audience. We need to remember that these verses could only be recited melodiously in a vilambit/gamaka style. In addition, they gave the actor enough liberty to explore both the lyrical and musical aspects of the metrical verse. They could not only be sung and expanded but could also be repeated as refrains. However, a majority of the audience were ordinary, illiterate people. Verse format was too pedantic a style for them. Hence, folk tunes were introduced to cater to their taste and the dialogues were written in both the standard and local varieties comprising a diglossia. There are also instances where bilingualism was used in place of diglossia.

The songs, making use of the ragas, but sung without any elaboration, were a characteristic of folk theatre. However, they were contained by the rhythmic beat of tabla/mridangam/dholak, the refrain–verse combination and a premediated trajectory. These songs used to follow the tunes of classical style music, both Hindustani and Karnataki. The songs bridged the gap that existed between the classical verse format and the folk tune/standard language/vulgar dialect format of the dialogues, and created a smooth intermediate zone. They also catered to the sensibilities of a newly emerging middle class who were familiar with English musicals, Parsi theatre and the Marathi *Sangeet Natak*. This musical format appears to be in continuity with medieval Bhakti sectarian communities in which the musical and lyrical aspects are extensively interwoven. In fact, both Sheshagirirao's *Shakuntalam* and Srikantheshagowda's *Pramilarjuniyam* systematically mention the tunes to be used for the songs. While *Shakuntalam*'s songs use tunes of famous Hindustani and Karnataki devotional (*bhakti*) songs and folk tunes, *Pramilarjuniyam* songs are based on tunes from Telugu devotional compositions. The very fact that the two texts were written and used in the northern and southern parts of Karnataka explains the sensitivity of the translators to their audience community. In a way, the emergence of such a hybrid format not only brought closer the segregated precolonial public spheres, namely, the royal, the religious and the open, but also helped in sensitizing the different spheres to each other.

Three distinct styles reflect three phases of the periodization of Kannada literature: the ancient Kannada (*hale-gannada*), medieval Kannada (*nadu-gannada*) and modern Kannada (*hosa-gannada,*) that applies equally well for other Indian literatures. While the vritta and kanda style predominantly represents the ancient (old) Kannada format (the ornate *campu* style) the songs represent predominantly the medieval Kannada format (bhakti poems and their singing tradition) and the prose style represents the modern Kannada format. As the latter part of the nineteenth century is also the period of the formation of Kannada identity, a reconceptualization of the Kannada literary tradition within the public sphere of theatre, involving its classical, medieval and modern periods was an urgent necessity. The first history of Kannada literature, albeit brief, written by F. Kittel, appeared in 1881.[31]

The discussion on the structuring of the translation process can be schematically shown in Figure 8.3. These adaptations were catering to three levels of audience, the elite, the newly emerging middle class and the folk, and made use of appropriate styles of metrical format, musical format and language variations.

Figure 8.3

Schematic Diagram Showing the Interrelationships Among the Metrical, Musical Styles and the Audience in the Nineteenth Century Theatrical Public Sphere

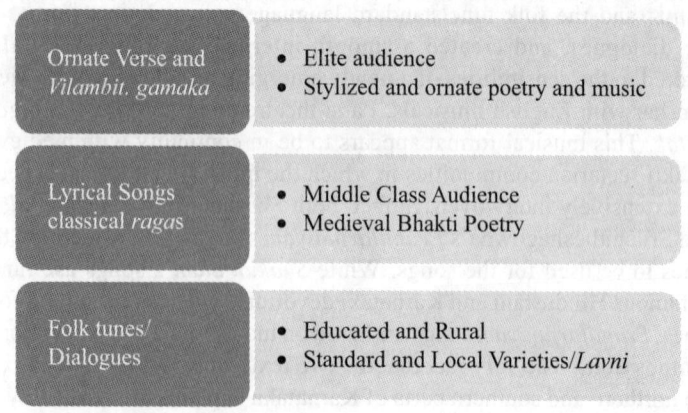

Ornate Verse and
Vilambit. gamaka
- Elite audience
- Stylized and ornate poetry and music

Lyrical Songs
classical *raga*s
- Middle Class Audience
- Medieval Bhakti Poetry

Folk tunes/
Dialogues
- Educated and Rural
- Standard and Local Varieties/*Lavni*

Source: Author.

In order to demonstrate the extendibility of the proposal made here, let us briefly take a look at Raja Laxaman Singh's translation of *Shakuntala Natak* and compare with the structure of the two Kannada translations that are previously discussed. Raja Laxman Singh, a notable figure in the pre-Bhartendu era, translated Kalidasa's *Abhijñānaśākuntalam* in Hindi in 1862–63 as *Shakuntala Natak*. There is a harmonious unification of verse, song and dialogue in the text. Laxman Singh uses *chaupai, sortha, sawai, kundaliya, chappai* as well as *shikharini* (Sanskrit metre), while the Sutradhar in the prologue sings songs using Dhrupad style of singing, *Bhairavi, Dhanasri* and *Basant* ragas. Laxman Singh also uses Braj Bhasha for the verse translation and Khari Boli for the dialogues. The *chhand* and music are interwoven in the play's text in an inherently complementary manner. Braj Bhasha and the metrical structure used in the text both render themselves fluently to the ornamental language (*alankara*), classical ragas and tunes. Although songs are absent from the text, one should not forget that for many such texts the songs were added when they were produced theatrically. A comparison of the three translations in terms of their linguistic and musical structures can be seen in Table 8.2.

Several translations of *Shakuntalam* during this phase in Marathi, Gujarati, Telugu and Tamil follow this scheme. A similar verse-song-folk/prose format could be seen in other Indian languages for several translations of Shakespeare. Many Marathi and Gujarati translations of Shakespeare during this period carry the prefix *Sangeet* suggesting that

Table 8.2

Table Showing the Comparison of Linguistic and Musical Structures in the Translations of Kalidasa and Shakespeare

STRUCTURE	KANNADA SHAKUNTALAM	KANNADA PRAMILARJUNIYAM	HINDI SHAKUNTALA NATAK
Introducing the character	*vritta, shatpadi*	*vritta, shatpadi*	–
Chanda: (*padya; elite*)	*vritta and kanada*	*vritta and kanda*	*doha, chaupai, sorthi, sawaiya, chaubola*
Folk	*caupadi*	Artificial folk: *lavani*	*basant, bahar*
Popular ~Classical (*pada, hadu*)	Semi-classical song	Semi-classical song	*shikharni* (Sanskrit meter)

Source: Author.

this format was the characteristic feature of translations during this period. For instance, in Marathi translations, *Romeo and Juliet* becomes *Sangeet Taravilas* (1880, trans. Dattatray Anant Keskar), *Sangeet Shashikala ani Ratnapal* (1882, trans. Narayan Bapuji Kanitkar), *Prataparao ani Manjula* (1882, trans. Eknath Vishnu Musale), *Sangeet Shalini* (1901), *Sangeet Tara Vilas* (1908, trans. Dattatraya Anant Keskar) and *Sangeet Mohan Tara* (1908). Thus, the early phase of modern Indian drama was a theatrical public sphere that, despite being simultaneously performed in several languages all over India, used more or less a multi-layered, hybrid structural format that was necessitated by the impact of colonial modernity, a need for the reformulation of classicism due to emerging nationalism and a need to incorporate the sensibilities of the heterogeneous audience.

Implications

The emergence of modern Indian drama and the new theatrical public sphere within which it was located was not fully modern European, nor classical Indian or indigenous folk. This is further problematized when we understand the precolonial public spheres and the transformations that took place that led to the emergence of the new theatrical public sphere.

The public sphere as a concept formulated by Habermas that puts forward bourgeois rational–critical debate centring on the developments in Britain, France and Germany during the seventeenth and eighteenth centuries in Europe has been extended to involve a plurality of independent publics. Such an understanding of public sphere is centred on literacy and print culture. As a consequence, discussions on the public sphere have been constrained to include precolonial Indian spheres. Hasan[32] strongly argues that multiple, contrasting public spheres were in existence in India during the medieval period.

The precolonial traditional public spheres in India consisted of the political (royal court), the religious (temple, dargah, *matha* and so on) and the open (village fair, *mela*, urs and so on) spheres. However, they were fairly segregated and were not overlapping in nature except for certain syncretic spaces. With the advent of colonial modernity, nationalism and identity formations, we notice the emergence of a print-culture-centred public sphere. Bakhle[33] points out the need to posit a musical public sphere looking into the emergence of an identity of national music consequent to the formation of music appreciation groups, learning of music through academic schools and institutions, and the canonization of music. Indian classical dance, in particular *Bharatanatyam*, appears to have followed a similar trajectory. As with music and dance, there is a need to posit a theatrical public sphere that took shape during the mid-nineteenth and early twentieth centuries in India. This essay suggests that a new public sphere involving a variety of hybridities was the characteristic feature of the nineteenth-century theatrical public sphere. The theatrical public sphere is not a new concept:

> In recent years, the public sphere as a conceptual construct has begun to mutate from a zone of bourgeois rational–critical debate to a plurality of independent publics, often formed around identity markers like gender, sexual orientation, ethnicity or class, or even by shared interests in cultural matters, as in the case of "the theatre-going public."[34]

There is a need to see theatre as a potential platform for discursive exchanges between a play, its audience, theatre artists, playwrights and the subsequent discussions. As the discussions and debates pertaining to the performance continue in print, conversations and mass media that includes scripto-centric, phono-centric and body-centric representations, the theatrical public sphere may be considered as one of the most effective public spheres for the communication and circulation of ideas. Theatre as a public sphere is actually a modification of public sphere theory from a focus on the political accomplishment of a single economic class to a potential situation or an institution in which diverse aesthetic and social epistemologies are present simultaneously. As de Tocqueville[35] observes,

> No literary pleasures are more accessible to the crowd than those that come from seeing a play. To experience them requires neither study nor preparation. They grip you in the midst of your preoccupations and your ignorance. When a class of citizens first begins to feel for the pleasures of the mind a love still half-uncivilized, it immediately takes to drama. The theatres of aristocratic nations have always been filled with non-aristocrats. Only in the theatre did the upper classes mingle with the middle and lower classes and agree, if not to accept their opinion, then at least to suffer them to express one.

Shifting the focus from a Euro-centric and language-centred understanding of translation, the discussion of the characteristic features of modern Indian theatre as a theatrical public sphere shifts the focus to the cultural context of the translating and performing languages, thereby advocating for a margino-centric and localized approach for the study of translation.

The hybridity involving classical, popular and folk on the one hand and verse, song and prose on the other as structural categories on which such a hybridity is constructed helps us to understand and appreciate not only the strategies and processes of early Indian theatre but also the techniques and models used by translators during this phase of translation. There is a need to revisit early adaptations as multi-layered constructions, making use of the comparative Indian perspective, incorporate transmediality and locate them within the intersecting zone of a composite cultural theatrical public sphere that involves colonial modernity, nationalism and regional identity formation. Thus, Shakespearean translations during the late nineteenth and early twentieth centuries, otherwise criticized as adaptations and unfaithful, are actually the cultural characteristics of a new theatrical public sphere that emerged during an important cultural turn from traditionality to colonial modernity in India.

Notes

1. A.N. Murthyrao, "Shakespeare and Karnataka." *Indian Literature* 7, no. 1 (1946): 63–72.
2. Sukanta Chaudhuri, *Shakespeare in India*. 2002, http://internetshakespeare.uvic.ca/Library/Criticism/shakespearein/india1.html, accessed April 2016.
3. Sakshi Soni and T.S. Satyanath, "Shakespearean *Mahabharata*: *A Midsummer Night's Dream* as *Pramilarjuniyam* in Kannada," in *Global World of Shakespeare Translations, Adaptation, Transformation*, ed. Abha Singh (Delhi: Prestige, 2015) 178–91.
4. Such justifications could be seen in the case of other genres, like the novel. Padikkal Shivarama, (*Nāḍu-nuḍiyarūpaka: rāṣṭra, Ādhunikate mattu kannaḍada modala kādambarigaḷu.* [Mangalagangotri: Mangalore University, 2001], 56–57) provides an instance of such a justification from the Preface of *Shringara Chaturyollasini*, a romance written by Gubbi Murigaradhya in 1896. Murigaradhya uses *hindumaryade*, "Hindu mannerism" to express the concept of cultural appropriateness.
5. T.S. Satyanath, "How does Shakespeare Become *Sekh Pir* in Kannada," *Translation Today* 1 no. 2 (2004), 44–102 and "Remapping Shakespeare in Kannada," in *Discourse on Translation in Kannada*, ed. P.P. Giridhar (New Delhi: Sahitya Akademi, forthcoming).
6. Nandi Bhatia, ed. *Modern Indian Theatre: A Reader*. (New Delhi: Oxford University Press, 2009).
7. Shanta Gokale, *Playwright at the Centre: Marathi Drama from 1843 to the Present* (Calcutta: Seagull, 2000).
8. Kathryn Hansen, "The Birth of Hindi Drama in Benaras, 1868–1885," in *Culture and Power in Benaras: Community, Performance and Environment, 1800–1990*, ed. by Sandria B. Freitag (Oxford: Oxford University Press, 1992), 62–92, Kathryn Hansen, "Parsi Theatre and the City: Locations, Patrons and Audiences," in *Sarai Reader 2002:*

The Cities of Everyday Life (Delhi: Centre for the Study of Developing Societies and Society for Old and New Media, 2002), 40–49 and Kathryn Hansen, "Languages on Stage: Linguistic Pluralism and Community Formation in the Nineteenth Century Parsi Theatre." *Modern Asian Studies* 37, no. 2 (2003): 381–405.

9. Ananda Lal and Sukanta Chaudhuri, ed. *Shakespeare on the Calcutta Stage: A Checklist.* (Papyrus, Kolkata, 2001).

10. Ania Loomba, "Shakespearian Transformations," in *Shakespeare and National Culture*, edited by John J. Joughin (Manchester: Manchester University Press, 1997), 109–41.

11. Sangita Mohanty, *The Indian Response to Hamlet: Shakespeare's Reception in India and a Study of Hamlet in Sanskrit Poetics* (doctoral dissertation, University of Basel, 2010).

12. D.A. Shankar, ed. *Shakespeare in Indian Languages* (Shimla: Indian Institute of Advanced Study, 1999).

13. Jyotsna G. Singh, "Different Shakespeares: The Bard in Colonial/Postcolonial India." *Theatre Journal* 41.4 (1989), 445–58; and Singh, ed. "Shakespeare and the Civilizing Mission," in *Colonial Narratives/Cultural Dialogues: Discoveries of India in the Language of Colonialism* (London: Routledge, 1996), 120–52.

14. Poonam Trivedi and Dennis Bartholomeusz, eds. *India's Shakespeare: Translation, Interpretation and Performance* (Newark: University of Delaware Press, 2005).

15. Mohanty, *The Indian Response to Hamlet.*

16. Hansen, "Parsi Theatre and the City," 381–405.

17. Mohanty, *Indian Response* to Hamlet.

18. This map is from Hina Khajuria's (2013) MPhil Dissertation *Inder Sabhha: Understanding Early Modern Indian Theatre and the Public Sphere.* I am thankful to her for consenting to make use of it here.

19. Although, Marathi and Tamil bibliographic information that I have is fairly extensive (Marathi: 78 translations till 1947, Patil 1993; and Tamil: 209 translations till 1982, Arul 1994), they are not comparable to the details I have in Kannada (119 till 2013; Satyanath forthcoming), which is more or less complete.

20. Sisir Kumar Das, *A History of Indian Literature: 1800–1910, Western Impact: Indian Responses* (New Delhi: Sahitya Akademi, 1991).

21. Some scholars mention the name of the translator as R. Krishnamacharya.

22. Dhurjjati Sarma, "Shakespeare in Indian: Colonial Modernity, Nationality and Regional Identities." (unpublished MPhil dissertation, Department of Modern Indian Languages and Literary Studies, University of Delhi, 2011).

23. There is also a refined translation of *Shakuntalam* that appeared as Kerala Verma's *Manipravala Shakuntalam* in 1882.

24. Sudipto Chatterjee, *The Colonial Staged: Theatre in Colonial Calcutta* (Kolkata: Seagull Books, 2008).

25. Sisir Kumar Das, *A History of Indian Literature: 1800–1910, Western Impact: Indian Responses* (New Delhi: Sahitya Akademi, 1991).

26. S. Balurao, ed. *Shekspiyarige Namaskara* (Delhi: Kannada Bharati, 1966).

27. Balurao, *Shekspiyarige Namaskara.*

28. Satyanath, "How does Shakespeare Become *Sekh Pir*," 71.

29. Himani Kapoor, "Mapping Shakespeare and Kalidasa: Early Indian Translations." (Lecture, University of Delhi and Shakespeare Society of India, Indraprastha College for Women, 7–9 March 2013).

30. For a detailed discussion, see Soni and Satyanath (2015).
31. Several Indian literatures witnessed the appearance of their first history of literature in print during this period.
32. Farhat Hasan, "Forms of Civility and Publicness in Pre-British India," in *Civil Society, Public Sphere and Citizenship: Dialogues and Perceptions*, eds Rajiv Bhargava and Helmut Reifiels (New Delhi: SAGE, 2005), 84–105.
33. Janaki Bakhle, *Two Men and Music: Nationalism in the Making of an Indian Classical Tradition* (Oxford: Oxford University Press, 2005).
34. Robert B. Shimko and Sarah Freeman, "Introduction: Theatre, Performance and the Public Sphere," in *Public Theatres and Theatre Publics*, eds. Robert B. Shimko and Sara Freeman (Newcastle upon Tyne: Cambridge Scholars Publishing, 2012), 1–19.
35. Alexis de Tocqueville, "Some Observations on the Theatre of Democratic Peoples," in *The American Stage*, ed. Laurence Senelick (New York: Library of America, 2011).

9

"Murmuring Your Praise":[1]
Shakespearean Echoes in Early Bengali Drama

Sayantan Roy Moulick and Sandip Debnath[2]

Prolegomenon

Kironmoy Raha says that it was to ease the tedium of English social life in India that theatre, in the Western sense of the term, made its inroad to Calcutta in 1775.[3] Soon, the need for a Bengali theatre, following the English model, was felt and it was poignantly expressed as early as 1826 in the editorial of *Shomachar Chondrika*:[4]

> In this vast city, various centres have already been established for the benefit and amelioration of the citizens which is unprecedented. But, unlike the English community, no public space has been created to provide them amusement.[5]

Brojendronath Bondyopadhyay in his book *Bongiyo Natyoshala* (playhouses in Bengal) comments that prior to the establishment of the Hindu College the Bengalis did not feel the need of a "European entertainment." An account of the impact of the education imparted by the college can be found in *Ramtanu Lahiri O Totkalin Bongoshomaj* (Ramtanu Lahiri and contemporary Bengal) by Shibnath Shastri. He documents the euphoria engendered by the lectures of Captain D.L. Richardson among his maverick students and his constant encouragement to visit the English theatres. Shakespeare became a cult figure in no time.

The following observation of S.K. Bhattacharyya reveals the precise nature of bardolatry among the early colonial moderns:

> While the English play-houses by their production of English, specially Shakespeare's, plays created an appetite for theatrical performances, the foundation of the Hindu College in 1816 and the teaching of Shakespeare by eminent teachers like Richardson created in the minds of the students—the intelligentsia of modern Bengal—a literary taste for drama as such, and taught them, not only how to appreciate Shakespeare critically, but also to recite and act scenes from his plays. This fashion spread to every academic institution.... So it came about that recitations from Shakespeare and production of Shakespeare's dramas became an indispensable part of English education and a popular item in all cultural functions.[6]

It is also pertinent to note here that the first Bengali theatre established by a Bengali, following that of Lebedeff on 27 November 1795, was by Proshonno Kumar Thakur. It was called Hindoo Theatre and it saw the performance of Shakespeare's *Julius Caesar* in the original and Dr H. H. Wilson's English translation of Bhavabhuti's *Uttar Rāmcharit* (the tale of Rama's later life) on the opening night of 28 December 1831. Hurro Chunder Ghose, a playwright, was in the managing committee of this theatre. Roughly twenty years later, the ambience became congenial for Gupta and Ghose to undertake the pioneering enterprises of presenting "Shakespeare in loincloths."[7]

Though the presence of English is indubitable, and the tradition of the reading and staging of Shakespeare did come as a result of foreign education, it is also equally important to consider Jasodhara Bagchi's observation: "[T]he initiative of learning English and reading English literature certainly did not come from the colonial masters"[8] as a reading of Macaulay's "Minutes on Indian Education" (1835) might lead us to surmise. Bagchi demarcates the "ambivalence in our approach to English studies,"[9] which helps us understand the dilemma we find in the plays of Jogendro Chondro Gupto and Hurro Chunder Ghose. Regarding the establishment of the Hindu College and its naming, Bagchi states:

> What the newly rising class demanded was an institution of English/ [W]estern learning that would at the same time be capable of upholding the orthodox Hindu social hierarchies. The paradox of both class formation and English studies in India is to be found in the naming of the new college of "modernisation" Hindu college. Stringent stipulations about Hindu caste and creed had to be fulfilled in order for one to be admitted to the college.... The literary reception of the west into Bengal

was a major part of the paradoxical class formation in Bengal under the colonial condition.[10]

It is in this context that the plays selected for this essay need to be read. However, we would first like to take a quick glance at the existing critical literature in order to justify our thesis. Most of the works that engage with the English/Western/Shakespearean impact on literatures in the Indian languages, though laudatory in their own right, study the influence of Shakespeare on the Indian stage and ignore the plays that were never performed. These critiques, thus, undermine the bold pioneering attempts of indigenizing Shakespeare—an omission that our essay endeavours to redress.[11] It was R.K. DasGupta who first articulated the literary importance of *Kirttibilash* and *Bhanumoti Chittobilash* towards an understanding of the renaissance in Bengal in his essay "Shakespeare in Bengali Literature" (1964). It was soon followed by Jasodhara Bagchi's article, "A Note on Bengali Translations of Shakespeare: 1850–1900" (1965), which devoted a brief section on the style and content of *Bhanumoti Chittobilash*. Bagchi makes no mention of *Kirttibilash*, as the plot does not follow any specific Shakespearean text. With these introductory remarks, let us now embark on a reading of the textual transactions.

Kirttibilash: The Shakespearean Absence–Presence

Published in 1852, Jogendra Chandra Gupta's play *Kirttibilash*, arguably the first tragedy in Bengali and also the first somewhat servile attempt to endorse Shakespeare on the Bengali stage in an indigenous form, was never performed. As Monindrolal Kundu in his book *Bangalir Natyochetonar Kromobikash* (Evolution of the aesthetics of Bengali dramaturgy) opines:

> It is not hard to locate the influence of Shakespeare's *Hamlet* on this play. Even so, the playwright's assay of depicting the intricacies of *Hamlet* in the framework of a legend has been a sorry plight.[12]

Gupta, in his covert reworking of *Hamlet*, has taken little but the overall structure and the tragic element of the play that goes against the *natak* tradition. Gupta indulges in a five-page long preface to his play in order to justify his pioneering resistance to and digression from the *natak* tradition. He critiques the Sanskrit tradition, which considered that a play should never end or conclude depicting the hero, an emblem of virtue incarnate, in a pitiful state or dead. Arguing in favour of the tragic over the comic, Gupta refers to Seneca, Shakespeare and Aristotle, and concludes, following an explicatory passage regarding the depiction of relationship between the sati and her husband, that "delight is momentary, but the impact of pathos lingers on."[13] The liberated Gupta also denies the general belief that the depiction of an ill-fated hero is unrighteous. We may also refer to the Sanskrit play *Urubhangam*, which ends with the death of Duryodhan on the stage, though the play, along with other plays of Bhasa, was officially rediscovered only in 1901 by T. Ganapati Shastri in a village in Kerala, near modern Thiruvananthapuram, as Sisir Kumar Das has pointed out.[14] However, as H.N. DasGupta states, the conclusion of the play does not go against the general character of Sanskrit drama because it "does not produce any grief in the minds of the audience." Duryodhan is punished for his misdeeds by death.[15]

Another departure from the indigenous tradition can be seen in the short exchanges in prose, relegating the lengthy lyrical utterances only to the *Nandi*, the expressions of intense emotion and the few aphoristic moral passages directed towards the audience. However, it must also be mentioned that the witty exchange between the Sutradhar and the *Nati* that follows Nandi, is in sync with the Sanskrit dramatic tradition. This conversation reveals the presence and influence of patriarchy. The position of women in the society and that of the Natis, their public and private space, can also be discerned as we read the following:

> Nati: My Lord; how will this shy woman recite *natok* at a social gathering. Notice that the lotus blooms in delight of the rising sun; but as darkness sets in, seeing its lord, the moon, and his accompanying stars, veils its visage and passes the night with the face downwards. So how will I perform among such amiable people?
>
> Sutradhar: Dear, such coyness of you is indeed delightful to me. But...the shyness of the wife of *Nata* and an old woman dressed as a young wife, are equally characters of ridicule.
>
> Nati: Lord, if hearing me recite will entertain the people, then I begin.[16]

Though the plot of *Kirttibilash* resembles *Hamlet*, we do not find the essential traits of Hamlet in the character of the protagonist Kirttibilash: his vacillation and his procrastination. The protagonist here undergoes a characteristic reversal.

Kirttibilash begins with the King eager to divest himself off the burden of kingship that cannot but remind one of the opening scene of *King Lear*. Just like Lear expressing his "darker purpose"

Know that we have divided

In three our kingdom; and 'tis our fast intent

To shake all cares and business from our age,

Conferring them on younger strengths, while we

Unburdened crawl toward death.[17]

We find Moharaja Chondrokanto confiding his intention to his minister:

> I grow old and so I find the regal burden tedious. My constant desire is to confer my responsibilities to one of my loved kin.[18]

When Kirttibilash soliloquizes about the injustices done by his stepmother, we recall Hamlet's disturbed speech: "Frailty, thy name is woman." However, unlike *Hamlet*, the Bengali play does not begin with darkness on stage and the introductory conversation of the Shakespearean text comes much later in the Bengali one. As for the fool or jester, as H. N. Das Gupta observes, "Almost invariably in all Sanskrit plays we come across a comic character (or *vidusaka*) who is a boon companion of the hero of the drama and pleases him by his witticisms and observations on some dramatic situations."[19] In this play the Shakespearean fool makes way for the Sanskritic *vidusaka*, Meghnath, the Bengali equivalent of Horatio, who takes up the role.

We must also mention that it is not just the Shakespearean influences that bridge the two plays in discussion here. As H. N. DasGupta avers, in the Sanskrit plays, the *devabhasha* Sanskrit is used as the formal and the royal language, whereas *prakrit* is used for conversations with those of low status. Following the same tradition, either consciously or otherwise, both the playwrights have used the *shadhu*[20] form for royal conversations and the *cholit*[21] form when the royal characters address those who are lower in rank.

Even given the weaknesses of *Kirttibilash*, any reader of the play would find R.K. DasGupta's summation apt:

> It is a tragedy and a poor tragedy. But its historical importance is great, greater than that of *Gorboduc* in the history of English tragedy. For the authors of *Gorboduc* were writing a tragedy at a time when Seneca had become popular in courtly and learned circles.... But the first Bengali tragedy appeared apologetically as a forbidden literary act. The first English tragedy was presented before the Queen at Whitehall. The first Bengali tragedy was never staged. Still the preface to *Kirtivilashnatak* is one of the most important documents in the history of the nineteenth century Bengali Renaissance.[22]

Bhanumoti Chittobilas and the Translational Trope

In the preface to his play *Bhanumoti Chittobilash* Hurro Chunder Ghose writes:

> In presenting this piece of dramatic composition to my indulgent readers,
> I would observe, that at the suggestion of an European friend of native
> education, I had originally undertaken the translation of Shakespeare's
> *Merchant of Venice*—a play, which, though inferior in some respect to
> Macbeth, Hamlet, Lear, and Othello, or perhaps to the First and Second
> parts of Henry IV, was considered the best for the purpose, for which the
> translation was avowedly undertaken by me. But the plan was abandoned
> before I had distanced the flight of *Jessica*, some of my learned friends
> having surmised that my performance was not likely to be popular, unless
> the mode in which it was done were altered. I took their advice and
> undertook to write it in the shape of a Bengali *Natuck*[23] or Drama, taking
> only the plot and underplots of the *Merchant of Venice*, with considerable
> additions and alterations to suit the native taste; but at the same time losing
> no opportunity to convey to my countrymen, who have no means of getting
> themselves acquainted with Shakespeare, save through the medium of their
> own language, the beauty of the author's sentiments as expressed in the best
> passages in the play in question. The sort of reception my *Natuck* is to meet
> with from the public, I can by no means divine or guess at, the work being
> of a novel character, professing, as it does, to be a Bengali *Natuck*, though
> written much after the manner of an English play. But should my work
> meet with their approbation, I would deem my labours amply rewarded,
> and, if thus encouraged, endeavour to devote my leisure hours to writing
> other works of a similar nature.[24]

"This piece of dramatic composition" is arguably, Bengal's, if not India's, first conscious endeavour to "translate" Shakespeare. But how are we to make sense of Ghose's pioneering attempt? Under which translational rubric does it fall? How does Ghose negotiate with the cultural traffic of translation? Is it simply an instance of adaptation, as it seems from the prefatory note? Should the play be considered merely an instance of the spectre of Shakespeare haunting the Bengali text? Or is it, to use Michel Garneau's neologism, a case of tradaptation[25] where any attempt of translation is always-already an adaptation? If it is an adaptation, then how much of *Bhanumoti Chittobilash* bears the imprint of *The Merchant of Venice*, the Shakespearean urtext? If it is a case of tradaptation, then how much of it is adaptation and how much of it is translation? Considering the recent advances in translation and adaptation studies, these are some of the questions with which any discerning reader of a translated text, particularly a text that is a maiden attempt to translate Shakespeare, would grapple. Before getting into the intricacies of translational politics and poetics, it would not be out of place to chart the unwieldy terrain of the category of translation itself. "Translation," as the Oxford English Dictionary (OED) defines it, is not only "the action or process of turning from one language into another; a version in a different language" but also "the expression or rendering of something in another medium or form;" the "[t]ransformation, alteration, change; changing or adapting to another use."[26] The definitions, however, seem to valorize the formal features of the process of translation and elide the socio-cultural grids. Of late, with the entrance of cultural studies into the domain of translational theory, the translation-scape has experienced a "cultural turn." In fact, the cultural dimension is of more importance than the formal features of the translation in the discipline of translational studies. For Homi Bhabha, one of the foremost cultural theorists of our time, "[t]ranslation is the performative nature of cultural communication."[27] Translation is not only interlingual but also an intercultural phenomenon. "[I]t is the 'inter'—the cutting edge of translation and renegotiation, the in-between space, that carries the burden of the meaning of culture."[28]

On the other hand, the Latin etymological root of "adapt"—*adaptāre*—means "to make suitable or fit (for a purpose)."[29] OED defines "adaptation" as "the action or process of altering, amending, or modifying something, esp. something that has been created for a particular purpose, so that it [is] suitable for new use." It glosses "adaptation" as "an altered or amended version of a text, musical composition, etc., (now esp.) one adapted for filming, broadcasting or production on the stage from a novel or similar literary source."[30] For Linda Hutcheon adaptation is "an acknowledged transposition of a recognizable other work or works;" "a creative and an interpretive act of appropriation/salvaging;" and "an extended intertextual engagement with the adapted work."[31]

Aware as Hurro Chunder Ghose was of the constraints of "translating" *The Merchant of Venice* in the primary sense of the term, in his enterprise to "cater to the native taste," he deploys a strategy that is indeed an approximation of the precolonial concept of "retelling." As Ayappa Paniker observes, in precolonial India, "translation was not understood as a literal word-by-word rendering of the original from the source language to the target language."[32] Prior to colonialism, translation in the Indian critical discourse was an act of transcreation. This detour facilitated

Ghose to accomplish his dual intentions to present the play in a familiar mode and maintain the Shakespearean flavour. Ghose draws upon Indian myths and relocates the play in the Indian discursive space. He adheres to an indigenous form of presentation—the *Natuck*—then prevalent in the theatrescape of Bengal. To recast the Shakespearean play in the mould of the Natuck, Ghose was liberal in his retelling. The transfer of emphasis from the world of trade and commerce to the domestic sphere is perceived in the altered title. This is very much in keeping with the Sanskrit dramatic tradition where, as H. N. DasGupta mentions, "the dominant sentiment [was] either erotic or heroic. All other sentiments found subordinate place."[33] With this shift, where Shylock's change of religion no longer remains the primary issue, it becomes imperative for Ghose to supplement the original Shakespeare play with necessary cultural correlatives.

The machineries of the Sanskrit dramatic tradition, namely, Nandi, Sutradhar and Nati have been introduced here. The Bengali has lyrical grace. To plot Shakespeare in the Indian socio-cultural grid, Ghose Indianizes the names of the characters. Portia becomes Bhanumoti, Nerrisa becomes Shushila and Jessica becomes Shoshimukhi. It is interesting to note that as the name Portia has both classical and biblical overtones; Bhanumoti too has Hindu mythological connections, *Bhanu* being the sun-god. Again, while the disguised Portia is addressed as "a Daniel come to judgment" in the trial scene, the disguised Bhanumoti receives the title Ramchandra, Ram being the hero of the epic Ramayana and a figure of integrity and wisdom. The introduction of a *raj-purohit* (the royal priest) and a *napit* (the Indian counterpart of the English barber, acquainted with the *vidhis* related to his profession) was essential to execute the Hindu rites on stage. Certain appellations have also been appended in order to maintain the social stratification. The setting has been shifted from Venice and Belmont to Gujarat and Ujjain respectively. However, Ghose's selection of the setting is not random. He has carefully chosen Gujarat as it was, like the medieval Venice, a renowned centre for trade. The choosing of the *Baniya* (trading) community to represent the Jews is also appropriate since in the nineteenth century the Baniyas were one of the chief money-lending classes apart from the Parsis. The practice of vegetarianism by the Baniyas also enabled Ghose to translate Shylock's denial to dine when invited: "You people are too sinful, flesh feeding, and sacrilegious," says Lokkhopati Rai, the Bengali Shylock. "What kinship can there be between us?"[34] Though Ghose criticizes the usurers, the play turns out to be a general indictment of a materialistic society.

In a striking departure from the original, Ghose's rendition, which opens with Chondraboli, the Queen and Bhanumoti's mother, terribly upset with the King for his dereliction of the obligations of a father, is indeed steeped in the Indian ethos. The idea that the reputation of a clan is contingent upon the timely marriage of the daughter is emphasized when she says, "If I remain calm, the family will earn a bad name."[35] But as the King later soliloquizes, he alludes to the Mahabharata and the havoc that the *swayamvara* wrought. Ghose, thus, justifies the departure that he makes in following Shakespeare. As Ujjain is mentioned in the Mahabharata, the allusions by Ghose to the epic become meaningful.

The preponderance of fate (vidhi, *adrista*, the divine desire, birth and rebirth, the devil and so on) and superstitious beliefs that are considered ominous (as the twitching of the right eye, the howling of the jackals at day and so on) are conspicuous throughout the play. Probably following the Jatra tradition, Ghose incorporates a song that is a sort of address to the audience instructing them to remain submerged in spiritual thoughts and spiritual thoughts only.

It is also interesting to note that, unlike Shakespeare's *The Merchant of Venice*, in this play the marriage of Bhanumoti takes place in the presence of all the courtiers and the traditions of a royal marriage in India have been minutely followed. Ghose rejects the immediate separation of the lovers on the day of the marriage. He allows them blissful moments of nuptial pleasure. Why does he depart from the Shakespearean text? Is it because his audience will not accept it as can be surmised from his preface? Or is it because he finds the portrayal of longing distasteful? The second enquiry might not be too out of place considering the erotic nature of the penultimate scene of Ghose's play, where the conclusive comment of Gratiano to keep safe Nerissa's ring gets a detailed treatment by the playwright.

Ghose's way of portraying women is interesting. While on the one hand he presents the image of an *ardhāngini*, of reciprocal relationship, of conjugation, not only in form but also in function, on the other, there are many signs of an unequal gendered relationship, of *pati parameshwar*—the husband as the supreme form of the divine. Though what Portia tells Bassanio,

One half of me is yours, the other half yours.

Mine own I would say: but, if mine, then yours,

And so, all yours.[36]

is the concept of ardhāngini in the Shakespearean mould, it would be quite wrong to conclude a difference in social perception in the portrayal of women—between that of Shakespeare and Ghose. Even so, none can deny a hint of the same. However, as we proceed, we perceive certain other elements of such complex gendering of identities. Desire gets gendered as Shushila expresses her confusion regarding Bhanumoti's desire to get into a man's guise. She says: "How, being a *rati*, would you become *madan*."[37] Rati and Madan cease to be just mythical characters sans life. A further violence committed by Ghose has been in his enquiry about the loss of chastity due to disguise. He cunningly makes Shushila ask Bhanumoti how she'll be able to sustain her own duty as a woman and a wife (*stri-dharma*) while attempting to save that of her husband. Let us take a look at three definitions of dharma. Monier-Williams, in his *Sanskrit–English Dictionary*, defines dharma-*rakshita* as one who is "protected"[38] while, the *Samsad Bengali–English Dictionary* of 1982 defines *stri-lokerdhormorokkha* as the "preservation of chastity" and *dhormonash* as the "ravishment of a woman's chastity, rape."[39] One may risk presuming that Ghose was not thinking much differently in the early Victorian times either. He further goes on to eulogize a sati following the scandalous portrayal of Bhanumoti expressing her desire to sleep with the Shastri, the disguised Portia. Following Shakespeare in such a debasement of Bhanumoti's and Shushila's *choritro* (character), we may read the section as a lengthy rebuttal, going against *The Merchant of Venice*, in order to preach the ways of god to men. It seems that it is his confession, seeking salvation for his deed of misrepresenting a "*pativrata* sati." The use of veils on the face and curtains on the stage are also stark departures. However, having marked these textual indentations of the male author, we still fail to grasp what Ghose really means when, digressing from the source text, he makes Bhanumoti retort to Charudotto—the Merchant—in 5.2, saying:

You are the friend of my husband.

So you presented your perspective of the women.

If the husband is clever the wife is more.

She saves her husband with her wit.[40]

Let us now have a look at the other aspects of social culture that are instilled in the matrix. Ghose criticizes the indifference of the people towards each other in this "*kolikal*."[41] The grace of greeting and inquiring about the well-being of the people we meet, of taking the seat following the elders, marks the play. We also find that a situation has been created where the demise of Lokkhopati Rai will make the bereaved daughter joyous in consideration of her monetary gains. The play has been structured in such a fashion that this happiness is considered to be no sin, but rather becomes a wish-fulfilment.

Following the indigenous tradition, Ghose adopts certain other changes as well. He introduces the messengers to announce the arrival of any person of high rank on the stage, maintaining the feudal hierarchy. He dispenses with all the Christian elements of the play and introduces the culture of rejoicing over the victory of truth, a kind of carnival atmosphere. He uses the style of Sanskritic word formation, to conjunct multiple words into one. He also makes use of pun and word plays in a more varied and profuse manner when compared to the Shakespearean original.

Ghose has also added some portions that, in the urtext, are supposed to be understood by the Shakespearean audience to have taken place behind the scenes. These additions by Ghose are no doubt deliberate expansions of the Shakespearean original in order to attain contemporaneity. Even so, since his avowed aim was to represent Shakespeare, he never quite lost sight of the original. Ghose's plot resembles that of Shakespeare's in all the major scenes and sections, conforming to what he has expressed through the preface. He also maintains the interplay of the main and the subplot following Shakespeare. The novel procedure through which Bhanumoti will get selected by means of the inscribed cascades, and that in the case of a wrong selection the suitor will lead a life of perpetual celibacy, has been translated by Ghose faithfully. The importance of royal blood of the suitor is prominently underlined in both the texts. Though the description of Jessica by Lorenzo in the translated text has turned more towards the beauty than the qualities of Shoshimukhi, there's not much deviation. The integrity of plot from the scene where Antonio seals the bond and the scenes that follow, till the trial scene has been retained by Ghose with the few changes of marriage sequences in between, and the exchange of the Italian tradition of masque with the Indian tradition of mask. The contents of the scrolls of fortune too show no difference from the original except in their prosodic features, the quatrains being converted into couplets. Though mentioned earlier that Ghose has done away with all the Christian elements of the Shakespearean play, the remark of Chandrasen—the Indian counterpart of Lorenzo, regarding "everything turning *bhodro*" in Gujarat, in 5.1 may be an insinuation of the christening of Shylock.

The music in the Shakespearean text gets transposed by the melody of the flute—an essential aspect of Hindu mythology. The symbols of piety and purity such as banana plants and mango leaves rested on the pitchers infuse the play. The play, thus, seems to be more of an attempt to reinforce the beliefs of the people against the scientific thinking and reasoning instilled by Western education than what the preface seems to claim—communication of the quintessential Shakespeare to the laity of Bengal. Translation, thus, as we can perceive from our reading of the text, is not a servile imitation of the urtext but turns out to be "an important axio-ideological factor in regulating the interaction between what we call literature and the other forms of social discourse."[42]

The Last Words

Having done with the exegesis of the plays in contention, we would now like to refer back to the title of our paper and conclude on a general note. Annie Brisset in her analyses of Québec theatres emphasizes on how national identity gets reinforced through translation: "Translation, then, becomes a matter of creating a Québécois work, in the true sense of the word, for not only has the title of the play been changed, the name of the author has changed as well."[43] And what is true for the Québec theatres can also be perceived to be a fact in the Indian context. The plays under consideration, we find, do not stand out as instances of absolute Bardolatry either. What happens in the process of these tradaptations is, to paraphrase Ganesh Devy, a transmigration of the soul of literature—the key element in the understanding of "translation" through the lens of Indian metaphysics. In Devy's words,

> The soul, or significance, is not subject to the laws of temporality; and therefore significance, even literary significance, is ahistorical in Indian view. Elements of plot, stories, characters, can be used again and again by new generations of writers because Indian literary theory does not lay undue emphasis on originality. If originality were made a criterion of literary excellence, a majority of Indian classics would fail the test. The true test is the writer's capacity to transform, to translate, to restate, to revitalize the original.[44]

Acknowledgement

We would like to thank Professor Swapan Kumar Chakravorty who, during his tenure as the Director General of the National Library of India, generously allowed us a full text photocopy of *Bhanumoti Chittobilash*. But for his help, this paper could never have been written.

Notes

1. Rabindranath Tagore, "Shakespeare," in *A Book of Homage to Shakespeare*, ed. Israel Gollancz (London: Humphrey Milford, Oxford University Press, 1916), 321.
2. All the translations from Bengali texts used in this essay are ours, whether primary or secondary.
3. Refer to his book *Bengali Theatre* (New Delhi: National Book Trust, 2001).
4. "A Bengali journal to propagate traditional Hindu religion" —says Sisir Kumar Das in *A History of Indian Literature: 1810–1910* (Delhi: Sahitya Akademi, 1991).
5. Quoted in Brojendronath Bondyopadhyay, *Bongiyo Natyoshala* (Kolkata: Viswabharati Granthalay, December 1944–January 1945), 5.
6. S.K. Bhattacharyya, "Shakespeare and Bengali Theatre," *Indian Literature* 7, no. 1 (1964): 29.
7. A reference to Jasodhara Bagchi's article "Shakespeare in Loin Cloths: English Literature and the Early Nationalist Consciousness in Bengal."
8. Jasodhara Bagchi, "Shakespeare in Loin Cloths," in *Rethinking English: Essays in Literature, Language, History*, ed. Swati Joshi (New Delhi: Trianka, 1991), 146.
9. Bagchi, "Shakespeare in Loin Cloths," 147.
10. Bagchi, "Shakespeare in Loin Cloths," 147–158.
11. While P. Guha-Thakurta in his book *The Bengali Drama: Its Origin and Development*, looks down upon Ghose's play and makes no reference of Gupta's, Brojendronath Bondyopadhyay in his book *Bongiyo Natyoshala* (Playhouses in Bengal), Prabodh Chandra Sen in his essay "Bengali Drama and Stage" and Sushil K. Mukherjee in his volume *The Story of Calcutta Theatres: 1753–1980* do but only mention these two playwrights and their works. Sisir Kumar Das in his essay "Shakespeare in Indian Languages" comments on the "Indianization" in Ghose's play but does not refer to *Kirttibilash*. On the other hand we have Hemendra Nath DasGupta's *The Indian Stage*, Kironmoy Raha's *Bengali Theatre*, Jyotsna G. Singh's "Different Shakespeares: The Bard in Colonial/Postcolonial India" and *Colonial Narratives/Cultural Dialogues: 'Discovery' of India in the Language of Colonialism*, and Sukanta Chaudhuri's "Shakespeare in India" (in Internet Shakespeare editions), where no reference has been made to either of these plays. It is clear that most of the critical output concentrates only on the plays that were staged.
12. Monindrolal Kundu, *Bangalir Natyochetonar Kromobikash: Prachin Theke Moddho-Unobingsho Shokabdo* (Kolkata: Shahityolok, 2000), 246. Translation ours.
13. Jogendra Chandra Gupta, preface to *Kirttibilash* (N.p., 1852).
14. Sisir Kumar Das, *A History of Indian Literature: 1911–1956* (New Delhi: Sahitya Akademi, 1995), 48.
15. Hemendra Nath DasGupta, *The Indian Stage* (New Delhi: Munshiram Manoharlal Publishers, 2002), 50.
16. Gupta, *Kirttibilash*, 2. Translation ours.
17. *King Lear*, ed. R.A. Foakes (Surrey: Thomas Nelson, 1997), 1.1. 36–40.
18. Gupta, *Kirttibilash*, 3.
19. DasGupta, *Indian Stage*, 53.
20. The chaste form of Bāṅglā.
21. The language, especially dialect, of the masses.
22. R.K. DasGupta, "Shakespeare in Bengali Literature," *Indian Literature* 7, no.1 (1964): 22–23.

23. *Natuck* is a spelling variant of the word *natak*. The Preface is written in both English and Bengali. The quotation is from the English version.
24. The italics in this quotation follow the original text.
25. "Michel Garneau, who produced a Quebec *Macbeth* in 1978, "chose a new term (tradaptation) that established a flexible midway stage between translation and adaptation, both acknowledging an allegiance to the Shakespearean text and asserting a desire to define a political sense of self-identity for Quebec, precisely by subordinating extraneous discourse like Shakespeare's." *Shakespeare and the Language of Translation*, ed. Ton Hoensellars (London: Thomson Learning, 2004), 16.
26. *Oxford English Dictionary Online*, s.v. "translation, *n*.," accessed 30 October 2012, http://www.oed.com/
27. Homi K. Bhabha, *The Location of Culture* (London: Routledge, 1994), 228.
28. Bhabha, *The Location of Culture*, 38–39.
29. *Oxford English Dictionary Online*, s.v. "adapt, *v*.," accessed 30 October 2012, http://www.oed.com/
30. *Oxford English Dictionary Online*, s.v. "adaptation, *n*.," accessed 30 October 2012, http://www.oed.com/
31. Linda Hutcheon, *A Theory of Adaptation* (New York: Routledge, 2006), 8.
32. Ayyappa Paniker, "Towards an Indian Theory of Literary Translation," in *Translation: From Periphery to Centrestage*, ed. Tutun Mukherjee (New Delhi: Prestige, 1998), 39–46, quoted in Shibani Phukan, "Towards an Indian Theory of Translation," *Wasafiri* 18, no. 40 (2003): 27, accessed 3 March 2013, doi:10.1080/02690050308589864.
33. DasGupta, *Indian Stage*, 51.
34. Hurro Chunder Ghose, *Bhanumoti Chittobilash* (Kolkata: Purnachandrodaya Press, 1853), 34.
35. Ghose, *Bhanumoti Chittobilash*, 3.
36. *Merchant of Venice*, ed. John Drakakis (London: Bloomsbury, 2010), 3.2.16–18.
37. Ghose, *Bhanumoti Chittobilash*, 146.
38. Monier Monier-Williams, *A Sanskrit–English Dictionary* (Delhi: Motilal Banarsidass, 1986), s.v. "dharma-rakshita."
39. Birendramohan Dasgupta, *Samsad Bengali–English Dictionary* (Kolkata: Sahitya Samsad, 1982), s.v. "*stri-lokerdharmaraksha*," "*dharmanash*."
40. Ghose, *Bhanumoti Chittobilash*, 207.
41. According to Hindu mythology, it refers to the fourth stage of a *yuga* or era. It is the age of evil.
42. Annie Brisset, "Translation and Parody: Quebec Theatre in the Making," *Canadian Literature* 117 (1988): 104, accessed 2 March 2013, http://canlit.ca/pdfs/articles/canlit117-Translation(Brisset).pdf
43. Brisset, "Translation and Parody: Quebec Theatre in the Making," 98.
44. Ganesh Devy, "Translation and Literary History—An Indian View," in *Post-Colonial Translation: Theory and Practice*, ed. Susan Bassnett and Harish Trivedi (London: Routledge, 1999), 187.

10
A Future Without Shakespeare

Jatindra K. Nayak

I discovered Charles and Mary Lamb's *Tales from Shakespeare* under very unusual circumstances in a village in Odisha. My brother, who studied English literature at Ravenshaw College, Cuttack, brought a copy of *Tales from Shakespeare* home and I used to leaf through the pages without being able to make sense of many of the sentences. My English teacher at the village school was very different from the Irish nuns who taught Shakespeare and Lamb to many Indian school students. He loved to teach us Tagore's famous poem "Where the Mind is Without Fear." He would read it aloud while wielding a sinister-looking cane and we would repeat the words of Tagore's poem with our minds full of fear. English, Tagore and the cane swishing in the air have therefore been fused into a single, seamless experience for me.

One of the earliest Odia translations of a Shakespearean play was titled *Premika Premikaa* and it was based on *Romeo and Juliet*. It was first serialized in the literary journal *Mukura* or the Mirror and came to be published in the form of a slim volume in 1908. The translator was Jagannath Ballabh Ghose who "most respectfully" dedicated this little book to The Hon'ble John Joseph Platel, Esquire, I.E.S, the district and session judge of Cuttack. It is, thus, clearly indicated that the translation has been undertaken by a loyal subject of the British Empire and the blessings of the colonial authorities are duly invoked. In the short preface Ghose informs the reader that most of the text corresponds to the original play. As Ghose states, "My story is not a faithful rendering of Lamb's story but it is based on it to a large extent. The rest I have translated from the original play." It is perfectly possible that Ghose might have been inspired by H.C. Rakshit, who presented prose versions of Shakespeare's plays in Bengali.

Let us look a little more closely at what Ghose does in his book. The book is divided into ten chapters with each chapter bearing a title in Odia and a quotation from the original English play. The chapter titles are as follows: *Prema Kalika* (the bud of love), *Bibaha* (the wedding), *Shokasambad* (sad news), *Tatnopadesh* (good advice), *Biday* (farewell), *Satirasahas* (the courage of chaste woman), *Harshabishada* (joy and grief), *Bisabriksha* (the poison tree), *Parinam* (outcome) and *Shanti* (peace). The chapter titles clearly indicate that the play has been presented as a moral tale involving human actions and their consequences. Each chapter provides a brief account of events in prose into which a brief exchange of dialogues between two characters is interpolated. However, reducing Shakespeare to a storyteller and the play to a prose narrative interspersed with dialogues does not simplify Ghose's task and leaves him with residual difficulties. In Ghose's hands certain elements get quietly transformed. Friar Lawrence becomes a *tapaswi* and the church is presented as an *ashram*. Juliet is referred to as a *sati* and the graveyard is presented as a *samadhimandir*. I have come across Ghose's translation/ retelling of *Comedy of Errors*, which was published in *Mukura* in the first decade of the twentieth century. It is titled *Bhranti Bilas* and I am not sure if it is based on a Bengali retelling of Lamb's *Tales* or on Iswarchandra Vidyasagar's translation of the same play into Bengali and bearing the same title. In all probability introducing Shakespeare to Odia readers through Lamb's *Tales* was part of a larger strategy. At this point of time, modernity in Odia literature was being negotiated through the assimilation of the plots of western works. In the latter half of the nineteenth century, Radhanath Ray inaugurated the process of modernizing Odia poetry by silently and unobtrusively reworking Ovid's *Atlanta's Race, Pyramus and Thisbe,* Shelley's *Cenci*, and many such western works. These were transposed to local settings and featured Odia heroes and heroines. By presenting a secular love story with a tragic ending in Odia literature, Ghose was contributing to this process of modernization.

I am tempted here to bring in a reference to a Chinese translation of Lamb's *Tales*, which was published in 1904 around the same time that Ghose is engaged in rewriting Lamb for the benefit of Odia readers and creating a space for more ambitious Odia translations of full-length Shakespearian plays like *Hamlet, King Lear,* and *Othello*. It would be interesting to see the way Lamb's *Tales* were appropriated in another Asian nation at a time when it was desperately trying to modernize itself after facing humiliation and defeat from a number of western powers. The translator's name is Lin Shu and the title of his Chinese translation of *Tales from Shakespeare* is *Yuvibian Yanyu*. Lin Shu saw translation as a tool of reform and his translation of Lamb was much more assimilative than that of Ghose. He gave the Shakespearean characters Chinese names and reworked the tales to make them express Confucian morality and a Chinese world view. Hamlet, for instance, is spared all psychological torment and is presented as a dutiful son who must kill his father's murderer. Juliet, whose skin is the colour of jade, displays little ardour or passion, and Portia loves Bassanio despite his poverty because he is possessed of the qualities of a literary scholar. The presence of the supernatural and of magic in Shakespeare's plays endears him to Lin because the west in Shakespeare's works does not appear very different from traditional China. Shakespeare convinces Lin that China's past need not be aggressively rejected: it resembles that of the west, which Chinese modernizers seek to emulate. At the same time, however, Lin, while translating Lamb's *Tales* into Chinese, takes the opportunity to introduce elements and ideas that were hitherto alien to China. The profession of the lawyer is one such element that the translation of *The Merchant of Venice* allows him to introduce. The other relates to the bringing out of a baby by surgically cutting open the abdomen of a woman. The third is the notion of a love that goes beyond filial affection or friendship.

I shall now turn to the central theme of my presentation that is the discussion of a more recent translation of tales from Shakespeare into Odia, *Shakespeare Kahanimala*, which was published in 1977. The translator, Basant K. Satapathy, was a well-known English teacher, a reputed short story writer, a critic and famous for his humour, which is laced with deep pathos. Even when he was a student in a school in a feudal state in Odisha in the early decades of the twentieth century, he had felt irresistibly drawn to English literature. As a young boy he rendered William Blake's "The Piper" and Thomas Hood's "I remember, I remember" into Odia. Later as a college teacher of English, Satapathy established himself as a charismatic teacher of Shakespeare. In his autobiography he gives a memorable account of his experience of teaching *Macbeth* and *King Lear* to undergraduate students and the innovative ways he had adopted to make Shakespeare accessible to Odia students. His account deserves to be quoted at length:

The day I joined the college as lecturer in English I walked into the class of fourth year students. The students told me, "We have brought the copies of the play, *Macbeth*. Please teach us that play." I borrowed a copy from them and started giving my first lecture in that college. The students listened to me with rapt attention and after giving them a broad outline of the plot, I recited:

If it were done, when it is done; I wish it were done quickly; but if assassination .... This enthralled the students and they started clapping joyfully.... Once the Principal of the college, Professor Pillai, went home on sick leave. At that time he was teaching *King Lear*. With his permission, I started teaching this text. I am extremely fond of teaching Shakespeare. I get carried away when I teach a play by Shakespeare. When I come out of the class the expression on my face makes people think that Shakespeare's ghost has possessed me. One day I was discussing the episode dealing with the reunion of King Lear and his youngest daughter, Cordelia. Lear said this to his daughter:

Thou art a soul in bliss,

But I am bound,

Upon a wheel of fire that my own tears

Do scald me like molten lead.

At another place in the text King Lear said this to Kent:

Let me wash my hand

They smack of mortality.

While teaching these two episodes I broke down and wept. Tears welled up in the eyes of all the hundred twenty eight students in the class.... It is impossible for a reader not to be deeply moved by the last scenes of Shakespeare. Who is left unmoved by Iago's speech in the famous "temptation scene"? Othello's speech which follows Iago's pierces one's heart:

If I do prove her haggard

Though that her jesses were my dear

Heart-strings

I'd whistle her off and let her down the wind

To prey at fortune.

But it was difficult to explain the meanings of lines like these to students without taking the help of Odia. So I often explained Shakespeare in Odia to students of B.A. and M.A. classes. This used to give me a lot of satisfaction and the students, for their part, benefited.

Satapathy went on to translate *Othello* into Odia, which was published posthumously. He also adapted a number of works written in English in Odia, which included James Synge's *Riders to the Sea* and Bernard Gilbert's *The Old Bull*.

On the face of it, his translation of Lamb's *Tales* is very different from Ghose's translation and, unlike Lin, he does not appear to be taking any liberty with the plot, characters or world view of the tales. He has chosen to translate 13 out of the tales in standard Odia although occasionally he cannot resist the temptation to bring in a few expressions in colloquial and idiomatic Odia. But, on the whole, he closely adheres to the words of the original text.

Why does his translation assume significance? I should like to show that, like Lin Shu, although he makes no attempt to Odianize or Indianize Lamb, Satapathy's translation of the *Tales* is informed by anxieties and concerns that deserve close attention today. This is because Satapathy meditates on a future without Shakespeare and on the alienation of the English teacher in post-independence India and offers solutions that will shock and provoke teachers of English in the Indian academia. This is the reason why I chose to dwell on this translation at some length.

I shall pay particular attention to the translator's preface because it is here that Satapathy takes pains to elaborate on his rather unconventional views. The preface titled "Why" is preceded by four epigraphs: the first is a quotation from a love poem in Odia by a Vaishnav poet, the second a quotation from the confession by Macaulay on the death of his sister, in which he tells her how literature has saved his life and his reason, the third by F.L. Lucas celebrating the power of poetry to make life bearable and the last a quotation from Kilingopolus. The last is particularly interesting for it focuses on the translator's craft:

> Translation requires a combination of learning and inspiration; the original must strike some vein in the translator so that he experiences some of the satisfaction of the original creation.

All these serve to indicate that, to Satapathy, translation is not a mechanical activity; it is invested with deep emotional significance. In the course of the preface, it will be clear how much emotional energy has been invested in the translation of the *Tales*. There are disturbing parallels between the life of the translator and Charles Lamb. Satapathy translated the tales to cope with his wife's mental instability and with her death. The preface begins by admitting that reducing Shakespeare's plays to stories robs them of their magic. The translator then goes on to say that ordinary readers lack the sincerity and concentration that Shakespeare's plays demand. He quotes Dr Samuel Johnson to convey the majesty of Shakespeare and leaves one in no doubt that he is a bardolator. Satapathy presents the *Tales* as only a gateway to Shakespeare and tells us how much they leave out.

After making these observations of a general nature, the translator turns his attention to the Indian context and asks rhetorically:

> How many Indians will have the luck to read Shakespeare in the original? Thousands of students who pass the matriculation examination may get an opportunity to read a couple of stories from Shakespeare in English and at college a few will read a play or two with the help of annotations.
>
> If you have not seen a tiger content yourself with seeing a cat. (Translation mine)

The *Tales* are cats and the original plays from which they are derived are tigers. But the tales are important for a very different reason and Satapathy's observations deserve to be quoted here. He now visualizes a future without Shakespeare in India:

> These tales will assume much greater significance when fanatic nationalists will drive out Shakespeare as they drove out the British and when the study of English literature will give way to the teaching of English as a language. (Translation mine)

How prophetic are these words. Over the last thirty years Shakespeare has lost his place of pride in many university syllabi. There was a time when only senior professors of English taught Shakespeare and junior teachers were denied this great privilege. Now the world has changed and, as Satapathy darkly predicted, communicative English threatens to displace the teaching of English literature in colleges and universities. Young lecturers in engineering colleges and management institutes never seem to tire of speaking of body language, short and long vowels, and accent neutralization.

It is almost as if Satapathy was ready to suggest desperate remedies. But these may make teachers of English intensely uncomfortable. In the preface, he refers to an experiment he once conducted in a classroom. After teaching undergraduate students a scene from Shakespeare's play *Othello*, Satapathy read out the part dealing with the same scene from his Odia translation of Lamb's tale. He noticed that students became suddenly more responsive and alert. This brings to mind Professor Avdesh Singh talking about teachers teaching Shakespeare in Hindi or Marathi and describing this activity as a kind of translation of Shakespeare. Is this a nightmare or does this open up new possibilities that we had never dared to explore?

However, the preface does not stop here. It goes a step further and makes a suggestion that is as provocative as the one Satapathy made earlier. And this suggestion is embedded firmly in the context of the translator's own life. Let me again quote from the preface:

> When I was a student of class eleven our headmaster taught us to enact the trial scene from *The Merchant of Venice* and the funeral scene from *Julius Caesar*. This was my first contact with Shakespeare. Later, in 1932, while studying in the intermediate class, I got an opportunity to get to know both Shakespeare and Charles Lamb. I came across a book which contained excerpts from Shakespeare's plays and Lamb's *Tales* and there were many illustrations in it to enliven the text. The book also provided the biographies of Shakespeare and Lamb. Reading the book filled my heart with feelings of adoration for Shakespeare and with compassion, love and pity for Charles and Mary Lamb. Shakespeare was a happy, healthy and prosperous man. Lamb was unlucky, unhealthy and poor. Shakespeare was a superman and Lamb was an ordinary man like us. (Translation mine)

Satapathy now draws our attention to the lessons he learnt from his long experience as a college teacher of English literature in India:

> After teaching English literature for over fifteen years I realize that if a teacher of English in India does research and writes hundreds and hundreds of papers in English it is very unlikely that they would get published in England or the U.S.A. But they would put their knowledge and love of English to good use if they place it at the service of their mother tongues and enrich them. (Translation mine)

Pragmatism? A counsel of despair? One does not know. I am reminded of the foreword that T.S. Eliot contributed to the Odia translation *of The Waste Land*, which was published in the late 1950s. In this, Eliot expressed the sincere hope that the translation would enrich Odia literature. Perhaps, Satapathy had something like this in mind when he reflected on the position of the teacher of English in a world from which Shakespeare has been banished by fanatic nationalists and replaced with communicative English by proponents of globalization.

The suggestions Satapathy made more than 30 years ago in the context of translating Lamb's *Tales* into Odia acquire a new resonance in the recent debate over the future of bilingualism or multilingualism in India, which was initiated by Ramachandra Guha in *Economic and Political Weekly*. Guha drew our attention to the steady erosion of the bilingual and multilingual culture prevailing until recently in India and pointed out that many now do their thinking, reading and writing in only one language in our country. Does Satapathy's prescription assume relevance in the context of this debate? I can only raise these questions. I hope the answers will come eventually.

Identity and the Politics
of Language

11

Does Shakespeare's Text Even Matter?

Preti Taneja

Commenting on the Kathakali *King Lear* performed at Shakespeare's Globe in 1999, Diane Daugherty writes, "Intercultural work is fraught with dangers. Colonial legacies frame it, economic imbalances complicate it, and orientalist accusations are barbs that Western artists who go this route will encounter."[1] More than a decade has passed since the Kathakali *King Lear* toured India and the UK; the manifestations of intercultural exchange since then through Shakespeare's works in translations into Indian languages and performance modes have proliferated, revealing various new joints and fissures in postcolonial relations between Britain and India. The question of how translation is presented to audiences who may or may not speak the source language *or* be familiar with the source text yet exist as a merging of two source cultures (in this case, India and England) has become more pressing. The introduction of technology onto the stage widens the debate. An update into the critical reception of the intercultural translations of Shakespeare that have taken place since the Kathakali *King Lear* is therefore timely and serves to reveal the state of understanding between the two cultures as it currently stands.

Jacqueline Lo and Helen Gilbert argue for a postcolonial approach to intercultural Shakespeare criticism: "In an age where cultural boundaries are continually traversed and identities are becoming increasingly hybridized, an intercultural theatre practice informed by postcolonial theory can potentially function as a site where this intersecting of cultures is both reflected and critiqued."[2] This statement serves as the framework within which this chapter tests Daugherty's claim against some recent negotiations of intercultural translations of Shakespeare's plays between the UK and India. In doing so, it discusses some current attitudes among theatre practitioners and critics towards translations into "other" languages and goes on to ask, "Does the text even matter?" Is the critic Russ McDonald correct when he claims, "Shakespeare in other words is not Shakespeare?"[3] In considering these questions, the essay reflects on the current state of postcolonial relations; how the "other" is perceived in the hybrid space created by intercultural theatre and across the still-contested site of Shakespeare's texts.

This space can be understood within parameters set out by Homi Bhabha as one that, "carries the burden of the meaning of culture."[4] It is therefore not the uncritical and unmediated expression of difference, depoliticized and abstract, which Lo and Gilbert have termed "masked indifference."[5] Bhabha goes on to argue that, postcolonial hybridity, and by extension intercultural theatre, is transgressive and reforming, and challenging as well as accepting and suggests how potential linguistic and cultural futures might evolve and be ushered in.

Mary Louise Pratt calls the hybrid space a "contact zone," a space of encounter, which "may be a site of violence, oppression and resistance or may be a site of closer, less antagonistic exchange, but it remains a theoretical space in which cultural difference can be explored."[6] Thus, it becomes necessary to evaluate politics of production and reception of intercultural theatre as only by doing so can a more grounded idea of the possibility and potential of Bhabha's open "interstitial future, that emerges in between the claims of the past and the needs of the present,"[7] that breaks apart notions of fixed identity and difference.

Language is one of the core sites on which identity is contested and reformed in postcolonial nations (and in this I include England). Susan Bassnett argues that translation itself "may be figurative, as a site of exchange, a hybrid space charged with multiple meanings."[8] With this in mind, I concentrate on questions raised by linguistic translations, the speaking and presentations of Shakespeare's texts in "other" accents. English has, of course, had a pervasive and fraught history in India—as the language of the colonizers, a compulsory mode for advancement through communication in the "master" language, taught by way of Shakespeare. Paul Friedrich argues that, above "all practical and logical advantages," and "despite their democracy and their Shakespeare," English in India maintains its "unforgettable association with British rule."[9] Keeping this in mind is crucial to the discussion that follows.

Lo and Gilbert call "the wide-scale imposition of imperial languages on non-Western peoples [...] an insidious form of epistemic violence."[10] A postcolonial framework considers the power dynamics of language use according to producers, directors, actors, audience and critics. The question of "whose values are heard and whose are silenced by the use of specific languages," is key.[11] Other questions that arise from a study of the productions in this chapter are neatly put:

> In addition, we might ask how linguistic translations are conducted and whose interests they serve: Does the translator function as a negotiator or a type of "native informant"? What happens to linguistic concepts that resist translation or adaptation? In terms of theatrical product, language issues are equally complicated: How do staged languages animate one another? Which carries the cultural authority? What happens to the performative features of verbal enunciation, particularly when stories from predominantly oral cultures are presented? How might we reread verbally silenced bodies in different ways?[12]

To propose some answers to these questions, I begin by considering the politics of production and reception of a landmark intercultural production: Dash Art's 2005/06 Indian *Midsummer Night's Dream*, directed by Tim Supple. Performed in seven different Indian languages, it offered the audience no translation to follow. In this sense it became almost non-verbal: the text submerged and reshaped to foreground the visual elements of the production, nevertheless, language remained a contested issue among critics, as I show. I go on to discuss Indian responses to the 2012 Globe to Globe festival's decision to prohibit the use of English, instead offering only screens with scene summaries to guide the audience through the plays. In contrast, Suman Mukhopadhyay's 2012 Bengali *King Lear* performed to an audience in New Delhi also used a screen, but one that re-translated into "Hinglish" the Bengali translation of the Shakespeare, to great, if unwitting postmodern effect. Finally, I briefly discuss some responses to the Royal Shakespeare Company's 2012 Delhi-set interpretation of *Much Ado About Nothing*, in which a pan-Asian cast performed Shakespeare's text with Indian accents to audiences in the Shakespeare heartland of Stratford-upon-Avon, before transferring to London's West End. This production, a translation of accent rather than language, reveals some striking attitudes towards the "other" that suggests that a dissolution of fixed notions of identity is still some way off when it comes to Shakespeare's text.

Royal Shakespeare Company Director Tim Supple's *A Midsummer Night's Dream* was commissioned and funded by the British Council in India in 2005, underlining the point that "when intercultural exchanges take place within the "non-West," they are often mediated through Western culture and/or economics."[13] On arrival in India, Supple told the sponsors he could not present the show in English.[14] He admits, "The kind of audiences the British Council wanted to attract would have preferred it to be in English."[15] Instead, Supple cast the play with Indian and Sri Lankan performers, and had it translated and performed in seven different languages including English. In this case it is unlikely that there were many in the audience who were able to understand every language used; however, no translation was offered into English, Hindi, Shakespeare's text or any contemporary dialect. Emily Linneman notes,

> This Babel of languages challenged the audience to access the play's meaning in new potentially innovative ways. As the audience and performers worked together to recreate the play's meaning, so the cultural value of Shakespeare was renegotiated and reinvigorated. The utopian primitivism of Supple's *Dream* enabled Dash Arts to present a challenge to Shakespeare's value as originator of the English language and offered the audience a spectacular, exotic, non[-]verbal Shakespeare—Shakespeare in other words, who was differed and different from the kind of Shakespeare normally presented at the RSC. The Indian culture presented in *Dream* may have been part of an idealised aesthetic but it also complicated and challenged the audience's response to Shakespeare's value was not only reaffirmed but reinvigorated through the process of performance.[16]

This positive response, though expressed in Western terms, ("exotic" and "Babel of languages"), highlights the best of the production's potential impacts. Nevertheless, the submergence of English and cultural makeup of the production begs postcolonial analysis.

With its English, and white, RSC director, a multilingual all-Asian cast and the submergence of the original text beneath layers of linguistic, spatial and physical translation, the production seemed to point to some a sort of acknowledgement and an implicit attempt at redressing a power balance formed under colonization. Shakespeare's text was highlighted by its very absence—interestingly cast against the linguistic of the middle-class, and therefore English-speaking, members of the Indian audience.

Yet Supple touches on what Jyotsna Singh has called an, "emphasis on effectiveness,"[17]—leaving the production to speak for itself as a whole. Supple did not want it to make postcolonial linguistic points and explained, "It was not the case that the mechanicals were Bangla speakers while the Theseus/Oberon and Hipolyta/Titania spoke proper Hindi and the magicals were from the South."[18] However, some of his choices did reference the imperial history of English in India and the corresponding aspiring Indian use of it. At the end of the play, Theseus and Hyppolyta spoke Shakespeare's text in what the production's official biographer Ananda Lal noted was "somewhat condescending" English, while the mechanicals "mispronounced and malapropized it."[19] He went on to observe that not only did this underscore language as a site of contested identity, it spoke to the endemic class and caste-based attitudes among the Indian audience. "Too often, we treat our artisans patronizingly as uneducated and unsophisticated; at best unintentional farceurs."[20]

Though Shakespeare's text was translated and became untranslatable in reverse, Supple sees his own contribution to the production as showing, among other things, an immense fidelity to Shakespeare's text. By this he means that an emphasis was placed on Shakespeare's intentions in the text at the basic level, keeping the verse in verse and the prose in prose. The text was not translated into modern Indian languages, but into the nearest poetic form closest to Shakespeare's time. The translations removed the play from the realm of the actors' own reality—they protested that they did not speak like that on a daily basis, if at all. The counter argument to this is that no one speaks like Shakespeare in contemporary English discourse.

The effect of what Indian critic Keval Arora calls Supple's "noble hearted egalitarianism,"[21] was twofold. Arora notes:

> The idea that languages are grounded in sociological cultural spaces and are imbricated in personal identity, that they shape memories of shared pasts and imagined futures, that they are as much bones of contention as means of contestations—none of these, on the evidence of the performance, seem part of Supple's plan.[22]

The first effect was that the poly-translations simply melted the different tongues into an amorphous mass and the audience were given permission to tune out. Arora said, "It's ironical that Supple's inclusivist gesture towards the individual actor ends up as an exclusionary experience for his spectators." Among audiences in India and abroad this caused some anxiety, that Shakespeare's text was not being treated with the respect that the language warranted.

Lal notes that, "for Indian audiences to whom Supple's *Dream* first played, the most resistant element may have been its polyglot script."[23]

He states that this protest had its roots in reverence for the "Bard's own English, which Indians may indeed regard as more sacrosanct than the English themselves do."[24] Supple describes the reactions of what he terms, "the Shakespeare Wallah generation,"[25] more used to the Shakespeare of Gielgud and Olivier, who demanded to know why he had not produced the play "in the original way."[26] He recalls that in India there were more objections to the fact that actors were not speaking in English than anywhere else that the production played in the world.

In the UK response, Supple noted a "patronising tone,"[27] from theatre critics, particularly when the production played in Stratford. Supple said, "There is an inbuilt prejudice against speaking Shakespeare and not in Queens' English—this is a problem with the text that the RSC has given us."[28] He and many others felt his production almost surpassed these issues, but even so, when the production toured to the States, he began to sit outside theatres and bet himself how long it would take for the first audience member to walk out. In San Francisco, Supple said it took three minutes. As they left, they remarked, "I didn't know it wouldn't be in English." The positive potential of the hybrid linguistic space to suggest new interpretations and meanings was not fully embraced by either source culture.

The reactions this production elicited and the challenges that such productions present to the sense of reverence for Shakespeare's original text might have been a salutary set of signs for Globe for the Globe festival director Tom Bird. At the WSF, which took place in London in 2012, the decision on language for the productions was definite—no English was to be allowed onstage. Artistic Director of the Globe Dominic Dromgoole argued that he wanted the invited directors to bring the shows as they would, for example, in Mumbai.[29] Bird recounts that Atul Kumar, director of the Hindi *Twelfth Night*, argued that his company theatre artists should therefore be allowed to use English because, as he rightly protested, that is the language they speak, but to no avail. It is striking that, particularly for postcolonial nations invited to take part, this guideline was emphatically promoted. It could be argued that this reversed the colonial dictum to enforce the learning and speaking of English in India—a keeping of the natives "native" while on English soil.

Certainly, Kumar felt strongly enough to ignore the guideline. His actors inserted English phrases into the production without the knowledge or blessing of the festival organizers. Those lines were in contemporary English, almost Hinglish, or English spoken with exaggerated Indian accents, as if to mock any reverence for the original text and the idea that there is a way Shakespeare "should" be spoken. They were performed in the spirit of buffoonery and yet the subtext spoke to long-standing language, identity and class politics between English and Hindi/Shakespeare, and his translators.

Malvolio was the perfect carrier for this. "We thought of giving him wrong English phrases, as in how someone in an Indian village would try and speak English, make a mess of it and still feel higher than everyone else,"[30] Kumar said. The use of English in this production therefore was clearly meant to challenge notions of cultural superiority—between Indians of different classes, between post-colonizer and post-colonized, and between those on the stage and those who commissioned them to be there.

In 3.4, Saurabh Nayyar was on stage as Malvolio wearing "yellow stockings, cross gartered" and waiting for Olivia. In a riposte to Maria (Trupti Khamkar) and Sir Toby (Gagan Riar), who is Malvolio's superior in terms of class hierarchy, Malvolio corrects their English and accuses them (in heavily accented Hinglish) of being "grammatically illiterate,"[31] showing his sense of superiority through his imagined prowess in the English language over theirs. Later in the play, as Malvolio thought of his life married to Olivia, Nayyar made a mockery of English and by implication, of those who pretend to have sahib-style manners. He described the clothes he would wear for Malvolio's wedding to Olivia swapping Hindi and English in the same breath, "*Sir pe pehnoonga bara sa crown. Aur sari duniya ko* I will look down."[32] (On my head I'll wear a big crown, and on the whole world I will look down.) The use of the word "crown" recalls a demand for obeisance to empire here and become sa subversion in that the crown was worn by Shakespeare's beloved underdog: the unwitting, nonprofessional fool.

A sense of pride in subverting Shakespeare's text and stretching the guidelines of the festival was evident. Amitosh Nagpal, who played Sebastian but also translated *Twelfth Night* into Hindi, interrupted the performance to address the Globe audience directly, saying, "Translation *ki job, ma kasam, itni* thankless job *hai yaar…mein aake liney suna raha hoon to kehrahe, 'Wah!* Shakespeare *kamal*!*"* (The job of a translator is truthfully a thankless one—I come and tell them a line and everyone says, "Wow, Shakespeare is the best!") In this he echoes the great Shakespearean German translator, August Wilhelm Schlegel, who spoke of his work as "a thankless task, in which one is continually tormented by ineluctable imperfections,"[33] and highlighted Shakespeare's dominance over all translation endeavours.

But Nagpal's real subversion was in undermining the idea of striving for "perfection" within his translation itself. Speaking only Hindi, he cracked colloquial jokes against the idea of Shakespeare's genius that monolingual English speakers in the audience would not understand. Interrupting the flow of the production he told the audience, "*Chalein to* Shakespeare *karletein Angrezi mein*! Thee, thy, thou, thou *karte karte* Gandhi *ke kapde chotein ho gaye...Chaliye theek hai, aap to* Shakespeare *dekhne aye hain to main* Sebastian *bun jata hoon, aur aapko* Shakespeare *sunata hoon.*"[34] *OK, fine. Let's do Shakespeare in English then! Doing 'thee, thy, thou' over and over has shrunk Gandhi's clothes! OK, well, you have come to watch Shakespeare so let me become Sebastian and give you some Shakespeare to listen to.* The joke works on several levels: against the authority of Shakespeare, against the reverence for Shakespearean English, against the mythology of a "saintly" Gandhi, against audiences who worship all these. "We are all just human," Nagpal seemed to be saying; "what we write and how we say it matters only as much as it does." He parodied the change from translator-for-hire to Sebastian in character by becoming formal in his stance and tone, befitting an actor with reverence for the text.[35] Later, Bird said that the hybrid result of Kumar and Nagpal's insertions added greatly to the humour and audience enjoyment of the play.[36]

Subverting the text was explicitly important for Sunil Shanbag, Director of the Gujurati *All's Well That Ends Well*, who was keenly aware of the historical and political subtext of the Globe to Globe festival. He said:

> The *fact* of the Globe to Globe festival shows how much the English still regard Shakespeare as a cultural extension of their relationship with the rest of the world, especially so with former colonies. So we do have to find ways to subvert that in a constructive and enriching way.[37]

In this he recognizes the fear expressed by some Western critics that the festival in itself was an act of cultural imperialism, that in "forcing" companies to do Shakespeare, a statement was being made.[38] That companies understood and subverted this was, however, sometimes lost on the UK's critics. Though Shanbag's production stayed within the guidelines set by the Globe, a part of his method was to use humour to critique Indian attitudes to Western modernity and Western attitudes to Indian traditional medicines.

> India has been struggling with tradition and modernity for some time now, and attitudes have been very ambivalent. Unlike in many, many societies, in India tradition has managed to hold its own rather well, adapting to, resisting, subverting modernity [...] and that's what we wanted to indicate. Gokuldas's

[the King of France] attitude to Western medicine is ambivalent. He is very impressed by Western doctors, and in fact refers to Heli's [Helena's] traditional medicine as outdated. At the same time he knows only too well the limitations of [W]estern medicine, and resents the way the English reject traditional Indian medicine. So it's a grey area, and that makes it even more interesting.[39]

Because of the lack of translation, some reviewers missed the subtlety and read the action simply as the character mocking Western methods. A number of reviewers did grasp and appreciate the ways in which Shanbag's translation strengthened the female characters in the play. However, Shanbag said this might be lost on Indian critics when the play moved back to India because in many cases they would not know the source text.

Such misinterpretations could be avoided by using the screen. The question of whether to use Shakespeare text or translate the "other" language back into contemporary English would arise. The Globe decided only to project scene summaries on the screen. The decision, according to Bird, had as much to do with the Globe's overall cultural experiment as it did with the dynamics of staging at the Globe, where a line-by-line translation would have resulted in a Wimbledon-like effect with the audiences' heads turning from screen to stage as if watching tennis, distracting the actors and each other.

The screen as a manifestation of the hybrid space offers potential and acts as the site upon which any cultural anxiety surrounding intercultural Shakespeare or hybrid productions, particularly in traditional spaces, might be projected. One such moment occurred at the Globe to Globe performance of Theatre Wallay/KASF's Urdu *Taming of the Shrew*. Actor Salman Shahid who played Baptista Minola/Mian Basheer came on to introduce the production, saying:

> Ladies and Gentlemen, we feel extremely honoured to be performing here, this is sacred space for actors from anywhere in the world. There are some things I would just like to tell you. A lot of it (the play) is told on those things (here he pointed to the screens), I haven't been able to exactly make out whether they are things or "thingies," (and here, the audience laughed at his self-deprecating English/Hinglish word play), but they are on both sides (of the stage). They give you also a synopsis of the play, a rough outline of what's happening because it's going to be hard times for English speakers.[40]

As the audience laughed a Western man in the mixed-ethnicity audience shouted out, "Not many here." Shahid responded with humour, "I'm not very sure whether that's a happy moment for us or not."[41]

In this exchange, the actor began by acknowledging reverence for Shakespeare and noting what performing on the Globe stage means to his company. Second, he referenced the screens as an imposition in the theatrical space of the digital age, which was nonetheless necessary in the theatre experiment. Most importantly, the audience member's position who wrongly assumed, perhaps because he could see so many brown faces around him, that there were "not many" English speakers present was undermined. In fact, most of the Urdu-speaking members in the audience would have been, at the very least, bilingual. In this short interchange, the anxiety of reception and uneasiness over the production, presentation and reception of foreign Shakespeares was spontaneously played out.

Though one critic in the UK newspaper the *Independent* wrote,

> You can see why Afghans, and Albanians, and Palestinians, and the citizens of pretty much every country in the world, might want to perform the works of the greatest playwright who ever lived, even though they have to perform them in another language. What's harder to understand is why British audiences would want to see the work of the greatest poet who ever lived without actually hearing the words.[42]

In fact, she went on to argue,

> More than 100,000 people have been to the Globe in the past six weeks to see all 37 of Shakespeare's plays in different languages, including recently the Israeli Habima Theatre Company's *The Merchant of Venice*. Some have seen all 37. Some have even stood for all of them. And 80 per cent of them, apparently, have never been to the Globe before.

If anxiety reared its head when the productions actually took to the stage or in the reviews, it did not prevent audiences from being open to the experience of Shakespeare in translation. In this the screens became part of the potential or may not have made a difference at all—as perhaps the Globe intended. It is important to note that even when people are bilingual, an ability to read English cannot be assumed.

A line-by-line translation was provided on a screen in Suman Mukhopadyay's 2012 Bengali *King Lear*, performed at the Bharat Rang Mahotsav festival in New Delhi. The production was a good example of the "empowering mimicry" model with the actors speaking in sonorous Bengali, while the costumes were approximations of what might have been worn on a Tudor stage. The screen translation was of the Bengali text, which was already a translation of the Shakespearean, not back to the original or even contemporary English, but to postmodern Hinglish.

For example: Kent's words to Oswald in 2.2.40 "I'll make a sop o'the moonshine of you," became, to the audience reading the English, "I'll make a *korma* out of you." Somewhere in the chain of translation, Shakespeare's "sop o' the moonshine" (a kind of milk custard) became, as John Dover Wilson and George Ian Duthie have it, "mincemeat,"[43] as in the popular English phrase "I'll make mincemeat out of you," meaning: I'll mess you up. This "mincemeat" in Bengali became *keema*, the Hindi word for minced meat, and this was translated on the screen as korma, perhaps to give a better flavour to the image.

Though Mukhopadyay had no involvement in the screen translation, yet it was an integral part of the audience experience of his play. Considered as a site of potential, the screen offers an insight into how subversive and persuasive it could be if a director integrated its use in the play's overall aesthetic. In a postmodern age, this is surely something worth considering: such experiments may introduce fresh perspectives on mainstream critical dialogue on intercultural Shakespeare translations and performances.

The RSC's 2012 *Much Ado about Nothing* provides an interesting counterpoint. The production, set in contemporary Old Delhi, was designed along the standard template of the English approximation of India: full of the inevitable bright pinks and reds and cacophonous noise, it offered the visual paradox of a modern city where time appears to be frozen. The cast included British Asian actors in traditional dress, yet they kept to Shakespeare's language—a further paradox for audience and critics. No screens were needed, but critical responses still felt the text had somehow been bastardized just by being placed in "other" mouths. Michael Billington in the *Guardian* wanted more emphasis on the Indian setting even as he urged the actors to pay increased attention to "narrative and verbal clarity"—Shakespeare's story and the speaking of his text.[44] Charles Spencer in the *Daily Telegraph* framed from the point of view of someone visiting India and commented on the delivery of the text in even more marked style:

> The company's delivery of Shakespeare's dense language, 70 per cent of which is in prose in this play, frequently offers more in the way of vigour than elegant clarity, while the scenes involving the supposedly comic night-watch are even more tediously unfunny than usual. But they will undoubtedly remind many Western visitors to India of frustrating encounters with the country's bureaucracy.

Implicit in this criticism is an appeal, drawn along lines of "us" versus "them," and based on the implied assumption that the Indian setting or the

Asian nature of the cast impacted on the proper delivery of Shakespeare's text. We are reminded of Ton Hoenselaars' view (echoed by Supple in his previously noted reference to the RSC delivery of Shakespeare) that:

> The ultimate paradox which the foreign Shakespeare initiative exposed was that, by desperately clutching at the "original" English like a household God, the English [have] really become alienated by [Shakespeare's] work, written in a language that ceased to be spoken almost 350 years ago.[45]

At the Globe, Bird believes this is inevitable, saying:

> Maybe not in our lifetime, but (Shakespeare's texts) are going to become redundant as all texts do, as they are performed more and more in traditional languages. Especially in India, where people are used to using a mix of languages.[46]

He added, "the benefit of not knowing the text or the language of performance is that you might grasp the pre-linguistic architecture of the play. By the point of performance, the text honestly didn't matter."

Does this in itself matter? The answer lies in the idea of the "pre-linguistic architecture," of the plays, on which there is agreement among the practitioners discussed here. Sunil Shanbag believes that "it is very easy to 'de-text' Shakespeare. His plots lend themselves to this." However, he wanted "to remain true to the text, to Shakespeare lyricism and make a political statement!" He asserts that whether "translators go for the spirit or the letter, whether it is performed in a mix of English or in a mix of Indian languages,"[47] the text continues to exist as the DNA of the production.

Japanese director Tetsuo Anzai notes, "The theatre maker's primary goal is not the communication of the literal meaning of the original text, but the recreation of the theatrical experience embodied there."[48] Anxieties around the sanctity of the text continue to be evoked in traditionalists by practitioners who thrive on experiments with language and form. Certainly in the Indian context, criticism by Western reviewers seems to be unable to lose its own culturally conditioned sense of what defines Indian performance culture: Bollywood. Shanbag recognizes that this is also a danger for Indian practitioners and audiences. "When we come from India the temptation to 'bollywood-ise' is ever present, especially now that Bollywood has been valorized by so many culture theorists, especially from the West."[49] Taking a critical approach to mass culture is, of course, a valid endeavour. However, a scan of the previews and reviews of the plays under consideration here shows that newspaper critics reviewing the Globe to Globe festival were taking a somewhat different tone.

Lyn Gardner in the *Observer* uses the term "all singing, all dancing" to describe what she called a "pretty one dimensional version"[50] (i.e., a Bollywood-esque) *Twelfth Night* and Emer O'Toole in *The Guardian* uses the same "all singing all dancing" phrase to describe the Shanbag's very different Gujarati *Alls Well That Ends Well.* In approach and tone, Shanbag, in fact, drew on Bhangwadi style theatre, suitable for the period he set the play in, which uses music and dance and cannot be compared to Bollywood.

Even in the critical responses to Supple's *Dream*, the *Daily Telegraph* and *The Times* found that Bollywood references in the play that, according to extensive production notes, certainly were not intended. Lal puts this down to "the Western critic's inherently problematising gaze,"[51] which also perceived the Globe to Globe festival itself either as an example of cultural imperialism (*The Guardian*, as previously noted) or at the risk of feeling "worthy," or "amateurish," the "kind of local arts event that's funded by the local council. Or worse, even like panto" (the *Independent*). Such attitudes undermine both the artistic value in the productions that veer away from Bollywood, and those who specifically draw on its rich traditions, which are in themselves hybrid. In an interview with the *Times of India*, Kumar said:

> *Twelfth Night* is not *Hamlet* or *Othello* or *Macbeth* or *King Lear*. It is more like Shakespeare version of a Bollywood blockbuster. Identical twins separated in shipwreck, cross-dressing, mistaken identities, unrequited love, high passion, sword fights and happy reunions are the themes that makeup the plot. Does this not sound like what we in India have all grown up with and still enjoy? In short, it is total entertainment and we chose to do it with dance and music.[52]

Ironically, the charge of "Bollywood" was largely absent from critical responses to this production in the UK press, perhaps because the genre was indeed so obviously referenced.

If some UK critics missed the ways in which the productions analysed here "spoke back" in postcolonial terms, others who covered the Globe to Globe festival marvelled at the universality of human experience encoded in Shakespeare's plays brought home to them by seeing those texts performed in "other" languages. They were able to grasp the "pre-linguistic" architecture of the plays through the success of intercultural theatre's presentation of hybridity.

Productions such as these, which take place along the West–East and North–South axis are categorized as "extracultural"[53] forms of intercultural theatre. As the analysis presented in this essay demonstrates, their purpose is to:

> Celebrate and even interrogate such differences as a source of cultural empowerment and aesthetic richness.... Extracultural theatre always begs questions about the power dynamics inherent in the economic and political location of the participating cultures, even if such questions are evaded in accounts of actual practice.[54]

It has not been my intention here to evade such questions, but to interrogate the responses to the challenges around power dynamics that recent intercultural theatre has raised. Translation, subversion and interrogating hierarchies of power are themes that mirror Shakespeare own priorities in the plays, as Caliban's often quoted lines in *The Tempest* attest:

> You taught me language; and my profit on't
>
> Is, I know how to curse. The red plague rid you
>
> For learning me your language!
>
> (1.2.365–67)

As Bassnett comments, "There is clearly no trust between master and slave, colonizer and colonized, and language reinforces the abyss that divides them." This essay has shown the state of current critical responses to intercultural translations as a means of highlighting their potential to reverse, even fill, that sense of the abyss with new tongues that may be heard as equal to one another.

Willson Harris writes of the potential of translations to "to tilt the field of civilisation so that one may visualize boundaries of persuasion in new and unsuspected lights to release a different apprehension of reality, the language of reality, a different *reading* of texts of reality."[55] Accepting that hybrid spaces can yield formations and meanings that are more than the sum of their parts allows for such productions to be taken on their own terms: not as a violation of "our" Shakespeare by "them," but as free standing artworks in their own right, even as they celebrate old meanings and provoke new ones that speak to present concerns. In this sense, productions cease to be representative of an attempt to overcome Shakespeare as a colonizing force, or as examples of a postcolonial approximation of colonial culture. In a critical and theatrical space that is open to possibilities, "hybrid sites of new meaning open up, new borders are encountered and crossed, often with surprisingly creative results." Such a space incorporates new technologies and tongues, actors and audiences can congregate from several languages and traditions, and Shakespeare can meet Bhangwadi or Bollywood, with differences nuanced and recognized even as they are radically re-imagined, re-presented and understood.

Notes

1. Diane Daugherty, "The Pendulum of Intercultural Performance: 'Kathakali *King Lear*' at Shakespeare's Globe," *Asian Theatre Journal* 22, no. 1 (Spring 2005): 52.
2. Jacqueline Lo and Helen Gilbert, "Toward a Topography of Cross-Cultural Theatre Praxis," *TDR: The Drama Review* 46, no. 3 (T175, Fall 2002): 46.
3. Ton Hoenselaars, *Shakespeare and the Language of Translation* (London: Arden, 2004), ix.
4. Homi Bhabha, *The Location of Culture* (London and New York: Routledge, 1994), 56.
5. Lo and Gilbert, "Toward a Topography," 46.
6. Susan Bassnett, *A Concise Companion to Postcolonial Literature* (Oxford: Blackwell, 2010), 92.
7. Bhabha, *The Location of Culture*, 219.
8. Bassnett, *A Concise Companion*, 92.
9. Paul, Friederich, "Language and Politics in India", *Daedalus, Current Work and Controversies* 91, no. 3 (Summer 1962): 557.
10. Lo and Gilbert, "Toward a Topography," 46.
11. Lo and Gilbert, "Toward a Topography," 46.
12. Lo and Gilbert, "Toward a Topography," 46.
13. Lo and Gilbert, "Toward a Topography," 36.
14. Tim Supple, personal interview, November 2012.
15. Tim Supple, personal interview, November 2012.
16. Emily Linneman, "International Innovation? Shakespeare as Intercultural Catalyst," in *Shakespeare Survey*, 64, ed. Peter Holland (Cambridge: Cambridge University Press, 2011), 13–24.
17. Jyotsna Singh, "*Local and Global 'Indian Shakespeares.*'" (lecture, Shakespeare Society of India and I. P. College, New Delhi, 7–9 March 2013).
18. Tim Supple, personal interview, November 2012.
19. Ananda Lal, "'We the Globe can Encompass Soon': Tim Supple's *Dream*," in *The Shakespearean International Yearbook, 12: Special Section: Shakespeare in India*, ed. Tom Bishop and Alexander C.Y. Huang, ed. emeritus Graham Bradshaw, special guest ed. Sukanta Chaudhuri. (Farnham: Ashgate, 2012), 71.
20. Lal, "We the Globe can Encompass Soon," 71.
21. Lal, "We the Globe can Encompass Soon," 73.
22. Lal, "We the Globe can Encompass Soon," 73.
23. Lal, "We the Globe can Encompass Soon," 77.
24. Lal, "We the Globe can Encompass Soon," 74.
25. Lal, "We the Globe can Encompass Soon," 74.
26. Lal, "We the Globe can Encompass Soon," 74.
27. Lal, "We the Globe can Encompass Soon," 74.

28. Lal, "We the Globe can Encompass Soon," 74.
29. Atul Kumar, Email interview, February 2013.
30. Atul Kumar, Email interview, February 2013.
31. *Twelfth Night*, or *Piya Behrupiya* dir. Atul Kumar, Globe Theatre, 27–28 April, 2012.
32. *Twelfth Night*, or *Piya Behrupiya* dir. Atul Kumar, Globe Theatre, 27–28 April, 2012.
33. Hoenselaars, *Shakespeare and the Language*, ix.
34. *Twelfth Night*, or *Piya Behrupiya* dir. Atul Kumar, Globe Theatre, 27–28 April, 2012.
35. In an email interview Atul Kumar emphasized that "this was improvised, not pre-planned."
36. Tom Bird, personal interview, February 2013.
37. Sunil Shanbag, Email Interview, February 2013.
38. Emer O'Toole, "Shakespeare Universal? No its Cultural Imperialism," *The Guardian*, 21 May 2012, accessed 14 March 2013, http://www.guardian.co.uk/commentisfree/2012/may/21/shakespeare-universal-cultural-imperialism/print
39. Sunil Shanbag, email interview, February 2013.
40. *The Taming of the Shrew*, dir. Haissam Hussain, Globe Theatre, London, 25–26 May, 2012.
41. *The Taming of the Shrew*, dir. Haissam Hussain, 2012.
42. Christina Patterson, "Lost in Translation: The Globe's Shakespeare Season Offers a Surprising Insight into Different Cultures," *Independent*, 7 June 2012.
43. Cambridge University Press, reissuing the Duthie and Wilson edition in 2012, notes, "John Dover Wilson's *New Shakespeare*, published between 1921 and 1966, became the classic Cambridge edition of Shakespeare's plays and poems until the 1980s," accessed February 2012, http://books.google.co.in/books/about/King_Lear.html?id=Xd6aQgAACAAJ
44. Michael Billington, "Much Ado about Nothing," *The Guardian*, 2 August 2012, accessed February 2013, http://www.guardian.co.uk/stage/2012/aug/02/much-ado-about-nothing-review
45. Hoenselaars, *Shakespeare and the Language*, 20.
46. Tom Bird, personal interview, February 2013.
47. Sunil Shanbag, email interview, February 2013.
48. Hoenselaars, *Shakespeare and the Language*, 13.
49. Sunil Shanbag, 2013.
51. Ananda Lal, "We the Globe can Encompass Soon," 75.
52. Ipshita Mitra, 'I wish I could do Hamlet all my life,' *Times of India*, 17 August 2012, accessed 9 September 2015, http://timesofindia.indiatimes.com/life-style/people/I-wish-I-could-do-Hamlet-all-my-life-Atul-Kumar/articleshow/15530848.cms
53. Lo and Gilbert, "Toward a Topography," 38.
54. Lo and Gilbert, "Toward a Topography," 38.
55. Bassnett, *A Concise Companion*, 86.

12

Utpal Dutt and *Macbeth* Translated

Naina Dey

Bengal's preoccupation with Shakespeare's plays is nothing new considering that early English productions took place in "garrison theatres" catering to the British colonists, the most popular being the Old Play House in Lalbazar Street, which was later occupied by Siraj-ud-Daulah during his attack on Calcutta in June 1756. In Calcutta, then the capital of British India, the earliest recorded performance is of *Othello* at the Calcutta Theatre in the Christmas season of 1780. Performances continued till the mid-nineteenth century chiefly at the Chowringhee and Sans Souci Theatres, though most of these performances were dependent on amateurs—British residents who performed exclusively for British residents. It is notable that *Macbeth* was enacted in 1814 at Chowringhee Theatre, an event duly recorded in the *Calcutta Gazette*. The amateurs who had "successfully" enacted the play were, in later years, joined by professionals. It is also remarkable that one-third of the audience on the evening of the performance were Bengalis.

In August 1848, Boishnob Choron Addy, an Indian actor, played Othello at the Sans Souci Theatre. Addy's role became an index of the first phase of the Indian appropriation of Shakespearean theatre. Also, touring British companies aroused great interest among the city's students, inspiring them to productions of their own. Interestingly, the tutors who educated Rabindranath Tagore at home made him translate all or parts of *Macbeth* when the poet was only 13. These were subsequently read out to

Ishwarchandra Vidyasagar, polymath, scholar and one of the architects of the Bengal Renaissance, who was also a Shakespeare translator.

The year 1893 witnessed the staging and translation of *Macbeth* by the period's renowned playwright, actor and director, Girish Chondro Ghosh. In later years, one also comes across translations by Shochindronath Sengupta, Nirendranath Roy and Basanta Kumar Roychoudhury, and in the twentieth century and after by Utpal Dutt, Ashok Mukhopadhyay and Ujjal Chattopadhyay.

Utpal Dutt's *Macbeth* was staged significantly on 27 September 1975 by People's Little Theatre, exactly three months after the Emergency of 26 June 1975 at Rabindra Sadan in Calcutta, as a cultural retaliation against the erstwhile authoritarian Congress regime under Prime Minister Indira Gandhi. One must take into account that Dutt found only those translations of Shakespeare's plays commendable that he thought were closest to the spirit of the original and were at the same time, supremely stageworthy—Jyotirindranath Tagore's translation of *Julius Caesar*, Sunilkumar Chattopadhyay's *The Merchant of Venice*, Poshupoti Bhattacharya's *Twelfth Night*, selected scenes from Nirendranath Roy's *Macbeth* (staged on 23 April 1952, Sreerangam) and Jyotindronath Sengupta's *Macbeth* (staged on 7 November 1954 by the Little Theatre Group at New Empire), his own *Othello*, *A Midsummer Night's Dream* and *Romeo and Juliet*—though according to Samik Bandyopadhyay, Dutt eventually found the literal translations of Nirendranath Roy and Jyotindronath Sengupta falling short of his purpose and, hence, chose to translate *Macbeth* himself. In both productions of *Macbeth* Dutt himself played the central character, though he had already played the protagonist in an earlier production in November 1951 by the Little Theatre Group. Dutt, however, had no faith in adaptations.

The 1951 production created quite a furore as Dutt after a brief stint at Gananatya Sangha, a theatre society that performed in the villages of Bengal, had returned to his own company the Little Theatre Group. The production was lauded by none other than the noted poet and journalist Saroj Dutta, in *Swadhinata* the organ for the Communist Party of India. Dutta specially commented on the narrow stage and bare props that in no way could diminish the quality of performance. The 1954 production of Jyotindronath Sengupta's translation, witnessed for the first time the participation of Sobha Sen, a talented artist and wife[1] of Utpal Dutt, as Lady Macbeth. Soon the PLT had to perform *Macbeth* in rural areas on request. In a 1972 interview, Dutt had commented on the reception of his production of *Macbeth* by the village audience:

I understood then, that they had travelled to the roots of Shakespeare's plays, without hindrance and the foreign attire, that they wore Scottish dress, they never took notice—because there Scotland, England, Bengal—the audience had become one, which only the power of a dramatist like Shakespeare could achieve.[2] (Translation mine)

In this essay I focus on Utpal Dutt's re-creation of *Macbeth* onstage, which he attempted in the 1975 production, which effected a transformation suited to a Bengali ambience that not only made Shakespeare a people's poet of all ages but reinforced Dutt's own Marxist ideology. This is made explicit in his book *Towards a Revolutionary Theatre* (1982):

> The Revolutionary Theatre must by definition, preach revolution, a radical overthrow of the political power of the bourgeois-feudal forces, a thorough destruction of their state machine.[3]

I will, in this regard, highlight a few aspects of the meticulous stage directions and end-notes that Dutt had incorporated into his translation of Shakespeare's play indicating movement, emotions, locations and language for the actors of his group for the sake of topical relevance that reveals the director-actor's awareness of an ever-changing dialectical process. These notes, in a more prosaic verse suited to Dutt's own age, are found in his own handwritten manuscript (reproduced in print by Thema). What is also notable in them is a greater reliance on actions and gestures than on elaborate stage props, which was the result of rigorous training in Geoffrey Kendal's travelling company.

By the time Dutt staged *Macbeth*, he was already a pioneering figure in modern *Indian theatre*. His Little Theatre Group (PLT), formed in 1949, had enacted a number of plays by Shakespeare, Shaw and Clifford Odets before immersing itself completely in highly political and radical theatre. Dutt's plays became apt vehicles for his Marxist ideology, visible in socio-political plays such as *Kollol* (sound of the waves, staged in 1965, Minerva), *Manusher Adhikare* (in the rights of man, staged in 1965, Minerva), *Louha Manob* (men of iron, staged in 1964, Presidency Jail), *Tiner Toloar* (the tin sword, staged in 1971, Rabindra Sadan) and *Moha-Bidroha* (the great revolt, staged in 1985, Rabindra Sadan). The subversive message of his play *Kallol*, based on the *Royal Indian Navy Mutiny* of 1946 irked the then *Congress* government of West Bengal and Dutt was jailed in 1965 and detained for several months. Thereafter, Dutt and his group were to face further hurdles while attempting to stage plays. In one of his accounts,[4] Dutt mentioned how on 26 June 1972, the management of Rabindra Sadan refused to allow PLT to perform *Tiner Taloar*. Again, after the immense success of *Dushswopner Nogori* (city of nightmares) in 1974 a case of treason was registered against the PLT. Dutt recollected how the police and "Congress-backed hooligans"[5] (translation mine) made successive attempts to jeopardize the performances of *Dushswopner Nogori* at at various places like Chandernagore, Bishwarupa Theatre in Calcutta and the Academy, and assaulted actors and spectators during a performance in Star Theatre on 26 August 1974.

In an interview given to Samik Bandyopadhyay in 1989, Dutt had stated:

> When we performed Shakespeare's *Macbeth*, we could understand that there could be no better play against despotism. There was no play appropriate enough to counter the emergency. Not till now.[6] (Translation mine)

Dutt used *Macbeth* as a strategy for political protest in the guise of enacting a "harmless" classic. He elaborates how his theatre company had selected *Macbeth* after careful deliberation:

> We all sat down and decided that it was time to strike. After the attack we sat down again and decided...now we must begin our austere practice of the classics. We have to do both. We must strike our enemy, and retreat. We would not keep on creating a din. That we felt was coarse political tactics.[7] (Translation mine)

The years 1957 and 1971 had witnessed the film productions of *Macbeth* by Akira Kurosawa and Roman Polanski, both of whom had explored not only the nature of ambition but also of political violence that was the outcome of dictatorship—and both were noted for manipulating their subject matter in accordance with contemporary relevance. While Kurosawa considered the self-destructive role of Japan in World War II, Polanski's *Macbeth* became a critique of the vested ambitions and perpetration of violence of the United States of America. Both filmmakers were, therefore, keen on highlighting the destructive nature of ambition and mindless violence. Similarly, Dutt was also responding to the twentieth-century preoccupation with Shakespeare's plays from the perspective of historiography, politics and verse-play. Dutt took into account the fact that within 50 years of *Macbeth's* composition, England had witnessed a macabre end to absolute monarchy. Therefore, while the tyrant could boast "There's not a one of them, but in his house/I keep a servant fee'd," his wronged subject bewailed "Each new morn,/New widows howl, new orphans cry; new sorrows/Strike heaven on the face." In the nightmarish condition of Scotland, Dutt saw the reflection of his own country as a terrorized state in the 1970s.

Utpal Dutt was perhaps the first to enter Bengali mainstream drama through translations of Shakespeare. On the other hand, by presenting Shakespeare in a regional Indian language, Dutt was also decolonizing the Bard. Therefore, in his translations we find dialectical oppositions between the colonial and postcolonial, the urban and the rural, and the Mediterranean exotic and the recognizable locale of the Indian villages. As Tapati Gupta comments:

> Dutt's productions amalgamated the past and present, mingled the east and the west. Western style and Indian taste and tradition. Dialectical oppositions crystallized into a common man's Shakespeare, for Dutt found Shakespeare ideally suited the tastes of the Indian masses, be it the Bengali middle-class of Calcutta or the village crowd. They were used to plays full of episodes, music, murders, dramatic happenings, poetic soliloquies, melodrama and fun. Such was the stuff of the traditional folk-plays or "jatra." These Shakespearean plays moved the crowd to tears and laughter. Utpal Dutt had trained into Shakespeare production through the hassles of a travelling company during his years with Geoffrey Kendal and could put up shows with only the most basic props, in almost Elizabethan surroundings, keeping his theory of theatrical dialectics in mind.[8]

Here I shall confine myself to discussing Dutt's transcreation of Shakespeare's *Macbeth*. I shall aim at showing his methods of transcreation, the means he adopted to make the play accessible to the ordinary Bengali middle-class without compromising the Shakespearean ambience, the concessions he made to the requirements of the stage and how he fitted them to his own ideological understanding of Shakespeare. While like any "good" translation that traditionally requires a complete transcript of the ideas of the original work while retaining the ease of original composition, Dutt's translation of *Macbeth* revealed a flavour that was distinctly cross-cultural as well as strictly methodical and highly innovative for the purpose of stage performance. Dutt developed the sparse stage directions of Shakespeare to highlight certain aspects of the play that he felt would add relevance to his political purpose. Therefore, the examples given here can be used as evidences of how Dutt regarded *Macbeth* not just as a play of unbridled ambition of one man, but as one in which ambition becomes a universal vice. Macbeth became for him a living epitome of sin as well as a tragic hero who was an unwitting victim of the very system he had devised for others to preserve his authority. Thus, *Macbeth* for Dutt had become more than a classic. Dutt was, of course, less interested in the nature of the supernatural than Shakespeare himself and, therefore, in 1.1 the "witches" of Shakespeare become simply "ek, dui, teen" (one, two, three). Specific stage directions seem to begin from 1.3, line 150:

> Macbeth: Give me your favour: my dull brain was wrought
>
> > With things forgotten. Kind gentlemen, your pains
> >
> > Are registered where every day I turn
> >
> > The leaf to read them.—Let us toward the King.—
>
> [To Banquo] Think upon what
>
> > hath chanced; and at more time,
> >
> > The interim having weighed it, let us speak
> >
> > Our free hearts to other.

On Dutt's stage, Ross and Angus exit after Macbeth says "Let us toward the King." Immediately after, Macbeth "seizing arm" tells Banquo aside "Think upon what hath chanced" obviously indicating their meeting with the witches that has fired Macbeth's ambitions.

At the beginning of 1.4 the directions are as follows:

1. Sols file & along footlights
2. King and princes enter U
3. On Duncan's sp. Sols. part and take position.

As Duncan begins to speak the sols. divide themselves into two rows and take positions on either side.

Duncan stands with his sons Malcolm and Donalbain on either side. Macbeth enters and advances towards Duncan. Ross and Angus stand on Macbeth's left, their backs to the audience. They kneel. When Duncan addresses Banquo as "Noble Banquo," all three stand up. As Duncan tells all to proceed "From hence to Inverness" the soldiers exit via upstage.

We notice how Dutt not only focuses on the meeting between Duncan, Macbeth and Banquo (Ross and Angus become the lesser lords due to their secondary positions onstage), but like Shakespeare puts emphasis on the Duncan's proclamation about Malcolm as future king, thus, perpetrating a dynastic legacy of which Dutt the Marxist would definitely have disapproved.

In Dutt's manuscript, in 1.5 Lady Macbeth is "seated" while reading her letter in front of a fire. After "Yet I do fear thy nature," she would tear the letter "and exit right of fire." She sits down again saying "Hie thee hither" and rises suddenly in her excitement on hearing the news from the messenger, saying "Thou'rt mad to say it," then composes herself, stands up, and then restrains herself. Again with "Come you Spirits" she stands up and places herself before the fire. The fire creates a visually chiaroscuro effect and has other symbolic implications. It may have signified hellfire for Dutt, while it intensified the element of the Gothic with Lady Macbeth's form silhouetted against it surrounded by menacing shadows. There is also the indication that the very thought of power corrupts.

In 1.6, according to Dutt's stage directions, Duncan enters upstage with soldiers, attendants. The soldiers divide themselves into two groups, stand on the left and the right in rows, scatter themselves at the back and front. Duncan stands almost centre stage. Macduff on the left, Macbeth and Fleance on the right, and Angus and Ross a little forward from the rest. Lady Macbeth kneels before Duncan and Banquo stands on the left downstage. Duncan says "See, see! Our honour'd hostess" and laughs (jokingly? ironically?)—and then "picks her up." The irony of the situation is as profoundly conveyed in Dutt's translation as it is in Shakespeare's text. In Shakespeare, both Macbeth and Fleance appear to be absent onstage. Dutt does not mention the physical position of Lennox.

In 2.4 Dutt introduces "Peasant 2 with sickle tied to pole" a character not found in the "Patropatri," that is, the list of dramatis personae in the published translation, but was presented during performance onstage. Dutt cuts away the portion "On Tuesday last,/A falcon, towering in her pride of place,/Was by a mousing owl hawked at, and killed" from the Old Man and gives it to the peasant, in a significant change on the part of Dutt, as the peasant becomes a representative of the faceless masses that now assumes an identity of its own. As Macduff and Ross engross themselves in discussions about the naming of the new king and his coronation, both Old Man and Peasant 2 leave the stage.

Scene 3.4, known as the banquet scene, becomes a key scene for Dutt. The scene opens with the nobles standing and all sit down after Macbeth's first greeting. Then saying "Ourself will mingle with society," Macbeth "comes down" from upstage. The "Service begins" after Lady Macbeth's greeting. As Macbeth converses with the First Murderer at the door "RD"/ right downstage, his wife moves towards the gathering in front. Dutt especially enhanced the dramatic effect of the banquet scene with the standing, sitting, rising and again sitting down of the courtiers, as Macbeth raves and rants at Banquo's ghost while his wife tries to bring the situation under control. There is "confusion" as Macbeth challenges the ghost: "Take any shape but that, and my firm nerves/Shall never tremble" and as he advances towards the spectre, Dutt gives his instruction: "Thanes holding Macbeth cover Banquo's escape." When the ghost disappears, Macbeth says to his courtiers "Pray you, sit still" but "no one does." Rather they gather on the right and leave in "knots." After the guests leave backstage, Macbeth sits on his throne upstage, his wife sitting at his feet, and begins his speech: "It will have blood, they say: blood will have blood." Dutt's version is more of an active version than Shakespeare's and, therefore, more unified in impression. The scene becomes significant as it not only exposes Macbeth's crime and the futility of his pretences, but his vulnerability due to his crime as he cowers before Banquo's ghost.

Scene 3.6 was set by Shakespeare "Somewhere in Scotland." Dutt, however, situates it within the castle following the suggestion of the eighteenth-century critic Capell. Moreover, he introduces onstage (but not in his translation) "Peasants with hoe and sickle" who will speak portions of the conversation between Lennox and another lord, once again emphasizing the role of the proletariat in affairs of the state.

In 4.1, Dutt also does away with Hecate and conjoins two short speeches of the second witch, very significantly, to heighten the speed of action. Dutt was aware that this was an adaptation for a different clime and, hence, the action no longer required supernatural soliciting for Macbeth's final ruin.

Scene 4.3, another important scene for Dutt as a turning point in the play where the time comes to strike back, begins in "apron" outside the proscenium stage. Malcolm and Macduff enter from Right; Macduff moves straightaway to the centre. Malcolm sits on a block. The scene makes use of three blocks—both characters' sitting and rising, advancing towards each other, retreating and indicating their excitement, anger, doubts, grievances, belief and disbelief. For the director/translator, the ambitious Macbeth's downfall is of less significance than the relevance of this scene in depicting the nature of the despot and the quest for an able ruler. In stating the condition of Scotland under Macbeth's rule, "Each new morn,/ New widows howl, new orphans cry; new sorrows/Strike heaven on the face," Macduff presents a fascist authority that had by means of force curbed the freedom of the citizens.

Dutt did not translate or include the conversation between Malcolm and the doctor about the healing powers of Edward the Confessor whom Shakespeare had set up a contrast to the "Devilish Macbeth" "bloody-sceptred." Though conscious of the social and religious history of Shakespeare's plays, Dutt did not deem it fit to load his text with cumbersome details that are bound to be lost upon his own audience.

In 5.6 there is:

Battle—confusion. Battle. Clash

Upstage and Downstage.

Spread.

Macduff rushes out at Right.

One death—Samar.

Dutt is referring to one of his actors, Samar Nag who also doubled up as one of the three witches (a common practice in theatre groups since the time of Shakespeare).

In 5.7 Utpal Dutt shows the entry of Macduff after "two deaths" (one of Samar Nag, the other of Young Siward) in the fierce fighting in the battlefield. At the end of the scene Siward says "Enter, Sir, the castle." "The surrender" of Macbeth's castle at Dunsinane is presented ceremonially with the soldiers raising their "spears" to welcome Malcolm.

The last few pages of Dutt's manuscript contains a meticulous "music chart" and "music guide" where he uses the compositions of three revolutionary twentieth-century classical composers: Igor Stravinsky, Aram Khatchaturian and Dmitry Shostakovich. Especially notable is Dutt's use of Stravinsky's controversial *The Rite of Spring* (originally staged in Paris in 1913) to mark the impending murder of Duncan, which opens up further possibilities, for the audience will be left to wonder whose sacrifice Dutt is intending to project—Duncan's or Macbeth's?

The "properties" list is in three columns indicating where the items necessary for enactment are to be placed in the left and right wings and onstage.

Dutt plays with his medium, as in his hands Shakespearean characters speak stylized Bangla in verse used by the educated upper-class, whereas the witches speak a language that is unrefined and typical of rustics. Macbeth's letter to his wife is in formal "shadhubhasha." What is also notable is Dutt's use of words, which turn out to be "transcreations" than mere translations. In 1.3 the word "sailor," which means simply "mariner" or "seaman," becomes *majhimalla*, which includes the broader connotation of a "boatman," or "helmsman" or a headman," also meaning "husband" among the Santhalis, and significantly refers to socially backward castes who are exploited and oppressed. Thus, the "majhimalla" who is the "master o' th' Tiger" is also the "master" or "husband" of the woman (Dutt uses the rural slang word *maagi* for the wife, which also has connotations of "whore"), whom the witches (*Dakinigan*, a word from Hindu mythology and folklore for supernatural female creatures), plan to torment.

In 1.5 Lady Macbeth is addressed by the messenger as *Debi*—an appellation for an upper class/caste woman, but also meaning "goddess," invoking ironical overtones in the contrast with her demonical personage. The porter addresses Macduff and Lennox as *huzoor* using the Urdu appellation for "master" or authority, including upper class/caste social position.

As Shakespeare's Porter (2.3) speaks of having "napkins enough," Dutt's Porter/*Dwarpal* desires the *gamchcha*—a cheap, coarse hand-woven cloth used as a towel, usually by peasants and other workers.

In 1.6 Duncan's greeting Lady Macbeth as "honour'd hostess" is converted to *griholokkhi*, *Lokkhi* or Lakshmi, easily identifiable by an Indian audience as the Hindu goddess of the hearth, but a term better suited for the Victorian Angel in the House.

In 1.7 Banquo tells Fleance: "Hold, take my sword.—There's husbandry in heaven;/Their candles are all out," "candles" not translated in the equivalent "*mombaati*" but replaced by *prodip* meaning "lamp" in a more localized object.

In 2.2 "the multitudinous seas" become *saptasindhubari*, the seven seas of Hindu mythology, and the "yew" tree of 4.1 becomes *nagkeshar*, a familiar tree.

In 4.3 Malcolm tests Macduff's allegiance: "were I King,/I should cut off the nobles for their land; Desire his jewels, and this other's house:/And my more-having would be as a sauce/To make me hunger more." In Dutt's translation, "sauce," which is a taste enhancer, becomes *brahmirash*—Brahmi being the medicinal herb that improves memory and appetite—a term that is once again familiar to most Indians, but also one that enhances desire and ambition here.

The random samplings from Dutt's translation show how Dutt preserved the general structure of the acts and scenes but was at the same time played with the boundaries. In his essay "Shakespeare and the Modern Stage,"[9] Dutt had asserted:

A modern interpretation of Shakespeare...must typify Shakespeare's place, not in the past, but in the present life of the nation and of the world. It ought to constitute a perpetual reminder of the position that [the] fills in the present economy, and is likely to fill in the future economy, of human thought. A reminder for those whose growing absorption in the narrowing business of life tends to make them forget it and take Shakespeare merely as a hypocritical satisfaction of their aesthetic conscience.[10]

Utpal Dutt's philosophy of the theatre and the actor's craft were based upon his firm belief in Marxist dialectics, which he viewed as "a scientific principle and which declares that nothing in this universe is static, everything is always changing."[11] For him, Shakespearean drama became a constantly evolving concept, with the audience's attitude to it also changing all the time. Thus, Macbeth the tyrant's fall is inevitable as is the downfall of the tyrannical Congress regime. Dutt wanted to convey that if one king/ruler/regime is replaced by another it is the people of the country who will determine their futures. Dutt was also of the opinion that during Shakespeare's time events were much slower and so was the pace, and justifies his own mode of compressing scenes and omitting characters he felt were unnecessary for his purpose of speeding up the drama:

> We of this faster age must have our own modes. The director therefore must remember two points with regard to the spectator he is educating: first, the modern average citizen is already embittered with struggle, and expects to see a simplified world on the stage; he wants to see all his feelings reflected and a solution given, but not in the complicated and painful plane of his day-to-day life, he must feel heightened by appreciating the peculiar realistic, all art must be elevating. Secondly, in order to drive home the contents of the play, the director must disarm the peculiar prejudices of a modern crowd.[12]

However, during an interview given to Shaibal Mitra (published on 31 March 1991 in *Ajkal*), the actor had also bemoaned the changing mindset of the audience:

> *Macbeth* is not much different from the jatra. Yet jatra is no longer the same. A change has come in the audience's perspective. People have become dissociated from their cultural origins. It is now difficult for them to listen attentively to the pages of dialogue in *Macbeth* in order to enter its depths. They no longer have the patience. They want something to happen on stage, they want fights. They want to watch Macbeth and Macduff in conflict. What was the use of words, long speeches?[13] (Translation mine)

In his article "Translation, Transcreation, Travesty," Sukanta Chaudhuri is of the opinion that "the absorption of Shakespeare in an Indian framework marks at the same time the absorption of Indian dramatic discourse within a total colonial discourse," though he also found Utpal Dutt an exception who produced Shakespeare in more or less "straight" verbal translations, through theatrically and politically complex productions, routed through German and Russian responses to Shakespeare rather than the British-colonial. Chaudhuri also refers to the Bengali poet Jagannath Chakraborty's defeatist challenge to all possible translators:

> Translate me—someone, anyone.
>
> Tame me—someone, anyone.
>
> Insult me.
>
> Twist and bend the arrogant horns within me,
>
> Put a hangman's noose on my poetry....
>
> Rub out, if you can, my name,
>
> With an eraser from my skin....
>
> As though I were someone else, something else.[14]

I would add and conclude with Utpal Dutt's own response in his enigmatic verse titled "Sandeha" (doubt) found in his manuscript of *Macbeth*:

> One evening in the circle of the lamp-light
>
> Beholding the diverse plays and poems that I had composed
>
> I was overcome by a deep despondence.
>
> Have I said all that I had intended to?
>
> Or have they turned reverse in the mirror,
>
> Had the right hand become the left in the mind's illusion?
>
> (Translation mine)

Notes

1. When Sobha Sen first performed in *Macbeth* she was not married to Utpal Dutt.
2. Mukhopadhyay, Prabhatkumar. *Rabindrajibani* vol. 4 (1957; repr., Kolkata: Visva-Bharati, 2010), 51.
3. Prabhatkumar. *Rabindrajibani*, 163.
4. Utpal Dutt, "Dusswapner Shei Dinguli," *Epic Theatre* (August 2012): 6.
5. Dutt, "Dusswapner Shei Dinguli," 7.

6. Samik Bandyopadhyay, "Mukhabandha," to Utpal Dutt's translation of *Macbeth* (Kolkata: Thema, 2006), 1–2.
7. Bandyopadhyay, "Mukhabandha," 2.
8. Tapati Gupta, "Shakespeare, the Mediterranean & Utpal Dutt's Politics of Representation," *Journal of the Department of English*, University of Kolkata (1999–2000): 153–54.
9. Utpal Dutt, "Shakespeare and the Modern Stage," in *Epic Theatre: Subarnajayanti Sankalan* Vol. 1 (section: Natyabishayak Alochana O Shamalochana), ed. Arup Mukhopadhyay (Kolkata: Deep Prakashan, 1988), 283–90.
10. Mukhopadhyay, Arup. *Utpal Dutta: Jeevan O Sristhi* (New Delhi: National Book Trust, 2010), 283.
11. Gupta, "Shakespeare, the Mediterranean", 150.
12. Mukhopadhyay, *Utpal Dutta: Jeevan O Sristhi*, 288.
13. Mukhopadhyay, *Utpal Dutta: Jeevan O Sristhi*, 66.
14. Jagannath Chakravorty, "Translate Me," trans. Supriya Chaudhuri, in Visvanath Chatterjee (ed.), *Word for Word: Essays on Translation in Memory of Jagannath Chakravorty* (Papyrus, Kolkata, 1994), 2.

Shakespeare and Indian Icons

13

Tagore and Shakespeare
A Fraught Relationship

Radha Chakravarty

Rabindranath Tagore's engagement with Shakespeare at various stages in his life reveals a tangle of apparent contradictions. In the essay "Religion of the Forest,"[1] for instance, Tagore critiques Shakespeare for his apparent lack of sympathy with nature and blames this attitude on the cultural ethos of his times. "In *The Tempest*," he says, "through Prospero's treatment of Ariel and Caliban, we realize man's struggle with Nature and his longing to sever connection with her."[2] As for *Macbeth*, Tagore says that the world beyond the human is only represented through "a barren heath where the three witches appear as personifications of Nature's malignant forces." In *King Lear*, he argues, the storm on the heath merely echoes the human conflict in the play and "the tragic intensity of *Hamlet* and *Othello* is unrelieved by any touch of Nature's eternity."[3]

And yet, a few years before this, on the occasion of the Shakespeare tercentenary in 1915, Tagore had written a sonnet, a tribute to the Bard couched in poetic diction and the language of hyperbole, suggesting an attitude of simple admiration.[4]

> When by the far-away sea your fiery disk appeared from behind the unseen, O poet, O Sun, England's horizon felt you near her breast, and took you to be her own.
>
> She kissed your forehead, caught you in the arms of her forest branches, hid you behind her mist-mantle and watched you in the green sward where fairies love to play among meadow flowers.

A few early birds sang your hymn of praise while the rest of the woodland choir were asleep.

Then at the silent beckoning of the Eternal you rose higher and higher till you reached the mid-sky, making all quarters of heaven your own.

Therefore at this moment, after the end of centuries, the palm groves by the Indian sea raise their tremulous branches to the sky murmuring your praise.[5]

The attitudes reflected in these two pieces of writing are so contradictory that it seems hard to believe that both came from the same pen. In this paper, I examine Tagore's evolving attitude towards Shakespeare to argue that it was neither simple nor innocent, but always related in complex ways to personal, literary and political factors. Such a study can be valuable in at least three respects. First, it adds to our understanding of the colonial context that framed Tagore's perception of his relationship with Shakespeare. Second, it can be related to the evolution of Tagore's own creative theory and practice, his fluctuating reputation at home and abroad, and his troubled relationship with the critical establishment. Third, it serves as a window to Tagore's inner conflicts, the ruptures within his own self that he sought to negotiate through his writings. It then becomes possible to see the idea of "Shakespeare" as a construct imbued with multiple valences in Tagore's conceptual and critical vocabulary. This essay is not a comparative study of the similarities and differences between these two literary giants. Instead, through the prism of Tagore's responses, it attempts to evaluate some aspects of Shakespeare's significance as a point of reference in the emergence of Tagore as a founding figure of modern Indian literature.

Tagore's relationship with Shakespeare began early. He says that he was born at the confluence of three great movements, religious, literary and nationalist:

> I was born and brought up in an atmosphere of the confluence of three movements, all of which were revolutionary. I was born in a family which had to live its own life, which led me from my young days to seek guidance for my own self-expression in my own inner standard of judgement.[6]

In the enlightened, liberal, eclectic atmosphere of the Tagore home at Jorasanko, Shakespeare, along with other English poets, was consumed alongside wide range of Indian texts and other works in translation. In his autobiographical work *My Reminiscences*, Tagore recalls being stirred by "The frenzy of Romeo and Juliet's love, the fury of King Lear's impotent lamentation, the all-consuming fire of Othello's jealousy."[7]

In 1874, Rabindranath translated *Macbeth* into Bengali as instructed by his tutor Gyan Chandra Bhattacharjee. This early exercise in translation, though later dismissed by Tagore as an immature attempt, is nevertheless significant, for translation would later play a major role in the rise and fall of Tagore's international reputation. Tagore's familiarity with Shakespeare's play would also surface again, much later in his life, when he composed certain scenes of his dance drama *Chandalika*.

Tagore, in the early stages of his life, was deeply moved by "the passionate emotion in English literature," acknowledging the powerful influence of the English Renaissance dramatists: "man, then, seemed consumed with the anxiety to break through all barriers to the innermost sanctuary of his being, there to discover the ultimate image of his own violent desire."[8] His own early plays, such as *Raja o Rani* (1889) and *Visarjan* (1890), clearly show the influence of Shakespeare. Ananda Lal describes them as "elaborate five-act tragedies modelled after Shakespeare, replete with blood and thunder, declamation, palace intrigue, conflicts of love and duty, subplots involving foil characters, purple poetry spoken by the major roles and plebeian prose by lower-class characters."[9] Among other features, Tagore borrowed from Shakespearean drama the idea of representing violence and death on the stage—something alien to classical Sanskrit dramaturgy.[10] By and large, this indebtedness to Shakespeare was part of Tagore's overall acceptance of the norms of contemporary theatrical practice in Britain, reflected in the use of naturalistic settings, stage design and make-up in the early performances of Tagore's plays at the Jorasanko house.[11]

Although Tagore did not write a systematic critique of Shakespeare's works and their significance for him, comments scattered across his theoretical writings bear out the fact that he was deeply influenced by Shakespeare at this stage. In the preface to *Malini* (1892), he acknowledges the centrality of Shakespeare in the shaping of contemporary Bengali drama: "Shakespeare plays are always our dramatic model. Their manifold varieties and extensiveness and conflicts had captured our mind from the beginning."[12] In the essay *"Sahityer Pran"* ("Living Spirit of Literature", *c.* 1892) he says: "By subjecting the human being to a turmoil that shakes his very being, Shakespeare has bared his entire humanity to view.... In this, there is a high philosophical crest, from where the widest panorama of human nature becomes visible."[13] According to him, Shakespeare offers us "the perennial man...not merely the surface man" and this explains why "we look upon Shakespeare's portrayal of extraordinary and powerful feelings as more truthful than the exact portrayal of everyday life."[14]

In *"Manabprakash"* ("Manifestation of Humanity", *c.* 1892), Tagore makes several important statements. He points out how altered contexts and changing world views have also transformed literary expression: "[I]n olden days, there was a deep unity of opinion and attitude among the general public...Shakespeare and the ancient poets could easily envisage and represent the human being."[15] In contrast to this, he speaks of the fractured and divided self in the world of his own times: "Now,... [t]he inner world has become very complex, and the path, too, is very secret."[16] He declares: "it is not the individuality of the author, but the expression of humanity, that is the aim of literature.... Sometimes in one's own name, sometimes anonymously.... The writer is merely the means, it is humanity that is the goal."[17] It is this quality in Shakespeare that evokes his admiration. Tagore is often compared to the Romantics because of his intense empathy with nature but, here, he seems to move away from the lyrical impulse of romanticism, to endorse the idea of the literary text as a space for the articulation of general human and social realities rather than a manifestation of the artist's singular personality.

It is clear from Tagore's statements that at one stage in his career, he was heavily influenced by Shakespeare. Gradually, however, he began to move away from Shakespeare in his own creative practice and also in his critique of Western dramaturgy. *"Rangamancha"* ("The Theatre", 1902) marks a turning point in Tagore's approach to theatre. Here, he deplores the use of backdrops and stage props on the Bengali stage, blaming the trend on European influence: "Europeans cannot do without the truth of material fact. It is not enough for the imagination to delight their minds, it must make the imaginary simulate the actual and beguile them as it beguiles children."[18] He adds:

> The theatre we have fashioned in imitation of the West is a cumbrous and bloated object. It is hard to move and impossible to take to the common people's door: in it, Lakshmi's owl virtually obscures Sarasvati's lotus. It calls for the capital of the rich more than the talent of the poet and artist.[19]

Later, in *Creative Unity*, his criticism becomes even more stringent. He now targets the very intensity of emotion that he had earlier perceived as one of the strengths of Renaissance drama: "In the Western dramas, human characters drown our attention in the vortex of their emotions."[20] Here, Tagore simultaneously attacks multiple targets: emotionalism in Renaissance drama, the elaborate realism of contemporary European stagecraft and Indian imitations of those practices.

At work here is not only a literary impulse but a deeper political motive: to argue for a less submissive attitude towards the culture of the colonizer. In this respect, Tagore's comparison of *The Tempest* with Kalidasa's *Abhijñānaśākuntalam* remains a landmark. In "Shakuntala" (1902) he finds similarities between the two plays, but is more emphatic about the differences. About the two female protagonists, he observes:

> Shakuntala's simplicity, unlike Miranda's, is not girt around by ignorance.... Miranda's simplicity is not tested by fire: it does not encounter any conflict with worldly wisdom. We see her only in the first stage of development; Shakuntala has been shown by the poet in all stages, from first to last.[21]

Regarding the relationship between nature and the human world in the two plays, he remarks:

> We see Miranda in the midst of a wave-lashed, desolate, mountainous island; but she has no intimate relationship with nature on that island.... The island is only required for the plot; it is not essential to the character.... Shakuntala is not an isolated being like Miranda; she is linked in spirit to her surroundings.[22]

But what disturbs Tagore most about Shakespeare's play is its expression of what he calls the Western will to conquer and dominate: "In *The Tempest*, power; in *Shakuntala*, peace. In *The Tempest*, conquest through force; in *Shakuntala*, fulfilment through beneficent power. In *The Tempest*, interruption halfway through the process; in *Shakuntala*, cessation at its close."[23]

It is impossible not to notice the marked change of tone in Tagore's comments on Shakespeare at this stage in his life. What historical, literary and personal contexts account for this change of attitude? For one thing, there was the rising tide of nationalism in India and, with it, the need to construct an Indian literary canon to counter the rhetoric of Macaulay and Mill. Tagore's statements can also be read as a challenge to the literary establishment at home, to assert the need for a "modern" Indian literature inspired by indigenous tradition rather than an imitation of foreign models. In personal terms, Tagore felt the need to shore up his troubled reputation by positioning himself as the descendant of Kalidasa. In Tagore's construction of "Shakespeare," therefore, the personal is also the political. In the process of self-fashioning, he uses "Shakespeare" and "Kalidasa" as signifiers, to engage simultaneously with Western colonialism and Indian orthodoxy.

Tagore's autobiographical writings reveal his sense of historical location, because he locates the moment of his birth at the intersection of three important movements. A similar historical sense is at work in his understanding of Shakespeare. In "Shakuntala" and "The Religion of the Forest," Tagore projects Shakespeare as a representative of his culture and also as the product of a particular stage in history. He clarifies that his aim is "to show in his [Shakespeare's] works the gulf between Nature and human nature owing to the tradition of his race and time."[24] Amit Chaudhuri takes this for an instance of the colonized subject's return of the gaze. As examples of Orientalist discourse, he cites James Mill's critique of the Ramayana and the Mahabharata as fictions that are "extravagant," "unnatural" and "monstrous," written in a style characterized by "Inflation . . . repetition; verbosity; confusion; incoherence."[25] Amit Chaudhuri says that "Tagore turns Mill's rhetoric upon Shakespeare, claiming, in effect, Hellenic classicism as an essentially Oriental literary distinction and Orientalizing, in Said's sense of the word, Shakespeare and the European poets."[26] Tagore, Amit Chaudhuri says, was one of the first Indian poets to recognize the potential of the Orient (though a "Western" construct) as an idea useful for the anti-colonialist cause, regarding "the Orient and its unbroken past as a foundation, a point of origin and a parameter for the self and for creativity."[27] Amit Chaudhuri's argument is useful in highlighting Tagore's political and strategic use of Shakespeare and Kalidasa. He says: "Tagore wants to trace a lineage from antiquity to modernity, and from Kalidasa to, specifically, himself, and to use that lineage to rebuff the coloniser."[28]

Amit Chaudhuri's account, finely nuanced though it is, ascribes to Tagore a nativist nationalism that does not do full justice to Tagore's complex and finely nuanced response to the East/West encounter. Amit Chaudhuri focuses too narrowly on Tagore's critique of Shakespeare, without taking into account the presence of a contrary impulse in Tagore's writings, namely, a profound admiration for Shakespeare and a generally eclectic approach to questions of cultural difference. He does acknowledge that the polarization of "East" and "West" in Tagore's statements is not as simple as it appears, for the Orient that Tagore claims for himself includes several elements traditionally associated with European culture: "Easternness, in his work, is no longer incompatible with individualism, with the self-consciousness about the powers and limits of language, or the awareness of the transformative role of the secular artist."[29] Amit Chaudhuri argues that Tagore here is opposing a bourgeois orthodoxy in Kolkata and "conflating his identity as an Oriental and his vocation as a secular artist in doing so."[30]

This is valid up to a point, but remains a limited understanding of Tagore's argument, which needs also to be framed within broader issues such as humanism, and the relationship between man and his environment. Tagore's critique of Shakespeare sets him apart from other Bengali intellectuals such as Bankimchandra Chatterji and Sri Aurobindo, but his stance should not be read as shallow nativist nationalism. As Sukanta Chaudhuri argues:

> Rabindranath's differing view is not owing to parochialism of taste and certainly not to any cultural chauvinism. It is chiefly because of his understanding of the relation between humankind and nature and the place of violence and peace, power and contentment in human society and the cosmic order.[31]

Though Tagore became more critical of Shakespeare in his later life, he clearly found Shakespeare's influence hard to shake off. This ambivalence persists throughout Tagore's long and chequered career. While he critiques some of the features of Shakespeare's writings that strike him as embodying certain flaws in Western culture, he remains alive to the value of some aspects of Shakespeare's legacy. On issues of art and realism, for instance, he sometimes tends to regard Shakespeare as a touchstone. In 1928, commenting on his own play *King of the Dark Chamber* (the English version of *Raja*) Tagore says: "the human soul has inner drama, which is just the same as anything else that concerns Man and Sudarshana is not more an abstraction than Lady Macbeth."[32] Here, Shakespeare's Lady Macbeth acts as a point of reference in Tagore's attempt to explain the interiority of Sudorshana. Though Tagore had ostensibly moved away from Shakespeare in his later works, especially in his symbolic drama, readers also notice the influence of *Macbeth* on some scenes in the late dance drama *Chandalika*.

Tagore remains discriminating, though, in his choice of favourite Shakespeare texts. In the essay "Sahityer Mulya" ("The Value of Literature", *c.*1941), he dismisses *Venus and Adonis* and *Lucrece* as works of ephemeral value and makes it clear that he does not think much of *A Midsummer Night's Dream*. But he has a different opinion about characters such as Lear, Macbeth and Falstaff: "Shakespeare has opened the doors to the portrait gallery of human nature; there, through the ages, crowds will throng.... The value of *A Midsummer Night's Dream* may decline, but the impact of Falstaff will remain forever, constant and immovable."[33]

Tagore's later works testify to his continued admiration for some aspects of Shakespeare. In the novel *Shesher Kabita* (*Farewell Song*) the dialogues on poetry and love make it clear that he believes in an inclusive, liberal approach to the study of literature and that the language of love can cross the barriers of time and place. In relation to the orthodox critical establishment of his own land, he projects English literature in general and sometimes Shakespeare in particular as pointers to a more inclusive, eclectic approach to art that would liberate Indian literature from the shackles of tradition. In his memoirs, *Chhelebela (Boyhood Days)*, written shortly before his death, Tagore recalls the thrill of attending classes in English literature during his early stay in England. In his imagination, Shakespeare still remains emblematic of the richness of English literature.

In Tagore's later years, a turn away from Shakespeare thus runs parallel to, and sometimes clashes with, a continued admiration for the legacy of the English dramatist. This dual attitude expresses, at one level, some of the tensions and contradictions within Tagore's own psyche. In relation to the colonial enterprise, Tagore finds it necessary at certain moments to distance himself from Shakespeare as a representative of Western cultural and political domination in order to claim instead a place among the great Indian classics. Yet he also embraces "Shakespeare" as an epitome of internationalism and cosmopolitanism, and uses him as an example with which to critique the narrow, imitative practices of his contemporaries in Bengal. In this respect, his willingness to accommodate Shakespeare becomes a token of Tagore's own syncretic world view; for, ultimately, through this process of inner conflict, Tagore's thought gestures at a recognition of the need to rise above limiting binaries. A fragmented self, he struggles for wholeness. In a divided world, with a divided vision, he nevertheless understands the need to look for overarching commonalities as a way of surmounting petty differences. For this quest, too, Shakespeare provides him with a model.

Tagore's writings also reveal a strong level of identification with the poet from elsewhere. At times, for instance, he regards Shakespeare as a signifier of the fickleness of fame, something Tagore himself had experienced. But in the survival of Shakespeare through the ages, he also finds living proof of the writer's ability to rise above his circumstances and of the power of art to outlive passing fashions in taste. Tagore's understanding of Shakespeare's relevance to India involves the recognition of the capacity of the creative imagination to travel beyond geographical boundaries and cultural divisions. This form of cultural border-crossing had been Shakespeare's achievement, but it was something Tagore, too, had accomplished. With *Gitanjali* and the Nobel Prize, Tagore's works had also triumphantly crossed the barriers between nations, to achieve international acclaim. Hence, Tagore's poetic tribute to Shakespeare bears a strong personal resonance as well as a utopian message regarding the power of literature to connect different cultures. In Tagore's encomium, Shakespeare, first embraced by England as her own progeny, eventually soars above the local realm to inhabit the mid sky, "making all quarters of heaven" his own. And ultimately, crossing the boundaries of space and time, his words arrive at the Indian shore, and find a welcome there:

> Therefore, at this moment, after the end of centuries, the palm groves by the Indian sea raise their tremulous branches to the sky murmuring your praise.

In this tribute to Shakespeare's trans-cultural significance, we see a mirror image of Tagore's own aspiration for a place in the international galaxy of literary luminaries.

Notes

1. Rabindranath Tagore, *Creative Unity* (London: Macmillan, 1922).
2. Rabindranath Tagore, *Creative Unity*, 60.
3. Tagore, *Creative Unity*, 60.
4. In 1915, the Shakespeare Tercentenary Committee published a special volume to commemorate the Bard. Eminent literary figures from across the world contributed to this volume. Tagore contributed his sonnet to Shakespeare at the request of the organizers. The Bengali version had appeared in *Sabuj Patra* (December 1915/January 1916) and was later included in *Balaka* (39).
5. Rabindranath Tagore, "Shakespeare," *A Book of Homage to Shakespeare*, ed. Israel Gollanz (Oxford: Humphrey Milford, Oxford University Press, 1916), 321. Accessed on 7 March 2016. https://archive.org/stream/bookofhomagetosh00golluoft/bookofhomagetosh00golluoft_djvu.txt
6. Rabindranath Tagore, "Autobiographical," in *The Essential Tagore*, ed. Fakrul Alam and Radha Chakravarty (Cambridge, MA: Harvard University/Belknap Press, 2011), 41.
7. Rabindranath Tagore, *My Reminiscences* (London: Macmillan, 1917), 18–82.
8. Tagore, *My Reminiscences*, 181–82.
9. Ananda Lal, "Introduction to Tagore's Plays," in *Rabindranath Tagore: Three Plays*, trans. Ananda Lal (Kolkata: M.P. Birla Foundation, 1987), 19.
10. See, for example, Prabhatkumar Mukhopadhyay, *Rabindrajibani*, vol. 4 (1957; Kolkata: Visva-Bharati, 2010), 170, 294.
11. Lal, "Introduction," 28.
12. Rabindranath Tagore, introduction to *Malini*, in *Rabindra Rachanabali* 5 (Kolkata.: Govt. of West Bengal, 1961), 485. Cited in Das, "Shakespeare in Indian Languages," in *India's Shakespeare: Translation, Interpretation and Performance*, eds. Poonam Trivedi and Dennis Bartholomeusz (New Delhi: Doris Kinderslay, 2006), 46–47.

13. Tagore, "Sahityer Pran," (Bengali; 1892) in *Rabindra Rachanabali* 13 (Kolkata: Visva-Bharati, 1961), 848.

14. Rabindranath Tagore, letter to Lokendranath Palit, July 1892, trans. Visvanath Chatterjee, in "Tagore as a Shakespearean Critic," *Tagore Studies* (1972–73), 20.

15. Tagore, "Sahityer Pran," 851.

16. Tagore, "Sahityer Pran," 854.

17. Tagore, "Sahityer Pran," 855.

18. Rabindranath Tagore, "Rangamancha," (The Theatre) trans. Swapan Chakravorty, in *Rabindranath Tagore: Selected Writings on Literature and Language*, eds. Sisir K. Das and Sukanta Chaudhuri (New Delhi: Oxford University Press, 2001), 98. "Rangamancha" was published in December 1902/January 1903 in *Bangadarshan*, and later included in *Bichitra Prabandha* (1907).

19. Tagore, "Rangamancha," 99.

20. Tagore, *Creative Unity*, 50. V. Chatterjee, in "Tagore as a Shakespearean Critic," argues that Tagore, while he appreciated Shakespeare's "powerful portrayal of infinite passion", voices a preference for serenity over sound and fury.

21. Rabindranath Tagore, "Shakuntala," trans. Sukanta Chaudhuri, in *Rabindranath Tagore: Selected Writings on Literature and Language*, eds. Sisir K. Das and Sukanta Chaudhuri (New Delhi: Oxford University Press, 2001), 240.

22. Tagore, "Shakuntala," 240.

23. Tagore, "Shakuntala," 251.

24. Rabindranath Tagore, "The Religion of the Forest," cited in Amit Chaudhuri, "Two Giant Brothers: Tagore's Revisionist Orient," in *Clearing a Space: Reflections on India, Literature and Culture* (Ranikhet: Black Kite, 2008), 136.

25. James Mill, cited in Chaudhuri, "Two Giant Brothers," 138.

26. Chaudhuri, "Two Giant Brothers," 138.

27. Chaudhuri, "Two Giant Brothers," 124.

28. Chaudhuri, "Two Giant Brothers," 136.

29. Chaudhuri, "Two Giant Brothers," 125.

30. Chaudhuri, "Two Giant Brothers," 125.

31. Sukanta Chaudhuri, introduction to *Rabindranath Tagore: Selected Writings on Literature and Language*, ed. Sukanta Chaudhuri (New Delhi: Oxford University Press, 2001), 9.

32. Tagore, *Letters to a Friend* (London: George Allen and Unwin, 1928), 49. Cf. *Letters from Java*, in *Visva-Bharati Quarterly*, old series, 6 (April 1928), 3, where Tagore insists that if a person mocks Javanese dancers for their apparent lack of realism, "he needs must also laugh at Shakespeare, whose heroes not only fight in metre, but even die to it" (cited in Lal, "Introduction," 44).

33. Tagore, "*Sahityer Mulya*" (1941), in *Rabindra Rachanabali* 14 (Kolkata: Visva-Bharati, 1961), 195–96. Translation mine.

14

Mapping Shakespeare and Kalidasa: Early Indian Translations

Himani Kapoor

Within the site of Indian literary studies, the names of Shakespeare and Kalidasa are often found together in the zone of translation. In the bibliographies of Indian-language translations of Shakespeare and Kalidasa, one finds names of translators recurring in the lists. The same translator is often found translating Shakespeare as well as Kalidasa in his native language, thus, bringing more or less simultaneously, both the canons into the vernacular public domain. The suggested interface between Shakespeare and Kalidasa, in fact, signifies a new hybridity that evolved within the late nineteenth and early twentieth-century discourse of colonial modernity, in which Shakespeare exemplifies the epitome of Western modernity and Kalidasa of Indian classicism, or what I call traditionality. This essay will attempt to map the processes of negotiating Shakespeare and Kalidasa as one of modernity versus tradition or classicism and the attempts at hybridization of both in the Indian literary and critical representations through a study of the late nineteenth and early twentieth-century translations.

The project of translation is generally perceived as a process of transfer of a particular text from one linguistic culture to another, centring on the question of fidelity. This essay seeks to look at the act of translation as a voluntary choice made by a translator and the resultant transaction between the attitudes of two different writing cultures and places that are at the centre of the translation activity. Moreover, by subsuming the translator and the publishing agencies in the nineteenth-century public sphere, the essay approaches the Shakespeare–Kalidasa exchange from the periphery to the centre. Therefore, I begin by charting out the translators, publishers and places where translation occurred and then discuss the individual translations.

Theoretical Preliminaries

William Jones was the first to refer to Kalidasa as the "Shakespeare of India."[1] Consequently, for the Orientalist school, Kalidasa's drama became the epitome of the Indian literary tradition. Following Jones' translation of *Abhijñānaśākuntalam*, critics note that Kalidasa's heightened canonical status brought about a significant change of attitude towards Indian literature within Orientalist studies. *Shakuntalam* was received with such critical acclaim that, in the nineteenth century, 46 translations of the play in 12 different languages followed Jones' translation. The analogy first made by him between Shakespeare and Kalidasa was to be made throughout *Shakuntalam's* reception in Europe.[2] Thus, for Europe, *Shakuntalam* became the window to view and judge Indian literature and culture. Dorothy Figuera demonstrates that *Shakuntalam's* discovery not only "opened up boundaries of humanism but also fostered a widespread revaluation of national literatures." She elucidates this point further by stating that in Italy Giovanni Berchet introduced the play and showed to what lofty heights such "folk" poetry could ascend, even if it neglected strict Aristotelian rules.[3] Thus, *Shakuntalam* undeniably becomes one of the first texts that led to the figuration of India on the world map.

The following is an extract from the preface to *Sacontala or The Fatal Ring,* the first translation in English by William Jones in 1789.

> At length a very sensible Bráhmen, named Rádhácánt, who had long been attentive to English manners, removed all my doubts, and gave me no less delight than surprise, by telling me that our nation had compositions of the same sort, which were publickly represented at Calcutta in the cold season, and bore the name, as he had been informed, of plays. Resolving at my leisure to read the best of them, I asked which of their Nátacs was most universally esteemed; and he answered without hesitation, Sacontalá, supporting his opinion, as usual among the Pandits, by a couplet to this effect: "The ring of Sacontalá, in which the fourth act, and four stanzas of that act, are eminently brilliant, displays all the rich exuberances of Calidása's genius." I soon procured a correct copy of it; and, assisted by my teacher Rámalóchan, began with translating it verbally into Latin, which bears so

great a resemblance [367] to Sanscrit, that it is more convenient than any modern language for a scrupulous interlineary version: I then turned it word for word into English, and afterwards, without adding or suppressing any material sentence, disengaged from the stiffness of a foreign idiom, and prepared the faithful translation of the Indian drama, which I now present to the publick as a most pleasing and authentick picture of old Hindû manners, and one of the greatest curiosities that the literature of Asia has yet brought to light.[4]

Jones' preface clearly demonstrates that, from the very first reading itself, Kalidasa was thought to be the greatest poet of the Indian subcontinent and *Shakuntalam* his masterpiece—"of the same sort were publickly represented at Calcutta,"—the likes of Shakespeare. Jones' work was following his own discovery that Sanskrit belonged to the Indo-European language family. Therefore, whether it was Jones' own judgement or just a passing introductory reference that he made, the commentaries and interpretations that followed definitely borrowed from this analogy— whether to refute it or to ascribe to it. Goethe, Monier Williams, Bankim Chandra Chatterjee and even Shri Aurobindo all contributed to the development of the Shakespeare–Kalidasa interface.

For India of the late eighteenth century, the analogy proved to be a threshold for beginning a critical discourse. On the one hand, the cultural exchange was significant for the process of Indian identity formation, and on the other, the Shakespeare–Kalidasa comparison became the site for the intersection of colonial modernity and Indian traditionality perceived as classicism, the later criticisms and comparisons being built upon this dichotomy. This point will be elaborated later.

Interestingly, the earliest forms of modern drama in the Indian terrain were Shakespearean plays essentially meant for an English audience. Indian dramatic literature was still in the process of evolving, though its seeds were already sprouting by the mid-nineteenth century. It has been observed that the earliest of this dramatic literature followed two distinct strands: first, the exploitation of the available popular and folk traditions with some adjustment with classical drama and, second, the creation of dramatic literature on the European model. Both strands were active, functioned and coexisted, even as each remained distinct from the other.[5]

While there is evidence of folk theatre in most Indian languages, it is also noteworthy that, by the early twentieth century, modern Indian theatre had changed a lot because of the emergent colonial modernity. The interesting characteristic of this early modern Indian drama is the synthesis of European modernity and Indian classicism/traditionality. In order to understand this, we need to take a look at the process of construction of a historical past for India, while repeatedly pointing out that India lacked history and a concept of a historical past.

It was around the mid-eighteenth century that Orientalists such as William Jones and Henry Thomas Colebrooke endorsed the idea of the golden Indian past situated in the remote, uncharted Vedic time. This view was later contradicted by the nineteenth-century colonial historians like James Mill who debunked the idea of the golden past and saw India and the Indian society as nothing but peculiar. The later Indian (swadeshi) scholars, hence, felt a deep need to dramatically reconstruct history in order to create a different self-image.[6] This new consciousness was an amalgamation of elements both from the golden (Vedic) past and from the European modernity as perceived by them.

The Orientalist–Anglicist debate is not limited just to the area of history and history-writing. The issue seeped deep into the Indian psyche. Natalie Robinson Sirkin and Gerald Sirkin in "The Battle of Indian Education: Macaulay's Opening Salvo Newly Discovered" point to the repercussions in India with respect to Western education. What is interesting about the perception of Western education is that along with being anti-tradition it was, importantly, economically empowering and thus, a more useful option.

> Unfortunately, in their opposition to cultural imperialism, the Orientalists became the unwitting perpetuators of economic imperialism: Their program of Indian studies would produce no body of men trained to replace the British in administering government and managing a modern economy. The Orientalists' education program was a program for the maintenance of the status quo; it was a traditional education for a small elite. In this choice between cultural and economic imperialism, the Bengalis were not at all ambivalent. Whenever they were given an opportunity to express their preferences, they over-whelmingly chose English and a modern education. The ancient culture embodied in the Sanskrit and Arabic literature could be safely left a little longer in the hands of the pundits and the moulavies, where it had rested for so many centuries; the rising middle class of Bengalis wanted economic advancement.[7]

The ideas of "traditionality" and "modernity" therefore go beyond their conventional meanings. Since precolonial India was looked at as being traditional, conservative and stagnant, the concept of the "modern" itself was associated with ideas of anti-tradition. Yet, despite the overwhelming influences of Western modernity, the entrenched concepts of tradition and the modern provided the basis for ideologies and movements.

Yet, despite being ideological opposites, the traditional and the modern may not necessarily be mutually exclusive entities. In fact, towards the late nineteenth century, the "modern" itself for the Indian scholar conceived of a synthesis of the Western and the indigenous traditional. The history of Shakespeare's reception and representation in India may be regarded as an example of this divide between the "traditional" and the "modern." Many of Shakespearean translations into Indian languages are found to be executing the English story in the Indian setting and with Indian signifiers and names. Hence, it is not just a coincidence that many early translators in Indian languages have attempted to translate both Shakespeare and Kalidasa.

The Shakespeare–Kalidasa overlap signifies a complex cultural manoeuvre of Indian dramatists during the late nineteenth and early twentieth centuries. Within all the processes of hybridization, we see a conspicuous attempt to synthesize colonial modernity with Indian classicism/traditionality. How is this process of bringing together modernity representing new knowledge systems, and traditionality representing classicism conceived by the Indian translators? In particular, how is this ambivalence revealed through the Shakespeare–Kalidasa interface?

In considering the data collected during my research in the zone of translation for this chapter, I have used the information available in the *Bibliography of Indian Literature* 1901–50, Volumes I, II, III and IV, published by Sahitya Akademi. The bibliographic information of Kalidasa and Shakespeare's translations have been put together and tabulated. Significantly, in case of seven languages, we have the instance of the same author translating both Shakespeare and Kalidasa. These languages are Assamese, Hindi, Kannada, Malayalam, Marathi, Sindhi and Tamil.[8] Table 14.1 contains the details of the name of the translator, the title of the translated work, the publishing agency, and the year and place of publication. The tabular format offers an overview of the comparative perspective of this study (See Appendix).

A study of the various components/processes of translations, such as titles, year of translation, translators and their background, publisher, purpose of translations and so on for both Shakespeare and Kalidasa will throw further light upon the nature of this process. Although there are several cases of the same translators working over a period of time, this piece of research concerns itself with translations from the late nineteenth and early twentieth centuries. Additionally, mapping the profiles of the translators has helped, to a significant extent, in understanding the process of this exchange. To begin with, I take up the cases of a few individual translators and then explore the case of the Hindi renditions of Shakespeare by Lala Sitaram.

A Note on the Translators

Kannada

Amongst the translations taken up in this essay, Basavappa Shastri's (1843–91) are the older and one of the first translations of *Shakuntalam* and *Othello* in Kannada. We see that within a decade he translates three plays of Kalidasa and goes on to translate one more of Shakespeare. We find that a majority of the plays have been published from Mysore, the capital of the princely state of Mysore. Additionally, he was patronized by the then maharaja of Mysore and a theatre company was engaged to perform these plays in the format of Parsi theatre. Basavappa Shastri's translation of *Shakuntalam* met with such success that it was later dramatized. His personal history also reveals an interesting detail about the system of court patronage during his time. After he was orphaned at the age of six he came under the royal tutelage of the Maharaja of Mysore. Thereafter, he became an exceptional scholar in Sanskrit, music and gamaka. The translation of *Abhijñānaśākuntalam* undertaken in 1883 was under court patronage. His translations became so successful that he was later conferred the title of "Abhinava Kalidasa" or the new/modern Kalidasa. Shastri in the 1880s translated five more plays from Sanskrit into Kannada, among which were two others by Kalidasa—*Vikramorvasiya* and *Malvikagnimitra*. It was in 1895 that he translated Shakespeare's *Othello* into Kannada. Interestingly, Shastri had no knowledge of English so a collaborator who was well versed in English co-authored his work. This work too, like *Shakuntalam*, was under court patronage and executed at the insistence of the maharaja of Mysore.[10]

The second translator taken up here, D. V. Gundappa (1889–1975) has been a well-known figure in Kannada literary history. Having more than 60 books to his credit he was awarded the Padma Bhushan by the government of India in 1974. Unlike Basavappa Shastri, Gundappa

Table 14.1

The Details of Kannada Translations of Shakespeare and Kalidasa[9]

Basavappa Sastri	*Abhijñānaśākuntalam*	Karnataka Sakuntala Nataka	1883	Mysore: Basavappa Shastri Granthamala
Basavappa Shastri	Malvikagnimitra	NA	1890s	NA
Basavappa Shastri	Vikramorvasiya	NA	1890s	Mysore: Prabodha Pustakamalaya
Basavappa Shastri & C. Subbarao	Othello	Shurasena Charitre	1895	Mysore GTA press
D.V. Gundappa	Macbeth	Macbeth	1936	Bangalore: Karnataka Prakatanalaya Verse translation
D.V. Gundappa	Henry VI	Jak Ked Dombi Dandhalaya Prahasana	1959	Mysore, Kavyakala
D.V. Gundappa	*Abhijñānaśākuntalam*	Geeta Shakuntalam	NA	NA

was not a court poet; his father was a lawyer and his forefathers had been in the service of the British for at least two generations, and he started learning English language at lower secondary level itself.[11] His translation of *Macbeth* is known to be the first faithful verse translation of Shakespeare. In fact, in the preface to the play, he emphatically reiterates not only his effort to retain Shakespeare in its original but also his resolve to take Indian epics to the West:

> I believe that this is necessary for the advancement of Kannada literature and the sensibility of the Kannada people and for the broadening of their vision of their world. If human civilisation and peace are to last, it is of foremost importance that different races of the earth attain a world vision. In order to achieve this, people in the west should read our epics, the Ramayana and the Mahabharata sympathetically as we must acquaint ourselves with their poetic tradition.[12]

Gundappa's translation of Kalidasa too was in a poetic form—his *Geetasakuntala* consists of selected verses from *Shakuntalam* in the form of thirty-five Kannada songs. Gundappa is one of the key figures associated with modern Kannada literature. Closely associated with journalism, he published papers both in English as well as Kannada. His translations of not only Shakespeare and Kalidasa but also of other authors of English and Sanskrit have been well received.

Literary scholars like Sukanta Chaudhuri have pointed out that Kannada's response to Shakespeare is in two ambivalent and parallel streams of sensibilities; the earlier one corresponding to the stage tradition and the later to the literary tradition. The two phases approximate the phases of adaptation and literary translations. A study of both Basavappa Shastri and Gundappa translating Shakespeare and Kalidasa suggests that hybridity was the practice and outcome both during the adaptation phase in performance as well as in the literary translations.

Sindhi

While Basavappa Shastri was a court protégé, Mirza Qalich Beg of Sindhi literature was of Georgian ancestry and his father had served in the court of the Talpur dynasty. He is known today as one of the biggest writers of Sindhi literature. Table 14.2 detailing the translation activity in the Sindhi language.

The very first Sindhi play, *Laila Majnu,* is acknowledged to have been written by Beg. He was inspired by the Urdu plays of Parsi theatre[13] and his plays were repeatedly staged in amateur theatres from time to time. Among all of Kalidasa's plays, *Shakuntalam* seems to be indisputably the most popular and it is after translating *Shakuntalam* in 1896 that Beg translated five plays of Shakespeare, most probably for dramatic

Table 14.2

The Details of Sindhi Translations of Shakespeare and Kalidasa

Mirza Qalich Beg	*Abhijñānaśākuntalam*	*Shakuntala*	1896
Mirza Qalich Beg	*The Merchant Of Venice*	*HusnaDildar*	1897
Mirza Qalich Beg	*King Lear*	*Sah Elia*	1900
Mirza Qalich Beg	*Cymbeline*	*Shamshad Mayana*	1908
Mirza Qalich Beg	*The Two Gentlemen of Verona*	*Aziz Ain Sharif*	1909
Mirza Qalich Beg	*Romeo and Juliet*	*Gulzar Ain Gulnar*	1909

productions, but all of them in the same decade. There is just a year's difference between the publication of *Abhijñānaśākuntalam* and of The *Merchant of Venice.*

Though the cases of the translators during the emergence of print culture show various shifts in the traditional systems of patronage,[14] but equally, the nineteenth century was still a time when court patronage significantly determined the nature of literature in print. The involvement of the dramatists on the other hand, showcases a popular demand on part of the audience who would be eager recipients of both Shakespearean and Kalidasa's plays. In fact, it has been noted that around the nineteenth century, the same drama companies or natak *mandalis* were involved with dramatizing, adapting and staging both Shakespeare and Kalidasa. Notable examples of these would be in the Marathi theatre pioneered by Anna Saheb Kirloskar and the Parsi theatre. Two playwrights who were involved in such a process have been discussed in detail.

Marathi

Like the Mirza in Sindhi, Govind Ballal Deval (1855–1916) in Marathi was also a playwright and had collaborated with *Shakuntal* (1890) of Annasaheb Kirloskar. An actor and playwright with the Marathi theatre pioneered by Annasaheb Kirloskar, he formed his own natak mandali in the 1890s. Subsequently, he produced an adaptation of Shakespeare's *Othello*, titled as *Jhunjarrao*. Deval wrote seven plays for the stage, of which six were adaptations: three were in Sanskrit and three in English. The most interesting feature of Deval's plays was that his plays were musical productions and became very popular in his time. The word *Sangeet* Natak itself signifies that these were musical plays and Deval is known to have written the songs for *Shakuntal*. In fact, *Shakuntal* was one of the plays that greatly helped in the popularization of the form of Sangeet Natak.

Table 14.3

The Details of Marathi Translations of Shakespeare and Kalidasa

Govind Ballal Deval	*Othello*	*Jhunjarrao*	1890
Govind Ballal Deval	*Vikramorvasiya*	*Vikramorvashiya*	1889

Source: Bibliography of Indian Literature 1901–50, Volumes I, II, III, IV published by Sahitya Akademi (1974).

Tamil

Pammal Sambandha Mudaliyar has been another well-known figure from Tamil drama. He is known to be the father of the Tamil dramatic movement and has produced hundreds of Tamil plays for the stage. The Tamil stage got a new direction thanks to him, it is believed. A lawyer by profession and also an actor like Deval, he wrote more than 80 plays, which were directed by him. His six volume work, *Metai Ninavukal* is seen to have contributed a lot towards the history of Indian drama in general.[15] Das also observes that this work was of great literary value not only for studies in the Tamil literature, but also because it brought in a change in the attitude of the publisher and the reader towards the printed text.

The information available about Kumaragurupara is scanty. However, Sambandha Mutaliyar not only translated several of the Shakespearean

Table 14.4

The Details of Tamil Translations of Shakespeare and Kalidasa

A. Kumaragurupara Atittar	Othello	Othello Uttaman	Madras. 1950
A. Kumaragurupara Atittar	The Rape Of Lucrece	Karpukannal	Madras, Allianceco. 1947
A. Kumaragurupara Atittar	Julius Caesar	Virasimhan	Madras, 1952. iii 87 p. 21cm
A. Kumaragurupara Atittar	Abhijñānaśākuntalam	Sakuntala Natakam	1938
P. Sambandha Mudaliyar	Cymbeline	Simhalanthan	Madras, 1929
P. Sambandha Mudaliyar	Hamlet	Amaladitya	Madras, 1931 (first pub 1908)
P. Sambandha Mudaliyar	Macbeth	Makapati	Madras, 1929 (first pub 1913)
P. Sambandha Mudaliyar	Abhijñānaśākuntalam	Sakuntala Natakam	Madras, 1938
P. Sambandha Mudaliyar	Malavikagnimitram	Malavikagnimitram	Madras, 1930
P. Sambandha Mudaliyar	Vikramorvasiya	Vikrama Urvasi	Madras, 1929

Source: Bibliography of Indian Literature 1901–50, Volumes I, II, III, IV published by Sahitya Akademi (1974).

and Kalidasa plays within the same decade but, indeed, a majority of them were intended for the stage.

Hindi

The following section will examine the biographical context of the various works undertaken by Lala Sitaram—translator, teacher, administrator and author.

Lala Sitaram—A Short Biographical Sketch[16]

Lala Sitaram, who apart from translating Shakespeare in Hindi had also translated six plays of Shakespeare in Urdu, was a very well-known figure of his time. Born in Ayodhya in 1861, Sitaram received his early education in Ayodhya and Fyzabad. Thereafter, he pursued a BA from Canning College, Lucknow and secured the first position in the university becoming the first student from Lucknow[17] to do so. This feat was celebrated with great jubilation in Lucknow in the Safed Baradari.[18] A host of lucrative opportunities would have been available to him, but he chose to be a teacher.

Lala Sitaram's literary and poetic career took off soon afterwards. His art of composing ghazals in Urdu was noticed by the famous poet Ghulam Hasnain "Qadra" Bilgrami, whose *shagird* he forthwith became and took "Azm" as his *takhallus* or pen name. Interestingly, after one year of his service in Education, Sitaram himself destroyed his ghazals, deeming them "unbecoming of his profession."[19] Table 14.5 gives a detail of the all the work undertaken by Sitaram.

The long list of translations from Shakespeare and Kalidasa needs to be understood within the context of the changes in Lala Sitaram's professional career, his interests and his shift from Urdu to Hindi reflecting the Hindi–Urdu divide. Sitaram had started contributing towards literary journals even as a student. His writings found their way to *Avadh Punch* and *Avadh Akbar*.[20] During his tenure as the headmaster of schools in Sitapur, Kanpur (Cawnpore) and Meerut, he translated four of Shakespeare plays into Urdu: *King Lear* (*Shah Lear*), *Comedy of Errors* (*Bhul Bhulaiya*), *Much Ado about Nothing* (*Daam-e-Muhabbat*), *and The Tempest* (*Hawai Tilism*).

His son (Kishor) recalls that the most interesting feature of these translations was that they were the "first to be printed on good paper and

Table 14.5

Details of Sitaram's Works

			Lala Sitaram: Timeline and Works
Year	Place	Language	Work/Translation
Before 1879		Urdu	*Friends in Council* - Arthur Helps (with Mirza Sajjad Husain)
		Urdu	Contributions to *Awadh Akbar (on Scientific subjects and Mathematics)*
		Urdu	Contributions towards *Awadh Punch*
1880–82	Sitapur, Meerut, Cawnpore	Urdu	King Lear "*Shah Lear*"
		Urdu	Comedy of Errors "*Bhul Bhulaiya*"
		Urdu	Much Ado about Nothing "*Daam-e-Muhabbat*
		Urdu	The Tempest "*Hawai Tilism*"
1883–91 Benaras	Benaras	Hindi	Contributed towards *Kashi Patrika*
		Hindi	*Meghdutam*
		Hindi	*Nagananda*
1891–93 Faizabad	Fyzabad	Hindi	*Kumarasambhava*
		Hindi	*Raghuvamsha*
		Hindi	*Ritusanhara*
			Rasakusumakara,
1893–1916	Cawnpore and Ayodhya	Hindi	*Kiratarjuniya*
		English	*Our Ancient Theatre*
		English	*Volumes on Mathematics*
1921	Ayodhya	English/ Hindi	*Selections of Hindi Poetry (7 vols)*
	Ayodhya	Urdu	*Akhlaqe-Afisqaratisi*
1937	Ayodhya	Hindi	*Ayodhya Ka Itihas*
1920	Ayodhya	English	*History of Sirohi Raj*
Shakespearean Translations			
1917	Allahabad	Hindi	*Apni Apni Ruci*
1915	Allahabad	Hindi	*Bhul Bhulaiya*
1925	Allahabad	Hindi	*Cymbeline*
1915	Allahabad	Hindi	*Hamlet, Denmark Ka Rajkumar*
1915	Allahabad	Hindi	*Raja Lear*

(Table 14.5 Contd.)

(Table 14.5 Contd.)

Lala Sitaram: Timeline and Works			
Year	Place	Language	Work/Translation
1915	Allahabad	Hindi	*Raja Richard Dvitiya*
1926	Allahabad	Hindi	*Macbeth*
1925	Allahabad	Hindi	*Bagula Bhagat*
1915	Allahabad	Hindi	*Manmohan Kajaal*
1931	Allahabad	Hindi	*Prem Kasauti*
1915	Allahabad	Hindi	*Jangal Mein Mangal*
1926	Allahabad	Hindi	*Othello Arhat Jhutha Sandeh*

in crown octavo size, which gave them the appearance of English books. For years later the vernacular books still continued to be printed on the *badami* paper in quarto size." The "vernacular" here is, of course, the translation of the canon, most probably introduced as the source material for students. Nevertheless, this observation marks out the special status of Shakespearean translations, both in terms of their reception as well as their marketability.

Sitaram's transfer to Benaras in 1883 brought about a significant shift in his literary interests. Hitherto he had written only in Urdu, but now his taste developed both in Hindi and Sanskrit literature. The Persio-Arabic words refer to the Persio-Arabic lexicon, which is absent in the sanskritized Hindi reproductions of his post Banaras period in the 1920s and 1930s.

He got acquainted with Bharatendu Harishchandra and was encouraged to pursue his work in Hindi. It is for *Kashi Patrika* that he wrote the Hindi verse translation of the *Meghdutam*. Around that time he also corresponded with F. Max Muller and G. Thibaut on behalf of Pandit Ram Mishra[21] as, unlike the Pandit, he was proficient in English. Later, the maharaja of Ayodhya, Sir Pratap Narain Singh,[22] became his patron and he translated many Sanskrit works into Hindi for the maharaja. Notable amongst these were Kalidasa's *Ritusanhara* and *Raghuvamsa*. The latter was dedicated to the Maharaja himself. Possibly, he kept working simultaneously on Shakespearean translations for Ramnayanlal Press, Allahabad.

Although Sitaram's literary output decreased after he was appointed the deputy collector of Cawnpore/Kanpur, yet his involvement with the sector of education was a lot fruitful for the twentieth century in general, because his writings were meant to be introduced into university

Table 14.6

Details of the Urdu Translations of Shakespeare Done Again for Hindi

Name of the Play	Urdu Title (1880–82)	Hindi Title (1911–20)
King Lear	Shah Lear	Raja Lear
Much Ado About Nothing	Daam-e-Muhabbat	Manmohan Ka Jaal
The Tempest	Hawai Tilism	Jangal Mein Mangal
Comedy of Errors	Bhul Bhulaiya	Bhul Bhulaiya

syllabi.[23] He planned to bring in the ancient knowledge systems into Hindi. Interestingly, his earlier translations of Shakespeare in Urdu were redone during his stay at Ayodhya. The Urdu translations of *King Lear, Much Ado about Nothing, Tempest* and *Comedy of Errors* were worked out again for Devnagari versions which were mostly published between the years 1911–20.

Table 14.6 shows the details of the Urdu Shakespearean plays redone by Lala Sitaram.

His revivalist attitude towards Hindi cannot go unnoticed either. Kishore writes:

> He had drawn up a scheme at Benares for translating into simple Hindi all that was to be had in the ancient Sanskrit learning of the Hindus and he felt that it should be the heritage of every Hindu to know what advances had been made in the various branches of learning in this country of ours....
> His chief idea in limiting his Urdu activities and adopting Hindi was that Hindi was the language of the masses and it was only through this language that he could hope to reach the desired objective. He had formed the idea of bringing out a series of six volumes in each of the following subjects: Our Ancient Epics, Our Ancient Theatre, Our Ancient Mathematics, Our Ancient Philosophy.

Although Sitaram was not able to complete all these planned volumes, this emphatic effort in reviving and making accessible in the simplest possible language, "Our Ancient…" demonstrates his vehement desire to bring in the traditional within the public domain and, many a times, using new and modern formats in popularizing the traditional.

In the Hindi literary sphere there could be a playwright like Agha Hashra Kashmiri who changes a tragedy, *King Lear*, into a comedy in three acts, *Safed Khoon* (1906), but, in turn, also creates a play with strong characterization with a twist at the end. Such transformations have been reported from other Indian languages too. There would be Harivanshrai Bachchan who translates only two plays, but substitutes the English blank verse with a Sanskrit metre *rola*, making his translation effective and powerful, or like Jayshankar Prasad who would exhibit the influence of Shakespeare in his own Hindi writings. Sitaram's approach is very different from all three: while he does not make an exceptional mark by way of his renditions, nevertheless he is one of the translators with the maximum number of Shakespearean translations into Hindi.

Translating Shakespeare during the time when he was first serving as the head master of a school, Sitaram's translations are typically "Indianized" not only in terms of the detail about places he uses, for instance the Italian cities in *Romeo and Juliet*, translated as *Prem Kasauti* (1931), are renamed Varnanagar and Manmathnagar. But unlike Agha Hashra Kashmiri who would be translating essentially for a dramatic production, hence, making amendments, Sitaram would stick to the story and act sequence and would in fact try Indianizing the poetic idiom too. This has significant implications for Shakespearean translations in Indian languages, as many early translations in Indian languages exhibit such a trend. Jagdish Prasad Mishra in his analysis of Sitaram's writings says,

> The translator (Sitaram) puts the sense of Shakespeare's plays into simple Hindi and tries to convey the meaning faithfully. But the prose of the translation is not able to capture the spirit of the original puns and quibbles… the translator's eyes are always fixed upon presenting the apparent meaning and not on bringing out beauties of the original.

Yet Mishra also notes that at places Sitaram does more than justice to the original.

For instance, Romeo's words, in *Romeo and Juliet* "He jests at scars that never felt a wound." have been translated as "Jisake paunva na phati bevai, so kya jaane pira parayi," an old Hindi adage well suited to the situation that marks Romeo's entry in 2.2.

At places Sitaram seems to supplement the translation with poetic verses, which might not be adequate in articulating the entire imagery. For instance, the song by Balthasar in *Much Ado about Nothing:*

> Sigh no more, ladies, sigh no more,
>
> Men were deceivers ever,
>
> One foot in sea and one on shore,

To one thing constant never.

Then sigh not so, but let them go,

And be you blithe and bonny...

In Sitaram, it is translated as *Manmohan ka Jaal:*

Kāhe mana bisūro re gorī

eto na socha karo apne mana

tuma sukumāra umira ke thorī

Bāta banāya manamoheṅ purusha saba

Karate chalāki tumheṅ gani bhori

Marsa sabai dagabāja janama ke

Nainā lagāya lain muha mori[24]

The use of colloquial language or a rhymed-verse translation, in what is usually designated as adaptation, however deviant it might be, points to the fact that indeed there is an attempt to "construct" a domestic identity. As Venuti explains in *"The Scandal of Translation"* that "not only do translation projects construct uniquely domestic interpretations of foreign cultures but, since these projects address specific cultural constituencies, they are simultaneously engaged in formation of domestic identities." One can thereby argue that while Sitaram would continually use the traditional, domestic idiom to interpret Shakespeare to its detail, his conscious use of Hindi as the second and final medium of the same plays first done in Urdu further contributes towards the ambivalent and complex domestic identities that are at play in the process of translation during this period.

While the English canon could be earlier used for educational purposes and, hence, needed to be translated into the then popular language Urdu, yet there is a compulsion to put the same English canon in a more "correct" language during the hey days of nationalism when the Hindi market was increasingly growing given the Hindi–Urdu divide. Sitaram attempts to put Kalidasa in the same language to propagate the traditional Hindi idiom. His case is only one among many others who would take a similar stance, given the biographical details of the translators.

The attempts to enrich modern Indian drama through translating Shakespeare and Kalidasa almost simultaneously, by the same translator, suggests a process of negotiating colonial modernity and classicism on the one hand and the process of construction of an Indian literary tradition that reflects its great classical past and an equally significant colonial modernity on the other. From the cases of the translators discussed previously it is apparent that the emergent scholarship in the late nineteenth and early twentieth centuries was trying to bridge the gap between Western modernity and Indian traditionality. Like them, there are other cases of translators and dramatists who attempted to democratize, in one idiom or the other, the drama of Shakespeare as well as Kalidasa. Given the amount of the data available and the diversity of the Indian literary terrain, it is difficult to come up with a single explanation for such processes in translation and hybridity. Yet, one way of explaining this would be that by the turn of the twentieth century the Indian concept of the "modern" was in itself a unity of the traditional/indigenous and the modern/Western. Also, with so many indigenous translators, publishers, patrons and institutions participating in the literary process and formulating the print public sphere, it is possible to say that the Shakespeare–Kalidasa interface may be considered to be of more historical and cultural value than literary. Shakespeare is often called an "accommodating ideal," which has time and again played its part in reviving and revitalizing the Indian stage practices. Perhaps Kalidasa too can be called an accommodating ideal that has enabled such scholars as Sitaram and others to exhibit their complex relationship with the "donor culture," and most importantly in the identity-formation process.[25]

The hybridity that has been discussed here has been problematized with Shakespeare becoming Shek Pir in Kannada, as observed by Satyanath (2004), in which the author makes use of a sketch by the famous Indian sculptor, painter, artist and freedom fighter R.S. Naidu. The sketch, reproduced from the volume *Sekpiarige-namsakara*, in this book, would sum up the consequences of the East–West encounter and thereby colonial modernity and Indian classicism aptly.[26] The composite nature of Shakespearean colonial modernity and Kalidasa's classicism appropriately visualized, would at the same time provide a subversive perspective of such a hybrid zone.

Appendix

Table A 14.1
Common Translators

Language	Translator	Original Text	Translated Title	Place/Publisher/Year
HINDI				
	Lala Sitaram	As You Like It	Apni Apni Ruci	Allahabad, Ramnarayanlal, 1917
	Lala Sitaram	Comedy of Errors	Bhul Bhulaiya	Allahabad, Ramnarayanlal, 1915
	Lala Sitaram	Cymberline	Cymberline	Allahabad, Ramnarayanlal, 1925
	Lala Sitaram	Hamlet Prince Of Denmark	Hamlet, Denmark Ka Rajkumar	Allahabad, Ramnarayanlal, 1915
	Lala Sitaram	King Lear	Raja Lear	Allahabad, Ramnarayanlal, 1915
	Lala Sitaram	King Richard II	Raja Richard Dvitiya	Allahabad, Ramnarayanlal, 1915
	Lala Sitaram	Macbeth	Macbeth	Allahabad, Ramnarayanlal, 1926
	Lala Sitaram	Measure For Measure	Bagula Bhagat	Allahabad, Ramnarayanlal, 1915
	Lala Sitaram	Much Ado About Nothing	Manmohan Ka Jaal	Allahabad, Ramnarayanlal, 1926
	Lala Sitaram	Romeo and Juliet	Prem Kasauti	Allahabad, Indian Press, 1931
	Lala Sitaram	The Tempest	Jangal Mein Mangal	Allahabad, Ramnarayanlal, 1915
	Lala Sitaram	Othello	Othello Jhutha Sandeh	Allahabad, Ramnarayanlal, 1915
	Lala Sitaram	Julius Caesar	Julius Kaisar	NA
	Lala Sitaram	Meghduta	Meghduta	NA*
	Lala Sitaram	Kumarasambhava	Kumarasambhava	NA

Lala Sitaram	*Rtusamhara*	*Rtusamhara*	NA
Lala Sitaram	*Meghduta*	*Meghdut*	Allahabad, National Press, 1917
Lala Sitaram	*Malvikagnimitra*	*Malvikagnimitr*	Kanpur, 1899
Lala Sitaram		*Malvikagnimitra*	Allahabad, Panchnatak-manimala
MALAYALAM			
A Govindapilla	*The Merchant of Venice*	*Venice-ile Vyapari*	Trivandrum, Travencore Priting Co, 1902
A Govindapilla	*Abhijñānaśākuntalam*	*Abhijñānaśākuntalam*	Trivandrum, Bhaskara Press, 1914
KANNADA			
Basavappa Sastri & C Subbarao	*Othello*	*Shurasena Charitre*	1895
Basavappa Sastri	*Abhijñānaśākuntalam*	*Karnataka Sakuntala Nataka*	1883
D.V. Gundappa	*Myakbet*	*1936*	Bangalore: Karnataka Prakatanalaya, 1936 Verse translation,
D.V. Gundappa	*Jak Ked Dombi Dandhalaya Prahasana*	*1959*	Mysore, Kavyakala,
D.V. Gundappa	*Geeta Shakuntalam*	*NA*	NA
TAMIL			
A Kumaragurupara Atittar	*Othello*	*Othello Uttaman*	Madras, 1950
A Kumaragurupara Atittar	*Rape Of Lucrece*	*Karpukannal*	Madras, Allianceco. 1947
A Kumaragurupara Atittar	*Julius Caesar*	*Virasimhan*	Madras, 1952. iii 87 p. 21cm
A Kumaragurupara Atittar	*Abhijñānaśākuntalam*	*Sakuntala Natakam*	1938
P. Sambandha Mudaliyar	*Cymberline*	*Simhalanthan*	Madras, 1929

(Table A 14.1 Contd.)

(Table A 14.1 Contd.)

Language	Translator	Original Text	Translated Title	Place/Publisher/Year
	P. Sambandha Mudaliyar	*Hamlet*	*Amaladitya*	Madras, 1931 (first pub 1908)
	P. Sambandha Mudaliyar	*Macbeth*	*Makapati*	Madras, 1929 (first pub 1913)
	P. Sambandha Mudaliyar	*Abhijñānaśākuntalam*	*Sakuntala Natakam*	Madras, 1938
	P. Sambandha Mudaliyar	*Malavikagnimitram*	*Malavikagnimitram*	Madras, 1930
	P. Sambandha Mudaliyar	*Vikramorvasiya*	*Vikrama Urvasi*	Madras, 1929
ASSAMESE				
	Atulchandra Hazarika	*Merchant Of Venice*	*Barijkomuar*	Shilong: Asamiya Sahitya Mandir (2nd ed), 1950
	Atulchandra Hazarika	*Sakuntala*	*Sakuntala*	Guahati: Asamiya Sahitya Mandir, 1948
SINDHI				
	Mirza Qalich Beg	*Merchant Of Venice*	*Husna Dildar*	1897
	Mirza Qalich Beg	*King Lear*	*Sah Elia*	1900
	Mirza Qalich Beg	*Cymberline*	*Shamshad Mayana*	1908
	Mirza Qalich Beg	*Two Gentlemen of Verona*	*Aziz Ain Sharif*	1909
	Mirza Qalich Beg	*Romeo and Juliet*	*Gulzar Ain Gulnar*	1909
	Mirza Qalich Beg	*Abhijñānaśākuntalam*	*Shakuntala*	1896
MARATHI				
	Govind Ballal Deval	*Othello*	*Jhunjarrao*	1890
	Govind Ballal Deval	*Vikramorvasiya*	*Vikramorvashiya*	1889

Note: NA*: Not Available.

Notes

1. Jones also writes, "All the other works of our illustrious poet, the Shakespeare of India, that have yet come to my knowledge, are a second play, in five acts, entitled Urvasí; an heroic poem, or rather a series of poems in one book, on the Children of the Sun; another, with perfect unity of action, on the Birth of Cumára, god of war; two or three love tales in verse; and an excellent little work on Sanscrit Metre, precisely in the manner of Terentianus; but he is believed by some to have revised the works of Válmic and Vyása, and to have corrected the perfect editions of them that are now current: this at least is admitted by all, that he stands next in reputation to those venerable bards; and we must regret, that he has left only two dramatick poems, especially as the stories in his Raghuvansa would have supplied him with a number of excellent subjects." William Jones, "Translator's Preface" in *Sacontala Or The Fatal Ring: An Indian Drama* (London: Charlton Tucker, 1870).

2. Dorothy M. Figuera, "Critical Reception and Methodology," in *Translating the Orient–The Reception of Sakuntala in Nineteenth Century Europe* (Albany, NY: State University Of New York Press, 1991).

3. Dorothy M. Figuera, *Translating the Orient: The Reception of Sakuntala in Nineteenth-Century Europe.* (New York: State University of New York Press. 1991).

4. William Jones, preface in *Sacontala or the Fatal Ring* (London: Charlton Tucker, 1870).

5. Sisir K. Das, *A History of Indian Literature: Western Impact: Indian Response, 1800–1910* (New Delhi: Sahitya Akadmy. 1991), 118.

6. Uma Chakravarty, "Whatever happened to the Vedic Dasi? Orientalism, Nationalism and a script for the Past," in *Recasting Women, Essays in Colonial History*, ed. Kumkum Sangari and Sudesh Vaid (New Delhi: Kali for Women, 1989), 27–87.

7. Sirkin, Natalie Robinson and Gerald Sirkin. 1971. "The Battle of Indian Education: Macaulay's Opening Salvo Newly Discovered." *Victorian Studies* 14, no. 4: 407–28. Available at http://www.jstor.org/stable/3825959

8. The data collected in the paper, pertaining to 1900–50 has been collected from the National Bibliographies. For data pertaining to the late nineteenth century, other sources have been relied upon, for instance for Sindhi, The *Anthology of Indian Literature*, KM George Vol. I, SahityaAkademi1994 provided the titles and the publication year. Therefore in many cases the publication agencies are not known. Though the table demands more discussion, only the relevant points pertaining to this paper have been made here.

9. Masti Venkatesh Iyengar another major author of modern Kannada also wrote several adaptations of Shakespeare and one play named "Kalidasa" in the 1950s.

10. The Maharajas play a major role in the process of not only learning and publishing scenario. Just like the maharaja of Myosore, the maharaja of Ayodhya, Narayan Pratap, too was a writer. Narayan Pratap's own work, *Rasakusumakararthat Sahityakaek Anutha Granth*, in which he was assisted and helped by Lala Sitaram a translator, taken up later in this chapter, is in itself an illustrious work with gilt prints and floral Victorian print art. The idea behind the work is to re-systematize his subjects of *rasa-nirupan* and *nayikabheda*. (Francesca Orsini, *Before the Divide: Hindu and Urdu Literary Culture* [New Delhi: Orient Blackswan, 2010], 267) Thus, not only were these rulers important for the system of court patronage at large but sometimes the patrons were involved with the process of modernizing the traditional.

11. G. Venkattasubbaiah, *D V Gundappa* (New Delhi: Sahitya Akademi, 2002), 12.

12. Guttal Vijaya, "Translation and Performance of Shakespeare in Kannada," in *India's Shakespeare* (Newark: University of Delaware Press, 2005), 110.

13. Das, *A History of Indian Literature*, 154.

14. Ulrike Stark, *An Empire of Books: The Naval Kishore Press and the Diffusion of the Printed Word in Colonial India* (New Delhi: Permanent Black, 2007), 11.

15. Das, *A History of Indian Literature*, 154.

16. The following biographical information was taken from the biographical sketch issued by Sitaram's son, K. Kishore in 1937, on Sitaram's death anniversary.

17. Founded in 1867, the Canning College was affiliated to the University of Calcutta, until 1921. In most probability, Sitaram would never have studied in Calcutta. His posting, as teacher and headmaster also remained in within the United Provinces.

18. The Safed Baradari was built by the last King of Awadh, Wajid Ali Shah, as an *imambara* in 1854. After it was annexed by the British in 1857, it was used for the British court proceedings. Therefore Sitaram's special convocation could take place there. As Kishore mentions, the ceremony was presided over by a British official.

19. Interestingly the same was done by another of his contemporaries and colleagues whom he was to work with in the court of Maharaja of Ayodhya. Jagannath Das 'Ratnakar', a well-known Braj Bhasha poet, is also supposed to have 'ripped and thrown away' his attempts at Urdu poetry. (Orsini, *Before the Divide*, 266).

20. Avadh Punch and Avadh Akbar were both journals published in the United Provinces. They form the most important examples of the early print culture in North India.

21. Pandit Ram Mishra Shastri was professor of Samkhya in Benaras College and was also heading a literary society of Benaras pandits. His association with Thibaut is documented by Henry Steel Olcott in *Old Diary Leaves 1878–83: The Only Authentic History of the Theosophical Society*. These closely linked circles of literary scholars both Indian and Western was a common phenomenon for the late nineteenth and early twentieth centuries.

22. The Maharaja of Ayodhya was himself a writer and had been a class fellow of Sitaram. A close association with a learned king can also be recalled in the case of Basavappa Shastri who had been the son of one of the ministers of the Maharaja of Mysore.

23. His "Selections from Hindi Poetry" a bilingual work in Hindi and English, in seven volumes was an outcome of his correspondence with Ashutosh Mukherjee, the vice chancellor of Calcutta University. Accordingly the work was also introduced to the syllabus of the university. While this work is noble not only because it involves a lot of primary research, but it is all the more interesting in terms of its bilingual form. It is notable that the university would include a bilingual form for propagating Hindi literature, which would be in its budding stages during that time. The "modern" and the traditional mingle here too.

24. Jagdish Prasad Mishra, *Shakespeare's Impact on Hindi Literature* (New Delhi: Munshiram Manoharlal, 1970), 44.

25. Furthermore it is important to see that even if it is not a single person translating both Shakespeare and Kalidasa, it is a general observation that some other translator deals with the other author with an insignificant time gap in between. It would be interesting to explore the role played by the theatre companies in commissioning the translations

26. The reference here, is reproduced from T.S. Satyanath, "How Does Shakespeare Become Sekhpir in Kannada," 2004, http://www.anukriti.net/tt/how_does.asp

Glossary

Adrista	The unperceived; specifically fate, luck or destiny
Alankara	Literally means ornamentation and refers to the science of figure of speech in Sanskrit and other medieval Indian literatures. *Alankara Shastra* is often equated with Indian poetics
Antaprakriti	Inner nature
Ardhangini	A female considered as composing half of the husband's body (self); thus, wife
Atmakatha	Memoirs
Bahiprakriti	Outer nature
Bahubali	A word which has its origins in Sanskrit. "Bahu" means arms and "bali" stands for strength. "Bahubali", therefore, refers to a person who has very strong arms or, as seen in *Omkara*, a man employed for his ability to strong-arm other
Basant	Also known as *Vasant(a)*, is a raga in classical Indian music usually that is performed during late evenings and during the spring season of the year
Bhairavi	An early morning *raga* in Hindustani classical music and is usually sung as the concluding item in a concert. In overnight performances of folk plays, songs in this *raga* are sung during early morning hours. *Bhairavi* in Carnatic classical music is quite different from that of Hindustani
Bhanu	The Sun-god. Chief of the eight great gods mentioned in *The Nāṭyaśāstra*, classified by Manmohan Ghosh in his introduction to the text, following Hopkin's *Epic Mythology*
Bharatanatyam	Refers to the dance tradition of temple courtesans (*devadasi*) that used to be performed in the temples of South India, which has been subsequently reformed during the early twentieth century to attain a modern and classical status

Bhodro	Polite, respectable
Bhodrolok	A respectable, middle class gentleman; carries connotations of civility and gentility
Bhoot	Ghost
Bhranti bilas/bilash	Comedy of Errors
Bibaha	Marriage
Biday	Farewell
Bisha briksha	A poison tree
Bishada	Sadness/melancholy
Bishwokobi	World Poet
Brahmirash	Juice of a herb with medicinal powers
Champu	A genre of *Kavya*, which is a mixture of prose (*Gadya*) and poetry (*Padya*), with prose interspersed among verse sections. It is popular in old and medieval Sanskrit, Kannada and Telugu literatures
Chaubola	A four-line meter in poetry extensively used in north India and in folklore
Chaupai	A four-line verse of poetry from the *Bhakti-Kal* in Hindi literature that makes use of units of four syllables
Chaupadi	A four-line meter that is usually sung, extensively used in Kannada folk and popular forms
Chhanda(s)	Refers to the metrical system of the *Vedas*, but also metrical system of medieval Indian literatures
Chhelebela	Childhood
Chokher Bali	Literally sand in the eye
Cholit	The language, especially dialect, of the masses. The "departure," signified by the root "chal," from the *sadhu* form, marks it off as a baser language used, and to be used, only by those in the lower strata
Choritro	Nature or disposition of a person as based on custom, ethics and values; thus, character
Dakinigan	A witch
Dargah	An Islamic sacred place representing the tomb of a Sufi saint and a venue for *Urs*, the death anniversary of the Sufi saint. A *Dargah* might also include a mosque, meeting rooms, Islamic religious school (madrassa), residences for teachers/caretakers, hospital, and other buildings for community purposes

Debi	The term denoting "goddess" could be used as means of addressing respectable women
Desi	Indigenous
Devabhasha	Literally, as mentioned in Mitra's *The Beginners Bengali–English Dictionary*, "the language of the gods, *Sanskrit*." However, the term has not been enlisted either in Monier-Williams's *A Sanskrit–English Dictionary* or in William Carey's *A Dictionary of the Bengali Language*
Dhanashri	A *raga* in Hindustani classical music that is usually performed in the early afternoon and presents a cheerful, happy mood
Dholak	A folk percussion instrument used in performances in several parts of India
Dhrupad	Refers to the oldest form of singing style in Hindustani classical music. It also denotes the verse form of the poetry as well as the style of singing
Doha	A two-line lyrical verse-format, which was extensively used by poets and bards in North India. It is also extensively used in folk theatre
Dronacharya	A character from the epic *The Mahabharata*, also referred to as Guru Drona, who was the royal preceptor to the Pandavas and Kauravas and was a master of advanced military arts
Dwarpal	A porter or gateman
Ebong	And
Ekalavya	A character from the epic *The Mahabharata*, a young prince of the Nishadha, the son of Vyatraj Hiranyadhanus, the king of the outcasts in the Kingdom of Magadha. Ekalavya aspired to study archery from Guru Dronacharya who refused to train him in spite of his skill. Deeply hurt but not broken or defeated, Eklavya didn't give up on his resolute will to master archery and collected the mud on which his *guru* walked, as a symbolic gesture of desire to follow his knowledge and footsteps, and later went into the forest and made a statue of Dronacharya under a huge tree. He began a disciplined program of self-study over many years and became an archer of exceptional prowess

Gamaka	Refers to an ornamental style of rendering Carnatic classical music. Medieval Kannada poetry's rendering is also called *Gamaka Vachana*, which is a melodious rendering of the verse (*padya*) set to classical ragas without the accompliment of percussion instruments
Gamchcha	A cheap, coarse hand-woven cloth used as a towel, usually by peasants and other workers
Griholokkhi	*Lokkhi* or *Lakshmi,* easily identifiable by an Indian audience as the goddess of the hearth
Guru	A teacher, a guide
Harsha	*Joy*
Huzoor	The Urdu appellation for "master" or authority, including upper class/caste social position
Izzat	Honour, reputation, prestige
Jati	A social group that forms a caste or a sub-caste amongst the Hindus. These castes/"jatis" are hereditary and stratified along the lines of purity and pollution
Jatra	An open-air rural opera or dramatic performance; a popular folk theatre form of Bengali theatre
Kallol	Sound of the waves
Kanda	Is a short four-line metrical verse found in ancient Kannada literature that is based on Prakrit metrical system, the *Matra Chandas*. Ornamental in language and music together, they were frequently used in Kannada Company *Nataks* to show actor's proficiency in singing
Kirtan	Refers literally to 'praise', 'eulogy'. Broadly refers to the singing of devotional compositions and performing of episodes of Bhakti hagiography. In medieval Kannada and Telugu literatures and in Carnatic music the term *Kirtane* also refers to Vaishnava compositions
Kolikal	According to Monier-Williams', it is "the last and worst of the four Yugas or ages, the present age, age of vice.... [It is] personified as the son of *Krodha,* 'Anger,' and *Hiṃsā,* 'Injury,' and as generating with his sister *Durukti,* 'Calumny,' two children, viz. *Bhaya,* 'Fear,' and *Mṛityu,* 'Death'." *Kolikal*, thus, symbolizes evil and chaos

Kundaliya	A six-line verse found in Braj Bhasha literature that literally means 'a coiled serpent'. This is because the stanza coils upon itself like a serpent, with its last word or phrase repeating the first word or phrase
Langda	In Hindi, "langda" is mildly offensive way of describing a person who is physically challenged by his lameness. In *Omkara*, "Landga" serves as a nickname for the Iago character which also indicative of a degree of endearment
Lavni	A folk genre of music and dance performed to the beats of percussion instrument *Dholki* and is popular in Maharashtra and parts of Deccan
Louha Manob	Iron men
Maagi	A derogatory term for "woman." Can be used to denote "prostitute."
Madan	The *Kama-deva*—divine incarnation of passion and love. Cf. Cupid
Madari	a juggler, a street performer, generally someone who plays and performs tricks with a monkey
Mahakavya	A great classical poem. Used here in the sense of an epic, referring specifically to the Mahabharata
Majhimalla	A "boatman" or "helmsman" or a "headman"; also meaning "husband" among the Santhalis
Manabprakash	Manifestations of humanity
Manusher Adhikare	In the rights of man
Matha	A monastic or similar religious establishment in Hindu sects and Jainism in South India. They were the centers of learning during the medieval period
Mela	A Sanskrit word meaning 'gathering' or 'to meet' or 'fair'. The term refers to all sizes of gatherings and can be religious, commercial, cultural, including the village fairs where a variety of exchanges, both material and other, use to take place. It was an important pre-colonial public sphere
Moha-Bidroha	The great revolt
Mombaati	Wax candle
Mridangam	A percussion instrument used in the performance of Carnatic classical music

Mukura	Mirror
Nagkeshar	A kind of flower or its tree
Nagra	A type of Indian shoe
Nandi	Invocatory songs in the praise of a deity presented as a mark of an auspicious opening to a drama. It has been considered as the most important of the *purvaranga* (preliminaries) of a Sanskrit drama. Refer to *Nātya–Mañjarī–Saurabha: Sanskrit Dramatic Theory* by G. K. Bhat for more details
Napit	The Bengali counterpart of an English barber. The Sanskrit equivalent is *Kshurin*. One who is acquainted with the customs related to his profession—*kshurakarman*—the act of shaving
Nata	According to *The Nātyaśāstra*, Nata is he who enacts "the affairs of men with the Sentiments, the States, and the Temperament." In the words of M. L. Varadpande, Nata is a "versatile theatrical personality." The word is derived from the root "nat" which means to dance and act and, as H. N. DasGupta points out, is the prakritized form of its Sanskrit root "nrit"
Nati	Specifically refers to the female counterpart of the Sutradhar and is supposed to be his consort. It is not used as a generic term to denominate the female characters in a play
Natok	In Indian theatrical tradition, the term refers to a play of the first order. It is the first of the ten *rupaka*s (drama, literally meaning "figurative"). Natok, in this sense, are especially erotic or heroic representations of myths or legends or historical anecdotes. However, the term has been used here in parlance with its present day usage, referring to any show or mimic representation or drama. For a detailed understanding, refer to *The Nātyaśāstra*; *Indian Theatre: Traditions of Performance* by Farley P. Richmond et al.; *Nātya–Mañjarī–Saurabha: Sanskrit Dramatic Theory* by G. K. Bhat and *A Sanskrit–English Dictionary* by M. Monier-Williams

O	And
Ore yehudi darao aaro kichu baki achche	Wait, Jew, there is something else
Padya	Refers to a verse in general, but specifically to verse that is sung in *Gamaka* style from *Kavyas* of medieval Kannada poetry
Parinam	Consequence
Patiparameshwar	The word stands as a combination of three words—*pati, param* and *ishwar*. Compounded together, they denote the husband considered as the supreme deity. In this sense, pati transcends its meaning of a "husband" and gets inflected with the ascriptions of "lord" and "master"
Pativrata sati	It refers to one who is "devoted" to her husband and is, therefore, a chaste woman
Pativrata	A chaste woman who reveres her husband and is faithful to him
Patropatri	Dramatis personae
Prachina O Nobina	The woman of old and the new woman
Prakrit	As defined by Monier-Williams', "original, natural, artless, normal, ordinary, usual.... [A]ny provincial or vernacular dialect cognate with Sanskrit (esp. the language spoken by women and inferior characters in the plays)"
Prem	Love; romantic love
Prema kalika	Bud of love
Premika	Male lover
Premikaa	Female beloved
Pretatma	A restless, unquiet spirit
Prodip	An oil-lamp
Purush probhu stree dashi	Man/the husband is the master, woman/the wife his servant
Raj-purohit	The chief priest of the royal office; usually the one who is commissioned as the foremost of the priests
Rangamancha	The stage or performing area
Rati	One of the two wives of Madan—the Kama-deva (while the other wife is Priti). Rati symbolizes the amorous pleasures, carnal desires and enjoyment borne out of union, especially legitimate
Sadhu bhasha	Refined form of Bangla language used in literary works or as formal address by educated upper-class Bengalis

Sadhu	The chaste form of the language "Bangla." The language adhered to "good, virtuous, honourable, righteous," and thus, chaste
Sahityer Mulya	The value of literature
Sahityer Pran	The soul of literature
Samadhi	Cemetery/grave
Saptasindhubari	Waters of the seven seas
Sati	The term generally refers to a good, virtuous and faithful wife. In specific use, it refers to the one who immolates herself by burning with her husband's corpse. Sati is also a name of the goddess *Uma*, an incarnation of splendour, light, fame, reputation and tranquillity
Satira Sahas	Courage of a chaste woman
Savai	Also known as *Savaiya*, which literally means one and quarter times. It is a form of poetry in Hindi literature that is written in praise of someone in which every verse is one and quarter times the length of common verse
Shadhubhasha	Formal, non-colloquial language
Shakespearer golpo tragedy o comedy ekotre	Shakespeare's stories, tragedies and comedies together
Shesher Kabita	The final or ultimate poem
Shikharini	An *Akshra-chandas* meter in Sanskrit with seventeen syllables with caesura (*yati*) after the seventh syllable
Shoka	Grief/bereavement
Sortha	A four-line meter used in the poetry of *Bhakti-kal* in Hindi literature
Stri-dhormo	The term is used here in the sense of moral as well as ethical duties and responsibilities of a woman as a wife. It is not used in the original meaning of menstruation or copulation
Sutradhar	In Manmohan Ghosh's translation, *The Nāṭyaśāstra* defines the character as "[o]ne who knows from the instruction of the Śāstra the principles (*sūtra*) of songs (*gāna*), instrumental music (*vādya*) and all the Recitatives, [and āll these] in conformity with one another." However, some scholars have connected the word with

	the puppeteer behind the *putul-nauch* (puppet-show), for the term stands as a combination of two words—sutra and *dhara*—literally, string and its holder. The present authors, however, do not attest the second view. For, the term sutra not only means string, but also refers to principles, conventions, rituals, as well as aphorisms. Likewise, dhara refers to bearing, observing and even preserving, and not just holding. Read in this sense, the description of the term Sutradhar is closer to its description in *The Nātyaśāstra*. Traditionally, and even in the plays in context, the Sutradhar is a male character who has as his female counterpart, supposed to be his wife, the Nati. For further deliberation, refer to *The Nātyaśāstra*; *The Indian Stage* by H. N. DasGupta; *History of Indian Theatre: Lokaranga, Panorama of Indian Folk Theatre* by M. L. Varadpande and *A Sanskrit–English Dictionary* by M. Monier-Williams
Swayamvara	Monier-Williams defines the term as "self-choice, the election of a husband by a princess or daughter of a Kshatriya at a public assembly of suitors." However, considered as a combination of *swayam* and *vara*, where the first word means "of one's own accord" and the latter one gets defined as "environing, enclosing" (not as a bridegroom as it is presently known to mean), it leads us to very different level of critical understanding where swayamvara loses its feminist stand and implies the confinement of a woman herself
Tabla	A pair of percussion instruments used in the performance of Hindustani classical music
Tamasha	A traditional form of Marathi theatre, often with singing and dancing, widely performed by local or travelling theatre groups within the state of Maharashtra, India
Tapaswi	Ascetic
Tatnopadesh	Sage counsel
Thakurmar Jhuli	Grandma's sack

Theyyam	It is a ritual primarily performed in the North Malabar region in Kerala in which various deities are worshipped. "Theyyam" is a word derived from the word *daivam*, meaning god and the word *attam*, meaning dance. It is the "dance of god" where the performers, necessarily from a lower caste, embody a god or an immortal spirit during the performance
Tiner Toloar	The tin sword
Urs	Arabic in origin and literally means 'wedding', the term suggests the death anniversary of a Sufi saint in the Indian context and takes place in the *Dargah*, the premises of a shrine or tomb in his name
Ustad	An expert or highly skilled person
Vidhi	As in Monier-Williams's *A Sanskrit–English Dictionary*, it is "a rule, formula, injunction, ordinance statute, precept, law, direction (esp. for the performance of a rite as given in the Brāhmaṇa portion of the Veda). Thus vidhis are considered sacred
Vidusaka	Etymologically, the word refers to one who transgresses and, thereby, defiles. A vidusaka is, as *The Nāṭyaśāstra* points out, "ready-witted, a maker of funs, and whose speech is always connected (lit. adorned) with the disclosure of extremely humorous ideas." The character, thus, can be conceived as an approximation to that of a jester. For more details, one may refer to *History of Indian Theatre: Lokaranga, Panorama of Indian Folk Theatre* by M. L. Varadpande
Vilambit	Refers to the introductory slow tempo in the performance of Hindustani classical music
Vritta	Refers to meters in the ancient Kannada literature that correspond to Sanskrit meters based on *Akshara Chandas*. They are usually four line meters with a fixed number of syllables and caesura (*yati*) after a fixed number of syllables.
Wah	Bravo
Wallah	A person in charge of, employed at, or concerned with a particular thing (used in combination): Here, Shakespeare wallah

Bibliography

All's Well That Ends Well, by William Shakespeare, directed by Sunil Shanbag. Globe Theatre, London, 23 May 2012.

Ancheri, Saumya. "Five Things About Atul Kumar's Hindi Version of *Twelfth Night." Time Out Mumbai,* 22 June 2012.

Angoor. Directed by Gulzar. Mumbai: A. R. Movies, 2008; originally released in 1982. DVD.

Arts Council England. "2012 Marks the World Shakespeare Festival and a New RSC Artistic Director." Accessed 5 July 2013. https://web.archive.org/web/20130609181248/http://www.artscouncil.org.uk/news/arts-council-news/2012-marks-world-shakespeare-festival-and-new-rsc-/.

Ashcroft, Bill, Gareth Griffiths and Helen Tiffin. *The Empire Writes Back: Theory and Practice in Post-Colonial Literature.* London: Routledge, 1989

Awasthi, Suresh. "Shakespeare in Hindi." *Indian Literature* 7, no. 1 (1964): 51–62.

Bagchi, Jasodhara. "A Note on Bengali Translations of Shakespeare: 1850–1900." *Jadavpur Journal of Comparative Literature* 5 (1965): 22–38.

———. "Shakespeare in Loin Cloths: English Literature and the Early Nationalist Consciousness in Bengal." In *Rethinking English: Essays in Literature, Language, History,* edited by Swati Joshi, 146–159. New Delhi: Trianka, 1991.

Baker, Shelly et al. "Review of Shakespeare's *The Tempest* (directed by Jatinder Verma for Tara Arts) at the Arts Theatre, London, January 2008" in *Shakespeare* 4, no. 1–4 (2008): 320–23.

Bakhle, Janaki. *Two Men and Music: Nationalism in the Making of an Indian Classical Tradition.* Oxford: Oxford University Press, 2005.

Balurao, S., ed. *Shekspiyarige Namaskara.* Delhi: Kannada Bharati, 1966.

Bandyopadhyay, Brajendranath. *Bongiyo Nātyoshālā.* Kolkata: Viswabhārati Granthālay, Poush 1351 BS.

Bandyopadhyay, Samik. "Mukhabandha." In Utpal Dutt's translation of *Macbeth,* 1–5. Kolkata: Thema, 2006.

———. "Utpal Dutt: An Interview by Samik Bandyopadhyay." In *Contemporary Indian Theatre: Interviews with Playwrights and Directors,* edited by Paul Jacob, 9–21. New Delhi: Sangeet Natak Akademi, 1989.

Barua, Navakanta. "Shakespeare in Assamese." *Indian Literature* 7, no. 1 (1964): 12–15.

Bassnett, Susan. *A Concise Companion to Postcolonial Literature.* Oxford: Blackwell, 2010.

———. *Translation Studies.* London: Routledge, 2002.

Bassnett, Susan and André Lefevere. *Constructing Cultures: Essays on Literary Translation.* Clevedon: Multilingual Matters, 1998.

Bassnett, Susan and André Lefevere, eds. *Translation, History and Culture.* London: Pinter, 1990.

Bassnett, Susan and Harish Trivedi, eds. *Post-Colonial Translation: Theory and Practice,* London: Routledge, 1999.

Basu, Asit. *Kolkatar Hamlet.* Kolkata: Jaatiyo Sahitya Parishad, 1989.

Basu, Bratya. *Hemlat.* Kolkata: Patralekha, 2007.

Basu, Shrabani. "The Play's the Thing." *The Telegraph India,* 13 May 2012. Accessed 30 July 2013. www.telegraphindia.com/1120513/jsp/7days/story_15482800.jsp#.Vd3nC-E4Hko

Bhabha, Homi. *The Location of Culture.* London and New York: Routledge, 1994.

Bharucha, Rustom. "Foreign Asia/Foreign Shakespeare: Dissenting Notes on New Asian Interculturality, Postcoloniality, and Recolonization." *Theatre Journal* 56, no. 1 (2004): 1–28.

———. *Rehearsals for Revolution: the Political Theatre of Bengal.* Honolulu: University of Hawaii Press, 1983.

Bhat, G. K. *Nātya-Mañjarī-Saurabha: Sanskrit Dramatic Theory.* Poona: Bhandarkar Oriental Research Institute, 1981.

Bhatia, Nandi. *Acts of Authority/Acts of Resistance: Theatre and Politics in Colonial and Postcolonial India.* Ann Arbor/New Delhi: The University of Michigan Press/Oxford University Press, 2004.

———. "Imperialistic Representations and Spectatorial Reception in *Shakespeare Wallah* (1)." *Modern Drama* 45, no. 1 (2002): 61+. Accessed 30 December 2013. http:// go.galegroup.com/ps/i.do?id=GALE%7CA97755086&v=2.1&u=inbhc&it=r&p= AONE&sw=w&asid=88d91f1a47ed40a7bbee4cc3f6a61293

———. ed. *Modern Indian Theatre: A Reader.* New Delhi: Oxford University Press, 2009.

Bhattacharyya, S. K. "Shakespeare and Bengali Theatre." *Indian Literature* 7, no. 1 (1964): 27–40.

Billington, Michael. "Cuts to the Heart." Review of *A Midsummer Night's Dream,* directed by Jatinder Verma for Tara Arts, Lyric Theatre, Hammersmith, London, *Guardian* 3 February 1997.

———. "*Much Ado About Nothing*-Review." Review of *Much Ado About Nothing* directed by Iqbal Khan for the Royal Shakespeare Company, Courtyard Theatre, Stratford-on-Avon, *Guardian* 2 August 2012. Accessed 3 March 2013. http://www.guardian.co.uk

———. "The Tempest, Arts Theatre." Review of *The Tempest,* directed by Jatinder Verma for Tara Arts, Arts Theatre, London, *Guardian* 12 January 2008.

Bird, Tom. Presentation at the Intercultural Symposium: Scholars and the Theatre Community Explore Shakespeare in Translation, London, 18–19 May, 2012.

Bishop, Tom and Alexander C.Y. Huang, eds. *The Shakespearean International Yearbook,* vol. 12. Special Section: "Shakespeare in India," Special Guest Editor, Sukanta Chaudhuri. Farnham: Ashgate, 2012.

"Blogging Shakespeare: Embracing Shakespearean Conversation in a Digital Age." *Shakespeare Birthplace Trust.* Accessed 20 October 2010. http://bloggingshakespeare. com/.

Boyd, Michael and Vikki Heywood. "Introduction." *Much Ado About Nothing* RSC programme brochure, 2012.

Brisset, Annie. "Translation and Parody: Quebec Theatre in the Making." *Canadian Literature* 117 (1988): 92–106. Accessed 2 March 2013. http://canlit.ca/pdfs/articles/ canlit117-Translation(Brisset).pdf

Burnett, Mark Thornton. *Shakespeare and World Cinema.* Cambridge: Cambridge University Press, 2013.

Cabaret, Florence. "*Indianizing* Othello: Vishal Bhardwaj's *Omkara.*" In *Shakespeare on Screen: Othello,* edited by Sarah Hatchuel and Nathalie Vienne-Guerrin, 107–21. Cambridge: Cambridge University Press, 2015.

Carey, W. *A Dictionary of the Bengali Language: Bengali-English.* New Delhi: Asian Educational Services, 1981.

Cartelli, Thomas. *Repositioning Shakespeare: National Formations, Postcolonial Appropriations.* London: Routledge, 1999.

Chag, Niraj. *Niraj Chag Composer and Musician.* Accessed 1 March 2013. http://nirajchag.com

Chakrabarti, Sudeshna. "Banga Rangamanche *Macbeth.*" In *Prekshapat: Macbeth* 400 (May 2006): 35–40.

Chakrabarty, Dipesh. "Witness to Suffering: Domestic Cruelty and the Birth of the Modern Subject in Bengal." In *Questions of Modernity,* edited by Timothy Mitchell, 49–86. Minneapolis: University of Minnesota Press, 2000.

Chakraborty, Bibhash. "Paanshaalaay Hamlet" (*Hamlet* in a Pub). In *Hamlet: A Collection of Articles on Anya Theatre production of Hamlet,* edited by Debashish Sau. Kolkata: Karigar, 2011.

Chakravarti, Paromita. "Modernity, Postcoloniality and Othello: the Case of *Saptapadi.*" *Remaking Shakespeare: Performance Across Media, Genres and Cultures,* edited by Aebischer Pascale, Edward J. Esche and Nigel Wheale, 39–55. United Kingdom. Palgrave Macmillan. 2003.

Chakravorty, Swapan. *Bangalir Ingreji Sahityochorcha.* Kolkata: Anustup, 2011.

———. "Rehearsing the Renaissance: Some Symptomatic Texts from Nineteenth-Century Bengal." In *Renaissance Reborn: In Search of a Historical Paradigm,* edited by Sukanta Chaudhuri, 114–30. New Delhi: Chronicle Books, 2010.

Chatterjee, Bankim Chandra. "*Prachina o Nobina.*" In *Bankim Rachanabali,* vol. 2, 249–54 Kolkata: Tuli Kolom, 1986.

———. "Shakuntala, Miranda *Ebong* Desdemona." In *Bankim Rachanabali,* vol. 2, 204–09. Kolkata: Tuli Kolom, 1986.

Chatterjee, Partha. *The Nation and its Fragments: Colonial and Postcolonial Histories.* Princeton: Princeton University Press, 1993.

———. "Two Poets and Death: On Civil and Political Society in the Non-Christian World." In *Questions of Modernity,* edited by Timothy Mitchell, 35–48. Minneapolis: University of Minnesota Press, 2000.

Chatterjee, Sudipto. *The Colonial Staged: Theatre in Colonial Calcutta.* Kolkata: Seagull Books, 2008.

Chatterjee, Sudipto and Jyotsna Singh. "Moor or Less: The Surveillance of *Othello,* Calcutta 1848" In *Shakespeare and Appropriation,* edited by Christy Desmet and Robert Sawyer. London: Routledge, 1999.

Chatterjee, Visvanath. "Tagore as a Shakespearean Critic." *Tagore Studies* (1972–73): 15–31.

Chaudhuri, Amit. "Two Giant Brothers: Tagore's Revisionist Orient." In *Clearing a Space: Reflections on India, Literature and Culture,* 122–139. Ranikhet: Black Kite, 2008.

Chaudhuri, Sukanta. Introduction to *Rabindranath Tagore: Selected Writings on Literature and Language,* edited by Sisir K. Das and Sukanta Chaudhuri, 1–21. New Delhi: Oxford University Press, 2001.

———. "Shakespeare in India." *Internet Shakespeare Editions.* Accessed 2 March 2013. http://internetshakespeare.uvic.ca/Library/Criticism/shakespearein/india1.html

———. "Translation, Transcreation, Travesty." http://www.stjerome.co.uk (last accessed 10 January 2013).

Chaudhuri, Sukanta and Chee Seng Lim, eds. *Shakespeare without English: The Reception of Shakespeare in Non-Anglophone Countries.* Delhi: Pearson/Longman, 2006.

Cochrane, Claire. "Engaging the Audience: A Comparative Analysis of Developmental Strategies in Birmingham and Leicester since the 1990s." In *Critical Essays on British South Asian Theatre*, edited by Graham Ley and Sarah Dadswell, 100–18. Exeter: Exeter University Press, 2012.

———. *Twentieth Century British Theatre Industry, Art and Empire*. Cambridge: Cambridge University Press, 2011.

Conversation with the Filmmakers. Performed by Ismail Merchant, James Ivory, Felicity Kendal, and Shashi Kapoor. New York: The Criterion Collection, 2004. DVD.

Daileader, Celia R. *Racism, Misogyny, and the Othello Myth: Inter-racial Couples from Shakespeare to Spike Lee*. Cambridge: Cambridge University Press, 2005.

Das Gupta, Hemendra Nath. *The Indian Stage*, vol. 2. Delhi: Munshiram Manoharlal, 2002; originally published 1944–46 in Kolkata.

Das, Sisir Kumar. *A History of Indian Literature: Western Impact: Indian Response, 1800–1910*. New Delhi: Sahitya Akademi, 1991.

———. *A History of Indian Literature: 1911–1956*. New Delhi: Sahitya Akademi, 1995.

———. "Shakespeare in Indian Languages." In *India's Shakespeare: Translation, Interpretation and Performance*, edited by Poonam Trivedi and Dennis Bartholomeusz, 42–65. New Delhi: Dorling Kindersley, 2006.

Dasgupta, Birendramohan. *Samsad Bengali–English Dictionary*. Kolkata: Sahitya Samsad, 1982.

Das Gupta, R. K. "Shakespeare in Bengali Literature." *Indian Literature* 7, no.1 (1964): 16–26.

Datta, Amresh. *Encyclopaedia of Indian Literature: Devraj to Jyoti*. New Delhi: Sahitya Akademi, 1988.

Daugherty, Diane. "The Pendulum of Intercultural Performance: Kathakali King Lear at Shakespeare's Globe." *Asian Theatre Journal* 22 no. 1 (2005): 52–72.

Davies, Andrew. "Culture: Rob's Career off to a Flying Start; Rob Mountford Has Already Starred in a Top Television Drama and Trod the Boards with the RSC—And He's Barely Been Out of Drama School Two Years. Andrew Davies Caught up with the Birmingham-born Actor En Route to Beijing." *Birmingham Post*, 11 June 2002. Accessed 1 August 2013. http://www.birminghampost.net

de Tocqueville, Alexis. "Some Observations on the Theatre of Democratic Peoples." In *The American Stage*, edited by Laurence Senelick. New York: Library of America, 2011.

Desmet, Christy, and Robert Sawyer, eds. *Shakespeare and Appropriation*. London: Routledge, 1999.

Dickson, Andrew. "World Shakespeare Festival: Around the Globe in 37 Plays." *Guardian*, 20 April 2012. Accessed 24 April 2012. www.theguardian.com/stage/2012/apr/20/world-shakespeare-festival-globe-theatre-rsc

Dionne, Craig, and Parmita Kapadia, eds. *Native Shakespeares: Indigenous Appropriations on a Global Stage*. Aldershot: Ashgate, 2008.

Dutt, Utpal. "Dharmatollar Hamlet." In *Gadya Sangraha* (Collected Prose), vol.1, edited by Samik Bandyopadhyay, 129–138. Kolkata: Dey's Publishing, 2004.

———. *"Dusswapner Shei Dinguli."* Epic Theatre *(August 2012): 4–8.*

———. "Hamlet o Janapriyota." In *Gadya Sangraha* (Collected Prose), vol.1, edited by Samik Bandyopadhyay, 61–67. Kolkata: Dey's Publishing, 2004.

———. "Little Theatre *o Ami*" (Little Theatre and I). *Epic Theatre* (May 1977): 48–72.

Dutt, Utpal, trans. *Macbeth* by William Shakespeare. Kolkata: Thema, 2009.

Dutta, Krishna and Andrew Robinson, eds. *Selected Letters of Rabindranath Tagore*. Cambridge: Cambridge University Press, 1997.

Eliot, T.S. "The Love Song of J. Alfred Prufrock." In *Selected Poems.* Bungay, Suffolk: Richard Clay (The Chaucer Press), 1982.

Fanon, Frantz. *Black Skin, White Masks.* London. Pluto Press, 1986.

Figuera, Dorothy M. *Translating the Orient: The Reception of Sakuntala in Nineteenth-Century Europe.* New York: State University of New York Press, 1991.

Gabriel, Theodore P.C. *Playing God: Belief and Ritual in the Muttappan Cult of North Malabar.* United Kingdom: Indiana University, Equinox Publishing Limited, 2010.

Gail, Kern Paster. *The Idea of the City in the Age of Shakespeare.* Athens, GA: University of Georgia Press, 1985.

Gardner, Lyn, "Twelfth Night—Review." *Guardian,* 30 April 2012.

Genette, Gérard. *Palimpsests: Literature in the Second Degree,* translated by Channa Newman and Claude Doubinsky. Lincoln: University of Nebraska Press, 1997.

Ghose, Jagannath Ballav. *Premika Premika.* Cuttack: The Union Printing Works, 1908.

Ghosh, Hurro Chunder. *Bhanumoti Chittobilash.* Calcutta: Purnachandrodaya Press, 1853.

Ghosh, Manmohan, ed. *The Nāṭyaśāstra: A Treatise on Hindu Dramaturgy and Histrionics.* Vol.1. Calcutta: The Royal Asiatic Society of Bengal, 1950.

Godwin, Richard. "That's Amara! Meet Amara Karam, Simon Pegg's Latest Leading Lady." *London Evening Standard,* 27 April 2012. Accessed 14 August 2013. *http:// www.standard.co.uk.*

Gokale, Shanta. *Playwright at the Centre: Marathi Drama from 1843 to the Present.* Kolkata: Seagull, 2000.

Gollancz, Israel, ed. *A Book of Homage to Shakespeare.* London: Humphrey Milford, Oxford University Press, 1916.

Golub, Spencer. "Between the Curtain and the Grave: The Taganka in the *Hamlet* Gulag." In *Foreign Shakespeare: Contemporary Performance,* edited by Dennis Kennedy, 158–77. Cambridge: Cambridge University Press, 1993.

Greenblatt, Stephen et al, eds. *The Norton Shakespeare.* New York and London: Norton, 1997.

Grimley, Terry. "Iqbal Khan Back at Birmingham Rep for East is East." *Birmingham Post,* 23 September 2009. Accessed 11 November 2012. http://www.birminghampost.net

Guha, Ramachandra. "Rise and Fall of the Bilingual Intellectual." *Economic and Political Weekly,* 23 January 2010.

Guha-Thakurta, P. *The Bengali Drama: Its Origin and Development.* London: Kegan Paul/ Trench/Trubner, 1930.

Gupta, Jogendra Chandra. *Kirttibilash.* n.p., 1852.

Gupta, Nidhi. "A Masala-tinged Poem, Sung to Perfection." *Sunday Guardian,* 2 September 2012.

Gupta, Tapati. "Shakespeare, the Mediterranean & Utpal Dutt's Politics of Representation." *Journal of the Department of English,* University of Calcutta (1999–2000): 150–63.

———. "'The Play's the Thing': Transcreating Shakespeare for the Stage." *Epic Theatre* (April 2003): 92–100.

Habib, M. A. R. *Modern Literary Criticism and Theory: A History.* New Delhi: Blackwell, 2008.

"Hamara Shakespeare: Shakespeare in Indian Languages." Prakriti Foundation. Accessed 25 January 2012. www.hamarashakespeare.com.

Hansen, Kathryn. "Languages on Stage: Linguistic Pluralism and Community Formation in the Nineteenth Century Parsi Theatre." *Modern Asian Studies,* 37, no. 2 (2003): 381–405.

Hansen, Kathryn. "Parsi Theatre and the City: Locations, Patrons and Audiences." *Sarai Reader 2: The Cities of Everyday Life,* 381–405. Delhi: SARAI, 2002.

Hansen, Kathryn. "The Birth of Hindi Drama in Benaras, 1868–1885." In *Culture and Power in Benaras: Community, Performance and Environment, 1800–1990*, edited by Sandria B. Freitag, 62–92. Oxford: Oxford University Press, 1992.

Hardiman, David. *Feeding the Baniya: Peasants and Usurers in Western India*. New Delhi: Oxford University Press, 1996.

Hasan, Mohammad. "Shakespeare in Urdu." *Indian Literature* 7, no. 1(1964): 132–39.

Hoensellars, Ton, ed. *Shakespeare and the Language of Translation*. London: Thomson Learning, 2004.

Huang, Alexa. "Global Shakespeares and Shakespeare Performance in Asia: Open-Access Digital Video Archives." *Asian Theatre Journal Special Issue: Asian Shakespeare 2.0* 28, no. 1 (2011): 244–50.

———. "Shakespeare 2.0." *Asian Theatre Journal Special Issue: Asian Shakespeare 2.0*. 28, no. 1 (2011): 1–5.

———. "'What Country, Friends, Is This?': Touring Shakespeares, Agency, and Efficacy in Theatre Historiography." *Theatre Survey* 54, no. 1 (2013): 51–85.

Hussain, Shai. "Much Ado About A Lot Of Things." *The Non Resident Indian*, 22 July 2012. Accessed 30 July 2013. www.the-nri.com/life/arts/much-ado-about-a-lot-of-things

Hutcheon, Linda. *A Theory of Adaptation*. New York: Routledge, 2006.

Ick, Judy Celine. "*Otelo*, Intercultural Spectatorship, and Ocular Proof." *Asian Theatre Journal Special Issue: Asian Shakespeare 2.0* 28, no. 1 (2011): 129–48.

Indian Literature. Shakespeare Number 7, no. 1 (1964).

Indian Shakespeare Quest. Directed by Patrick Mc Grady and presented by Felicity Kendal. Wavelength Films for BBC, 2012. Documentary.

"Internet Shakespeare Editions." *Shakespeare in India::*. N.p., n.d. 04 June 2014. Web.

Iqbal, Nosheen. "Much Ado About Delhi: RSC's Indian Shakespeare." *Guardian*, 1 August 2012. Accessed 2 September 2012. www.theguardian.com/culture/2012/aug/01/much-ado-rsc-indian-shakespeare

Jaggard, William. *Shakespeare Bibliography: A Dictionary of Every Known Issue of the Writings of Our National Poet and of Recorded Opinion Thereon in the English Language*. Stratford-upon-Avon: Shakespeare Press, MCMXI.

Jain, Nemi Chand. *Indian Theatre: Tradition, Continuity and Change*. New Delhi: Vikas Publications, 1992.

Kaliyattam, directed by Jayaraaj, Performed by Suresh Gopi, Lal, Manju Warrier and Biju Menon. Moserbaer, 1997.

Kapoor, Shashi with Deepa Gahlot. *The Prithviwallahs*. New Delhi: Roli Books, 2004.

Karanth, K. Shivaram. *Yakshagana*. New Delhi: Abhinav Publications, 1997.

Kaushal, J.N., ed. *Rang Yatra: Twenty-five Years of the NSD Repertory Company*. Delhi: National School of Drama, 1992.

Kendal, Felicity. "Felicity Kendal's Indian Shakespeare Quest." Telecast, Television, BBC, 16 May 2012.

———. Introduction to *The Shakespeare Wallah*, by Geoffrey Kendal with Clare Colvin, viii-x. London: Sidgwick and Jackson, 1986.

———. *White Cargo*. London: Michael Joseph, 1998.

Kendal, Geoffrey with Clare Colvin. *The Shakespeare Wallah*. London: Sidgwick and Jackson, 1986.

Kennedy, Dennis, ed. *Foreign Shakespeare: Contemporary Performance*. Cambridge: Cambridge University Press, 2004.

Kennedy, Dennis, and Yong Li Lan, eds. *Shakespeare in Asia: Contemporary Performance*. Cambridge: Cambridge University Press, 2010.

Khajuria, Hina. "Inder Sabha: Understanding Early-Modern Indian Theatre and Its Public Sphere." Unpublished MPhil dissertation, Department of Modern Indian Languages and Literary Studies, University of Delhi, 2012.

Knowles, Ric. *Theatre & Interculturalism.* Basingstoke: Palgrave Macmillan, 2010.

Kohli, Hardeep. "A Midsummer Night's Dream, Lyric Hammersmith, London." Review of *A Midsummer Night's Dream,* directed by Jatinder Verma for Tara Arts, Lyric Theatre, Hammersmith, London, *Herald* 5 February 1997.

Kott, Jan. *Shakespeare Our Contemporary.* London: Methuen, 1965.

Kundu, Monindrolal. *Bangalir Natyochetonar Kromobikash: Prachintheke Moddho-Unobingsho Shokabdo.* Kolkata: Shahityolok, 2000.

Lal, Ananda. "Introduction to Tagore's Plays." In *Rabindranath Tagore: Three Plays,* translated by Ananda Lal, 3–123. Kolkata: M.P. Birla Foundation, 1987.

———. "'We the globe can encompass soon': Tim Supple's *Dream.*" *The Shakespearean International Yearbook, 12: Special Section: Shakespeare in India* General Editors Tom Bishop and Alexander C.Y. Huang, Editor Emeritus Graham Bradshaw, Special Guest Editor Sukanta Chaudhuri. Farnham: Ashgate, 2012. 65–82.

Lal, Ananda, ed. *The Oxford Companion to Indian Theatre.* New Delhi: Oxford UP, 2004.

Lal, Ananda and Sukanta Chaudhuri, eds. *Shakespeare on the Calcutta Stage: A Checklist.* Calcutta: Papyrus, 2001.

Lamb, Charles and Mary. *Tales from Shakespeare.* Accessed 7 March 2010. http://www.gutenberg.org/files/573/573-h/573-h.htm

Lei, Bi-qi Beatrice, and Ching-Hsi Perng, eds. *Shakespeare in Culture.* Taiwan: National Taiwan University Press, 2012.

Leitch, Thomas. "Adaptation and Intertextuality, or, What isn't an Adaptation, and What Does it Matter?" In *A Companion to Literature, Film, and Adaptation*, edited by Deborah Cartmell, 87–104. London. Wiley-Blackwell, 2012.

Ley, Graham and Sarah Dadswell, eds. *British South Asian Theatre: A Documented History.* Exeter: Exeter University Press, 2011.

———. *Critical Essays on British South Asian Theatre.* Exeter: Exeter University Press, 2012.

Linneman, Emily. "International Innovation? Shakespeare as Intercultural Catalyst." In *Shakespeare Survey,* 64, edited by Peter Holland 13–24. Cambridge: Cambridge University Press, 2011.

Lo, Jacqueline and Helen Gilbert. "Toward a Topography of Cross-Cultural Theatre Praxis." *TDR: The Drama Review* 46, no. 3 (T 175, Fall 2002): 31–53.

Long, Robert Emmet. *James Ivory in Conversation: How Merchant Ivory Makes Its Movies.* Berkeley: University of California Press, 2005.

———. *The Films of Merchant Ivory.* New York: Harry N. Abrams, Inc, 1991.

Loomba, Ania. *Gender, Race, Renaissance Drama.* Delhi: Oxford University Press, 1992; originally published 1989 by Manchester University Press.

———. "Local Manufacture Made-in-India Othello Fellows: Issues of Race, Hybridity and Location in Post-colonial Shakespeares." In *Post-colonial Shakespeares,* edited by Ania Loomba and Martin Orkin, 143–63. London/New York: Routledge, 1998.

———. *Shakespeare, Race and Colonialism.* Oxford: Oxford University Press, 2002.

———. "Shakespearian Transformations." In *Shakespeare and National Culture,* edited by John J. Joughin, 109–41. Manchester: Manchester University Press, 1997.

Loomba, Ania and Martin Orkin. "Introduction: Shakespeare and the Post-Colonial Question." In *Post-Colonial Shakespeares,* edited by Ania Loomba and Martin Orkin, 14–32. New York: Routledge, 2004. Accessed October 17, 2013. E-brary.

Loomba, Ania, and Martin Orkin, eds. *Post-colonial Shakespeares*, 2nd ed. New York: Routledge, 2004.

Macaulay, Thomas Babington, *Minute on Indian Education*. Columbia University Archive, 1853.

Mayer, Claudia. "Notes on Design." Programme for *The Tempest*, Tara Arts, 2008.

McMullen, Marion. "Theatre: Bharti Patel Didn't Think She Would Ever do Shakespeare." *Coventry Telegraph*, 31. Aug. 2012. Accessed 14 August 2013. http://www. coventrytelegraph.net

Mehta, Chandravan C. "Shakespeare and the Gujarati Stage." *Indian Literature* 7, no. 1 (1964): 41–50.

Mendel, Arthur. "Hamlet and Soviet Humanism." *Slavic Review* 30, no.4 (December 1971): 733–47.

Ministry of Information and Broadcasting, Government of India, ed. *Indian Drama*. New Delhi: Publications Division, 1981.

Mishra, Jagdish Prasad. *Shakespeare's Impact on Hindi Literature*. New Delhi: Munshiram Manoharlal, 1970.

Mitra Majumdar, Dakshinaranjan. *Thakurmar Jhuli*. Kolkata: Mitra and Ghosh Publishers, 1984.

Mitra, Ipshita. "I Wish I Could do 'Hamlet' all my Life: Atul Kumar." *Times of India*, 17 August 2012. Accessed 30 July 2013. http://timesofindia.indiatimes.com/life-style/ people/I-wish-I-could-do-Hamlet-all-my-life-Atul-Kumar/articleshow/15530848.cms

Mitra, Subal Chandra. *The Beginners' Bengali-English Dictionary*. Calcutta: New Bengal Press, April 1955.

Modood, Tariq. "Immigrants, Settlers and Multiculturalism." *Twelfth Night* RSC programme brochure, 2012.

Mohanty, Sangita. 2010. "The Indian Response to Hamlet: Shakespeare's Reception in India and a Study of Hamlet in Sanskrit Poetics." Doctoral Dissertation, University of Basel, Basel.

Monier-Williams, Monier. *A Sanskrit–English Dictionary*. Delhi: Motilal Banarsidass, 1986.

Montaigne, Michel de. "On the Cannibals." In *The Complete Essays,* translated and edited by M.A. Screech, 228–41. Harmondsworth: Penguin, 1993.

Morris, Sylvia. "Round the Globe with Much Ado About Nothing." *Shakespeare blog* (blog), 6 August 2012. Accessed 30 July 2015. http://theshakespeareblog.com/2012/08/ crossing-the-globe-with-much-ado-about-nothing

Much Ado About Nothing, by William Shakespeare, directed by Iqbal Khan, Royal Shakespeare Theatre, Stratford-Upon-Avon, 6 August 2012.

Mukherjee, Sushil Kumar. *The Story of the Calcutta Theatres: 1753–1980*. Kolkata: K.P. Bagchi, 1982.

Mukhopadhyay, Arup. *Utpal Dutt: Jeevan O Shrishti*. Kolkata/New Delhi: National Book Trust, 2010.

Mukhopadhyay, Arup, ed. *Epic Theatre: Subarnajayanti Sankalan*. Kolkata: Deep Prakashan, 2014.

Mukhopadhyay, Prabhatkumar. *Rabindrajibani,* vol. 4. Kolkata: Visva-Bharati, 2010; originally published in 1957.

Mukhopadhyay, Tarun. *Bangla Natoke Poshchimer Alo*. Kolkata: Ebonga Mushaira, 2007.

Murthyrao, A.N. "Shakespeare and Karnataka." *Indian Literature* 7, no. 1 (1964).

Nabokov, Vladimir. *Bend Sinister*. New York: Henry Holt and Co., 1947.

Nayak, Jatindra K. "Storyteller, Poet, Playwright: Three Oriya Translations of Shakespeare (1908–59)." In *International Shakespearean Yearbook*, vol. 12: Special section, "Shakespeare in India." General editors Tom Bishop and Alexander C.Y. Huang, Editor emeritus Graham Bradshaw, Special Guest Editor Sukanta Chaudhuri, 53–64. Farnham: Ashgate, 2012.

Neely, Carol Thomas. "Women and Men in Othello." In *William Shakespeare's Othello*, edited by Harold Bloom, 79–104. New York: Chelsea House Publishers, 1987.

Nofil, Zafri Mudasser. "Hindi, Gujarati Adaptations Set to Wow World Shakespeare Fest." *DNA India*, 21 March 2012. Accessed 30 July 2013. www.dnaindia.com/entertainment/report-hindi-gujarati-adaptations-set-to-wow-world-shakespeare-fest-1665344

O'Toole, Emer, "Shakespeare Universal? No Its Cultural Imperialism." *Guardian*, 21 May 2012.

Olive, Sarah. *"All's Well That Ends Well."* In *A Year of Shakespeare: Reliving the World Shakespeare Festival*, edited by Paul Edmondson, Paul Prescott and Erin Sullivan, 33–36. London: Bloomsbury Arden Shakespeare, 2013.

Omkara, directed by Vishal Bhardwaj, performed by Ajay Devgan, Saif Ali Khan and Kareena Kapoor in the lead roles, supported by Vivek Oberoi, Naseeruddin Shah and Konkona Sen Sharma. Moserbaer, 2006.

Orsini, Francesca, *Before the Divide: Hindi and Urdu Literary Culture*. New Delhi: Orient Blackswan. 2010.

Owen, Jonathan. "Meera Syal: 'I Didn't Want to Reach 50 and be Full of Regrets'." *Independent*, 6 May 2012. Accessed 3 March 2013. http://www.independent.co.uk

Padikkal, Shivarama. *Nāḍu-nuḍiyarūpaka: Rāṣṭra, Ādhunikate mattu kannaḍada modala kādambarigaḷu*. Mangalagangotri: Mangalore University, 2001.

Panja, Shormishtha. "'In Search of a Local Habitation and a Name': Illustrations in 19th and 20th Century Bengali Prose Retellings of Shakespeare." In *The Shakespearean International Yearbook 13: Special Section, Macbeth*, edited by Tom Bishop, Alexander C.Y. Huang, Guest Editor Stuart Sillars, 35–52. Farnham: Ashgate, 2013.

———. "Intercultural Theatre and Shakespeare Productions in India." In *Routledge Handbook of Asian Theatre*, edited by Siyuan Lee, 504–509. London: Routledge, 2016.

———. "Lebedeff, Kendal, Dutt: Three Travelers on The Indian Stage." In *Transnational Mobilities in Early Modern Theater*, edited by Robert Henke and Eric Nicholson, 245–61. London: Ashgate, 2014.

———. "Not Black and White But Shades of Grey: Shakespeare in India." In *Shakespeare without English: the Reception of Shakespeare in Non-Anglophone Countries*, edited by Sukanta Chaudhuri and Chee Seng Lim, 102–16. New Delhi: Pearson Longman, 2006.

———. "Rabindranath Tagore's *Chokher Bali*: The New Woman, Conjugality and the Heterogeneity of Home." In *Signifying the Self: Women and Literature*, edited by Malashri Lal, Shormishtha Panja and Sumanyu Satpathy, 211–25. Delhi: Macmillan, 2007; originally published in 2004.

———. "Shakespeare on the Indian Stage: Resistance, Recalcitrance, Recuperation." In *Transnational Exchange in Early Modern Theater*, edited by Robert Henke and Eric Nicholson, 215–24. Aldershot: Ashgate, 2008.

Parekh, B.C. *The Future of Multi-Ethnic Britain Report of the Commission on the Future of Multi-Ethnic Britain* London: Profile Books, 2000.

Patel, Bharti. *Bharti Patel*. Accessed 28 July 2013. http://www.castingcallpro.com

Patil, Anand. *Western Influence on Marathi Drama: A Case Study*. Panaji: Rajhans Publications, 1993.

Patterson, Christina. "Lost in Translation: The Globe's Shakespeare Season Offers a Surprising Insight into Different Cultures." *Independent*, 7 June 2012.

Paul, Friederich. "Language and Politics in India." *Daedalus, Current Work and Controversies* 91, no. 3 (Summer 1962): 543–59.

Pavis, Patrice. *Theatre at the Crossroads of Culture*, 3rd ed. London: Routledge, 2001.

Peter, John. "The Tempest—Review." Review of *The Tempest,* directed by Jatinder Verma for Tara Arts, Arts Theatre, London. *Sunday Times,* 20 January 2008.

Phillips, John W.P. "Shakespeare and the Question of Intercultural Performance." In *Shakespeare in Asia: Contemporary Performance.* edited by Dennis Kennedy and Yong Li Lan, 234–52. Cambridge: Cambridge University Press, 2010.

Phukan, Shibani. "Towards an Indian Theory of Translation." *Wasafiri* 18, no. 40 (2003): 27–30. Accessed 3 March 2013. doi:10.1080/02690050308589864.

Pillai, Kainikkara M. Kumara. "Shakespeare in Malayalam." *Indian Literature* 7, no. 1 (1964): 73–82.

Prasher, Kalyani. "Why Atul Kumar is House Full." *Yahoo News,* 5 March 2014. https://in.news.yahoo.com/why-atul-kumar-is-house-full-100141409.html

Pratt, Mary Louise. *Imperial Eyes: Travel Writing and Transculturation*. London: Routledge, 1992.

Punjani, Deepa. "Piya Behrupiya Play Review." *Mumbai Theatre Guide*, 17 August 2012. Accessed 30 July 2013. http://www.mumbaitheatreguide.com/dramas/reviews/19-piya-behrupya-hindi-play-review.asp#.dpuf

Pym, John. *The Wandering Company: Twenty-One Years of Merchant Ivory Films*. London: British Film Institute Publishing, 1983.

Raha, Kironmoy. *Bengali Theatre*. New Delhi: National Book Trust, 1980; originally published in 1978.

———. "Old Calcutta." *Enact* 107 (1975): 108.

Rajadhyaksha, M.V. "Shakespeare in Marathi." *Indian Literature* 7, no. 1 (1964): 83–94.

Rajamannar, P.V. "Shakespeare in Telegu." *Indian Literature* 7, no. 1 (1964): 127–31.

Rao, A.N. Moorthy. "Shakespeare in Kannada." *Indian Literature* 7, no. 1 (1964): 63–72.

Rohera, Draupadi. "Gujarati at the Globe." *Hindustan Times*, 20 May 2012. Accessed 30 July 2013. www.hindustantimes.com/entertainment/gujarati-at-the-globe/article1-858462.aspx

Roy, Parama. "Reading Communities and Culinary Communities: The Gastropoetics of the South Asian Diaspora." *positions: east asia cultures critique* 10, no. 2 (2002): 471–502. Accessed 16 October 2012. Project Muse.

Rumbold, Kate. "*Much Ado About Nothing*." In *A Year of Shakespeare: Reliving the World Shakespeare Festival*, edited by Paul Edmondson, Paul Prescott, and Erin Sullivan, 149–152. London: Bloomsbury Arden Shakespeare, 2013.

Ryuta, Minami, and Poonam Trivedi, eds. *Re-playing Shakespeare in Asia*. New York: Routledge, 2010.

Sangari, Kumkum and Vaid, Sudesh. *Recasting Women: Essays in Indian Colonial History*. New Delhi: Kali for Women, 1989.

Saptapadi, directed by Ajoy Kar, performed by Suchitra Sen, Uttam Kumar, Chhabi Biswas and Chaya Debi. Moserbaer, 1961.

Saraiya, Indu. "The Shakespearewallah's Remembrance of Things Past." *The Sunday Statesman* (Kolkata), 3 June 1984.

Sarkar, Tanika. *Hindu Wife, Hindu Nation: Community, Religion and Cultural Nationalism.* Delhi: Permanent Black, 2001.

Sarma, Dhurjjati. "Shakespeare in Indian: Colonial Modernity, Nationality and Regional Identities." Unpublished MPhil dissertation, Department of Modern Indian Languages and Literary Studies, University of Delhi, 2011.

Satapathy, Basant. *Mane Pade,* Bhubaneswar: Sikshasandhan, 2008.

———. *Othello* in *Chhayakalpa,* Cuttack: Agraduta, 2013.

———. *Shakespeare Kahanimala,* Cuttack: Agraduta, 1977.

Satyanath, T.S. "How does Shakespeare Become *Sekh Pir* in Kannada." *Translation Today* 1, no. 2 (2004): 44–102.

———. "Remapping Shakespeare in Kannada." In *Discourse on Translation in Kannada,* edited by P.P. Giridhar. New Delhi: Sahitya Akademi, forthcoming.

Sawant, Purvaja. "Theatre Review: Piya Behrupiya." *Times of India,* 5 April 2013. Accessed 30 July 2013. http://timesofindia.indiatimes.com/entertainment/hindi/bollywood/news/Theatre-Review-Piya-Behrupiya/articleshow/19378329.cms

Schlote, Christine. "Finding our Own Voice" An Interview with Jatinder Verma." In *Staging New Britain Aspects of Black and South Asian British Theatre Practice,* edited by Geoffrey V.Davis and Anne Fuchs, 309–20. Brussels: Peter Lang, 2006.

Sen, Prabodh C. "Bengali Drama and Stage." In *Indian Drama,* edited by Ministry of Information and Broadcasting, Government of India, 41–58. New Delhi: Publications Division, 1981.

Shah, Naseeruddin. *The Anupam Kher Show—Kucch Bhi Ho Sakta Hai.* Colors Television, 3 August 2014, by Anupam Kher.

Shakespeare Wallah. Directed by James Ivory. New York: The Criterion Collection, 2004; originally released in 1965. DVD.

Shakespeare, William. *Hamlet: The Arden Shakespeare,* edited by Harold Jenkins. London/New York: Routledge, 1992.

———. *King Lear,* edited by R. A. Foakes. Arden Shakespeare, 3rd ser. Surrey: Thomas Nelson, 1997.

———. *The Merchant of Venice,* edited by John Drakakis. Arden Shakespeare, 3rd ser. London: Bloomsbury, 2010.

———. *The Norton Shakespeare,* edited by Stephen Greenblatt Walter Cohen, Jean E. Howard and Katherine Eisaman Maus. New York/London: W.W. Norton, 1986.

Shankar, D.A., ed. *Shakespeare in Indian Languages.* Shimla: Indian Institute of Advanced Study, 1999.

Sharma, Madhav. *Madhav Sharma.* Accessed 28 July 2013. http://www.madhavsharma.com

Shastri, Shibnath. *Ramtanu Lahiri O Totkalin Bongoshomaj.* Kolkata: S. K. Lahiri, 1909.

Shimko, Robert B and Sarah Freeman. "Introduction: Theatre, Performance and The Public Sphere." In *Public Theatres and Theatre Publics,* edited by Robert B. Shimko and Sara Freeman, 1–19. Newcastle upon Tyne: Cambridge Scholars Publishing, 2012.

Sillars, Stuart. "Image, Word, Authority in the Early Modern Frontispiece." In *Word, Image, Text: Studies in Literary and Visual Culture,* edited by Shormishtha Panja, Shirshendu Chakrabarti and Christel R. Devadawson, 10–21.Delhi: Orient BlackSwan, 2009.

———. *The Illustrated Shakespeare 1709–1875.* Cambridge: Cambridge University Press, 2008.

Singh, Jyotsna G. "Different Shakespeares: The Bard in Colonial/Postcolonial India." *Theatre Journal* 41, no.4 (1989): 445–458. Accessed 3 March 2013. doi:10.2307/3208007.

———. *Colonial Narratives/Cultural Dialogues: 'Discovery' of India in the Language of Colonialism.* London: Routledge, 1996.

————. "Wooing and Wedding." *Much Ado About Nothing*. RSC programme brochure, 2012.

Singh, Jyotsna G., ed. "Shakespeare and the Civilizing Mission." In *Colonial Narratives/ Cultural Dialogues: Discoveries of India in the Language of Colonialism*, 120–52. London: Routledge, 1996.

Singh, Jyotsna G. and Gitanjali G. Shahani. "Postcolonial Shakespeare Revisited." *Shakespeare* 6, no. 1 (2010): 127–38. Accessed 3 March 2013. doi:10.1080/17450911003743603.

Smith, Peter J. "*Twelfth Night*." In *A Year of Shakespeare: Reliving the World Shakespeare Festival*, edited by Paul Edmondson, Paul Prescott and Erin Sullivan, 221–23. London: Bloomsbury Arden Shakespeare, 2013.

Soni, Sakshi and T.S. Satyanath. "Shakespearean *Mahabharata*: *A Midsummer Night's Dream* as *Pramilarjuniyam* in Kannada." In *Global World of Shakespeare Translations*, Adaptation, Transformation, edited by Abha Singh, 178–91. Delhi: Prestige, 2015.

Spencer, Charles, "Much Ado About Nothing, Noel Coward Theatre," *Daily Telegraph*, 1 October 2012.

Stark, Ulrike. *An Empire of Books: The Naval Kishore Press and the Diffusion of the Printed Word in Colonial India*. Permanent Black, 2007.

Subramanyam, Ka. Naa. "Shakespeare in Tamil." *Indian Literature* 7, no. 1 (1964): 120–26.

Sunder Rajan, Rajeswari, ed. *The Lie of the Land: English Literary Studies in India*. New Delhi: Oxford University Press, 1992.

Syal, Meera. "Global Vision's Good Medicine." Review of *A Midsummer Night's Dream* by Jatinder Verma, Tara Arts, Lyric Theatre, Hammersmith, London. *The Express*, 31 January 1997.

Tagore, Rabindranath. *Creative Unity*. London: Macmillan, 1922. http://www.gutenberg. org/files/23136/23136-h/23136-h.htm

————. *Letters to a Friend*. London: George Allen and Unwin, 1928.

————. "Manabprakash." In *Rabindra Rachanabali* 13, 850–55. Kolkata: Visva-Bharati, 1961; originally published *c*.1892 in Bengali.

————. *My Reminiscences*. London: Macmillan, 1917.

————. "Rangamancha" (The Theatre), translated by Swapan Chakravorty. In *Rabindranath Tagore: Selected Writings on Literature and Language*, edited by Sisir K. Das and Sukanta Chaudhuri, 95–99. New Delhi: Oxford University Press, 2001.

————. "Sahityer Mulya." In *Rabindra Rachanabali* 14, 195–96. Kolkata: Visva-Bharati, 1961; originally published 1941 in Bengali.

————. "Sahityer Pran." In *Sahitya*, *Rabindra Rachanabali* 13, 846–50. Kolkata: Visva-Bharati, 1961; originally published *c*.1892 in Bengali.

————. *"Shakespeare."* In *A Book of Homage to Shakespeare*, edited by Israel Gollanz, 321. Oxford: Humphrey Milford, Oxford University Press, 1916. https://archive.org/ stream/bookofhomagetosh00golluoft/bookofhomagetosh00golluoft_djvu.txt

————. "Shakuntala," translated by Sukanta Chaudhuri. In *Rabindranath Tagore: Selected Writings on Literature and Language*, edited by Sisir K. Das and Sukanta Chaudhuri, 237–51. New Delhi: Oxford University Press, 2001.

————. *The Essential Tagore*, edited by Fakrul Alam and Radha Chakravarty. Cambridge, MA: Harvard University/Belknap Press, 2011.

Thakur, Vikram Singh. "Shakespeare Reception in India and The Netherlands until the Early Twentieth Century." *CLCWeb: Comparative Literature and Culture* 14, no. 2 (2012), 1–9. Accessed 25, October 2013. http://dx.doi.org/10.7771/1481-4374.1958

The National Bibliography of Indian Literature 1901–1950, 4 vols. New Delhi Sahitya Akademi, 1974.

The Taming of the Shrew, directed by Haissam Hussain, Globe Theatre, London, 25–26 May, 2012.

Tibbetts, John C. "Backstage with the Bard: Or, Building a Better Mousetrap." *Literature-Film Quarterly* 29, no. 2 (April 2001): 1–23. Accessed 31 December 2013. www.johnctibbetts.com/PDFs/Backstage%20With%20The%20Bard.pdf

Trivedi, Harish. "Shakespeare in India: Colonial Contexts." In *Colonial Transactions: English Literature in India*, 10–28. Manchester: Manchester University Press, 1995.

————. "Translating Culture vs. Cultural Translation." *91ˢᵗ Meridian* 4, no. 1 (Spring 2005). Accessed 3 March 2013. http://iwp.uiowa.edu/91st/vol4-num1/translating-culture-vs-cultural-translation.

Trivedi, Poonam. "'Filmi' Shakespeare." In *Narratives of Indian Cinema*, edited by Manju Jain, 229–48. Delhi: Primus Books, 2009.

————. "Introduction". In *India's Shakespeare: Translation, Interpretation and Performance,* edited by Poonam Trivedi and Dennis Bartholomeusz, 13–39. Delhi: Pearson Longman, 2006.

————. "Shakespeare and the Indian Image (nary) Embo(y)ment in versions of *A Midsummer Night's Dream.*" In *Replaying Shakespeare in Asia*, edited by Poonam Trivedi and Minami Ryuta, 54–75. New York: Routledge, 2010.

————. "Shakespeare in India." *MIT Global Shakespeares.* Accessed 18 April 2012. http://globalshakespeares.mit.edu/blog/2010/03/20/india/.

————. "Why Shakespeare is…Indian." *Guardian*, 4 May 2012. Accessed 5 May 2012. http://www.theguardian.com/stage/2012/may/04/why-shakespeare-is-indian.

Trivedi, Poonam and Minami Ryuta, eds. *Replaying Shakespeare in Asia*. New York: Routledge, 2010.

Tsui, Kam Jean. "Rewriting Shakespeare: A Study of Lin Shiu's Translation of *Tales from Shakespeare.*" MPhil thesis submitted to University of Hong Kong, 2008.

Twelfth Night, by William Shakespeare, directed by Atul Kumar, Globe Theatre, London, 27 April 2012.

Vatsyayan, Kapila. *Traditional Indian Theatre: Multiple Streams*. New Delhi: National Book Trust, 2005.

Venning, Dan. "Cultural Imperialism and Intercultural Encounter in Merchant Ivory's *Shakespeare Wallah.*" *Asian Theatre Journal* 28, no. 1 (Spring 2011): 149–67. Accessed 16 October 2012. Doi 10.1353/atj.2011.0000.

Venuti, Lawrence, ed. *The Translation Studies Reader*. London: Routledge, 2000.

Verma, Jatinder. "A Chronology for Shakespeare's *Dream*–Our First Production in Tara's 20ᵗʰ Year." Programme for *A Midsummer Night's Dream*, Tara Arts and Lyric Theatre Hammersmith, 1997.

————. "Cultural Transformations." In *Contemporary British Theatre*, edited by Theodore Shank, 55–61. Basingstoke: Macmillan, 1996.

————. "Director's Vision." Programme for *The Tempest*. Tara Arts, 2008.

————. "The Merchant of Venice." Programme for *The Merchant of Venice*, Tara Arts, 2005.

————. "The Shape of a Heart." In *Alternatives within the Mainstream: British Black and Asian Theatre,* edited by Dimple Godiwala, 383–89. Newcastle: Cambridge Scholars Press, 2006.

Vincent, Pheroze L. "Piya Behrupiya is up Delhi's Alley." *The Hindu*, 12 August 2012. www.thehindu.com/features/.../piya-behrupiya-is.../article3754223.ece

Vishwanathan, Gauri. *Masks of Conquest: Literary Study and British Rule in India*. London: Faber and Faber, 1990; originally published 1989.

Wal, Aradhna. "The Bard Goes Glocal." *Tehelka–India's Independent Weekly News Magazine*, 1 September 2012. Accessed 30 July 2013. www.tehelka.com/2012/08/the-bard-goes-glocal/.

Williams, Raymond. *The Country and the City*. New York: Oxford University Press, 1973.

Wolf, Matt. "Globe to Globe: All's Well That Ends Well, Shakespeare's Globe." *theartsdesk*, 25 May 2012. Accessed 2 September 2012. www.theartsdesk.com/theatre/globe-globe-alls-well-ends-well-shakespeares-globe-0

World Shakespeare Festival. *RSC*. Accessed 2 April 2012. www.worldshakespearefestival.org.uk/.

Worthen, W.B. "Drama, Performativity and Performance." *PMLA* 113, no. 5 (Oct. 1998): 1093–107.

Year of Shakespeare "Year of Shakespeare." Shakespeare Birthplace Trust, University of Birmingham, and University of Warwick. Accessed 18 April 2012. http://yearofshakespeare.com

About the Editors and Contributors

Editors

Shormishtha Panja is Professor of English and Director, Institute of Lifelong Learning, University of Delhi. She received her BA in English (Hons.) from Presidency College, Kolkata, and her PhD from Brown University, where she was awarded the Jean Starr Untermeyer Fellowship. She has been awarded a Fellowship at the Folger Shakespeare Library and a Mayers Fellowship at the Huntington. She has taught at Stanford University and IIT-Delhi and has been invited to lecture at universities in the USA, UK, Canada and Australia. She has been the President of the Shakespeare Society of India from 2008 to 2014.

Her books include *Shakespeare and the Art of Lying* (ed.), *Shakespeare and Class* (co-ed.), *Word Image Text: Studies in Literary and Visual Culture* (co-ed.) and *Signifying the Self: Women and Literature* (co-ed.).

Babli Moitra Saraf is the Principal of Indraprastha College for Women, University of Delhi, where she is an Associate Professor in the Department of English and heads the department of Multimedia and Mass Communication. She received her MPhil degree in English and PhD in Sociology. She is fluent in several Indian and foreign languages and is a published translator. *La Preda e altri Racconti* (Einaudi 2004) and *La Cattura* (Theoria 1996) are Italian translations of the Bengali activist–novelist Mahasweta Devi's works in collaboration with Maria Federica Oddera. Her work *Rajouri Remembered* (2007), is a translation of oral history and documents from Hindi, Urdu and Punjabi, recounting the effects of the Partition of India in the state of Jammu and Kashmir. She has published in the field of Translating and Interpreting Studies. She is on the editorial board of *Translation: A Transdisciplinary Journal*, and of *Saar Sansaar*, dedicated to Hindi translations directly from foreign languages.

Moitra Saraf has been a scholar under the Indo-Italian Cultural Exchange Program, Visiting Scholar under the Fulbright-Nehru International Education Administrator Program, a Research Associate and Visiting Faculty at the NIDA School of Translation Studies. She received the Distinguished Teacher Award of the University of Delhi, the Amity Women Achiever in Education Award, the 27th Dr S. Radhakrishnan Memorial National Award for Teachers and the Distinguished Alumnus Award from St. Stephen's College, Delhi, for Lifelong Pursuit of Excellence.

Contributors

Thea Buckley is studying for her PhD in English at the Shakespeare Institute, University of Birmingham, supervised by Professor Michael Dobson. Her research interests include Indian Shakespeare film and performance, intercultural Shakespeare and Shakespeare in education. She works at the Royal Shakespeare Company and is a co-editor of the *Shakespeare Institute Review*. Her work on Asian Shakespeare productions has been published internationally in *A Year of Shakespeare* (2013), *Cahiers Elisabethains* (Autumn 2013) and *Multicultural Shakespeare* (2014).

Paromita Chakravarti is Professor, Department of English, Jadavpur University and has been Director, School of Women's Studies, Jadavpur University, Kolkata. She completed her doctoral studies on early modern discourses of madness from the University of Oxford. She has been a Visiting Fellow at the Universities of Oxford, Liverpool and Hyderabad. Her book, *Women Contesting Culture*, co-edited with Professor Kavita Panjabi was published in 2012.

Radha Chakravarty is a writer, critic and translator. She has co-edited *The Essential Tagore* which was nominated the Book of the Year 2011 by Martha Nussbaum. She has translated Tagore, Bankimchandra and several contemporary Bengali writers into English. She is Professor of Comparative Literature and Translation Studies at Ambedkar University, Delhi.

Claire Cochrane is Professor of Theatre Studies at the University of Worcester in the UK where she both teaches and directs Shakespeare as well as other early modern drama. She holds her MA and PhD from the Shakespeare Institute of the University of Birmingham. In addition to publishing widely on Shakespeare in performance including her first monograph *Shakespeare and the Birmingham Repertory Theatre 1913-1929* (Society for Theatre Research, 1993), she specializes in twentieth and twenty-first century British regional theatre history. Her most recent monograph is *Twentieth Century British Theatre Industry, Art and Empire* (CUP, 2011). She also writes extensively on developments in Black British and British Asian theatre and audiences. Her most recent publication is *Theatre History and Historiography Ethics, Evidence and Truth*, a collection of essays co-edited with Jo Robinson (Palgrave, 2016).

Sandip Debnath is Assistant Professor in the Department of English, GLA University, Mathura. His areas of interest are modern Indian drama, Shakespeare and cultural studies.

Naina Dey teaches at Maharaja Manindra Chandra College, University of Calcutta. Her books include *Macbeth: Critical Essays, Edward the Second: Critical Studies, Real and Imagined Women: The Feminist Fiction of Virginia Woolf and Fay Weldon, Representations of Women in George Eliot's Fiction* and a book of poems, *Snapshots from Space and Other Poems*. She was awarded the Excellence in World Poetry Award, 2009 by the International Poets Academy, Chennai in 2009.

Paramita Dutta, MPhil, PhD, from Jadavpur University, is currently working as Assistant Professor in the Department of English at Rammohan College, Kolkata. Her research interests include Shakespeare and Renaissance studies, Shakespeare and film, Shakespeare in India, Indian theatre and she is also fond of writing short stories and learning foreign languages. She has presented papers nationally and internationally and her recent international publications include an article on Tagore's *Bidaay Abhishaap* in the anthology *The Politics and Reception of Rabindranath Tagore's Drama: The Bard on the Stage* (Routledge, 2015) and a short story titled 'The First Time' in the collection *Emanations 2+2=5* (International Authors, 2015).

Himani Kapoor pursued an MPhil from the Department of Modern Indian Languages and Literary Studies, Delhi University. Her dissertation was entitled "Mapping Translations of the Bhagwad Gita." She is currently working as an Assistant Professor of English at Amity University, Gurgaon.

Trisha Mitra is a student of the University of Delhi. She holds an MPhil degree from the Department of English, University of Delhi. She is currently a guest lecturer at the Department of Germanic and Romance Studies, University of Delhi, where she is teaching undergraduate students.

Jatindra K. Nayak is Professor of English, Utkal University, Odisha. Educated at Ravenshaw College, Cuttack and Merton College, Oxford, he won the KATHA Translation Award in 1997 and the Hutch-Crossword Book Award in 2004. He has co-translated Fakir Mohan Senapati's classic Odia novel *Chha Mana Atha Guntha* (Six Acres and a Third; 2005, 2006) into English. His other publications include the English translations of the Odia novels *Yantrarudha* (Astride the Wheel, 2003) and *Desa Kala Patra* (A Time Elsewhere, 2009). The thematic collections that he has edited include *Reminiscences: Excerpts from Oriya and Bangla Autobiographies* (2004), *Meeting the Mahatma: Gandhiji's Visits to Orissa* (2006) and *Memory, Images, Imagination* (2010).

Sayantan Roy Moulick is an independent researcher. He was, until recently, a guest lecturer in the Department of English at Vidyasagar Evening College, University of Calcutta.

T. S. Satyanath is a former professor at the Department of Modern Indian Languages and Literary Studies, University of Delhi. His areas of interest are comparative Indian literature, translation studies, folklore studies and cultural studies.

Preti Taneja is a Research Fellow in Global Shakespeare at the University of Warwick and Queen Mary, University of London. She holds a PhD in creative writing from Royal Holloway, University of London with a focus on *King Lear* in colonial and postcolonial India. She is a winner of the BBC/AHRC's New Generation Thinker award for outstanding research and broadcast skills.

Index